JUSTIN POLLARD

Justin Pollard read archaeology and anthropology at Cambridge. He is an historical writer and consultant in film and TV. His credits include the films *Elizabeth* and *Atonement* and the BBC TV Drama *The Tudors,* as well as more than twenty-five documentary series such as Channel 4's *Time Team.* He is a writer and researcher for *QI* and the author of seven books including *The Interesting Bits* and *Boffinology.*

SECRET BRITAIN

The Hidden Bits of Our History

JUSTIN POLLARD

JOHN MURRAY

First published in Great Britain in 2009 by John Murray (Publishers)
An Hachette UK Company

First published in paperback in 2010

1

A CIP catalogue record for this title is
available from the British Library

ISBN 978-1-84854-199-3

Typeset in Sabon MT by Palimpsest Book Production Limited,
Falkirk, Stirlingshire

Printed and bound by Clays Ltd, St Ives plc

John Murray policy is to use papers that are natural, renewable
and recyclable products and made from wood grown in sustainable
forests. The logging and manufacturing processes are expected to
conform to the environmental regulations of the country of origin.

John Murray (Publishers)
338 Euston Road
London NW1 3BH

www.johnmurray.co.uk

For Graham, Sharon, Elodie, Olivia and Katy

It was the secrets of heaven and earth that I desired to learn.

Mary Shelley, *Frankenstein* (1818)

CONTENTS

10 Secret Truths

11 Secret Tricks

12 Secrets of the Grave

13 Secret Places

17 Commercial Secrets

INTRODUCTION

This little book tells some of the more surprising and, I hope, less well-known stories from our history, which are all, in their way, secret. But it is not a book of conspiracy theories, or at least the conspiracy theories in it all concern events long past and, as such, there is no real need to panic. Rather than arousing alarm, this volume is designed for the odd moment when a small fragment recovered from the treasure chest of our past might entertain you. You can read some or all of it in any order – it makes no real difference – and take each story as seriously or as lightly as you may. It is the literary equivalent of a box of chocolates, which, I suppose, makes me the Milk Tray man of historians, rather appropriately, given the subject matter.

It is in the nature of such a work that in an effort to include a greater breadth of stories I have had to do so at the expense of detail in each account. If you would have liked to know more on any one then you have my apologies but I hope these little nuggets might equally inspire you to delve further into whatever it is that takes your fancy. Personally I think that any one of the stories gathered here would make a fine book in itself and, if I had time, I'd write them all.

Britain is a country as full of secrets as it is full of history. We have whole hidden cities beneath our feet, mysterious towers on our coastline and even coded messages concealed in the very names given to our fields. And that's before we even start looking at the people who lived here. They have been, and probably remain, a mischievous bunch, fond of tricks, prone to dallying, eccentric in habit and sometimes inspirational in the face of an enemy. As much room as possible has been found for all of them in this book's darker corners, where they lurk in lost villages, concealed boatsheds and underground vaults. I very much hope that you enjoy seeking them out. Catch them if you can.

MAY CONTAIN NUTS

These stories have been gathered over nearly two decades from a variety of sources, ranging in accuracy from the contemporary words of those who were actually there to the reminiscences of those who once 'danced with a man who danced with a girl who danced with the Prince of Wales', as it were. Even the eyewitness accounts vary as much as modern witness statements, not necessarily from a desire to deceive but through the variability of memory and the changes that inevitably occur in each retelling. Second-hand sources are also prey to the vagaries of fashion as styles of storytelling come and go and historians change their minds as to what the interesting bits in any event actually were.

To get to the bottom of each story I have hence tried to trace it to a source recorded as close to the event as possible, in many cases written by people who were at least there or claimed to be there. Whether you agree with their opinions or not, I hope you will enjoy their stories and forgive their occasional flights of fancy. If there is anything here that you know to be factually wrong, however, I do hope that you will let me know.

Justin Pollard
Wyke, 2009

1

Secret Games

It was beautiful and simple as all truly great swindles are.

O. Henry, *Gentle Grafter* (1908)

The Berners Street Hoax

It began very early, around five on a November morning (sources differ as to the exact day) in 1809 outside 54 Berners Street, a quiet middle-class part of London just to the north of Oxford Street and the home of one Mrs Tottenham. The doorbell rang and the maid answered. There standing before her was a sweep, wishing her the compliments of the day and saying he had come, as requested, to sweep the chimneys.

Except no request to sweep the chimneys had been sent. Indeed, the maid assured him that the chimneys were in excellent condition. So the disappointed workman went on his way. A misunderstanding, certainly, but hardly an event worth writing home about. However, a few moments later the doorbell rang again, and another sweep presented himself with the same story. Then another. And another. There were twelve in all.

With the final sweep dispatched the maid no doubt rather hoped the worst of the day was behind her, but she was very wrong. No sooner had the tide of sweeps receded than a fleet of coal carts rumbled into view, each with a large delivery of coal for number 54 – an order that the maid, and Mrs Tottenham herself, assured them had not been placed, by them at least. Already traffic was becoming congested around Berners Street as at this date Oxford Street (then Oxford Road) could be approached only from east or west via a labyrinthine series of small lanes. This, however, was just the beginning.

Hot on the heels of the coalmen came the cakemakers – each carrying large 10-guinea wedding cakes, which, they said, had been ordered and were to be delivered on this particular day to the said house. They too were sent away empty-handed to declarations that Mrs Tottenham, a widow, had no intention of remarrying, and certainly not on the day in question. The legion of cakemakers were merely the faintest intimation of the flood of tradesmen to come.

Doctors began calling at the house, presenting the letters that had summoned them. In their wake came apothecaries, surgeons and lawyers, followed by vicars and priests to minister to the resident within who, they had been told, was dying. Outside, a group of rather bemused undertakers, each with a bespoke coffin that had been ordered from them, waited to see just how many corpses might be brought forth from the building.

Mrs Tottenham and her maid, now somewhat rattled, pledged to all concerned that she was quite well and did not need so much as a single coffin, nor the last rites, nor even the ministrations of a physician.

Next to appear were the fishmongers, around forty in all, fulfilling orders for cod heads and lobsters. Behind them came bootmakers, dancing masters, shoemakers, haberdashers, hat-makers and butchers' boys. Over a dozen pianos had been laboriously brought, not to mention the 'six stout men bearing an organ', to add to the large quantity of furniture that was piling up on the doorstep. The roads around Berners Street were now severely congested, as delivery carts, disgruntled tradesmen and onlookers milled around in utter confusion.

The great and the good were also taking an interest. Through the heaving streets a carriage bore the Governor of the Bank of England and another entourage conveyed the chairman of the East India Company. Even royalty was represented in the person of the Duke of Gloucester in his silk-lined carriage. Finally the Lord Mayor of London himself rolled up as if to put the city's seal of approval on this scene of utter chaos.

It was not until evening that the crush of vehicles and the crowds of tradespeople and sightseers finally began to thin out and normality was restored. So what had really happened?

The secret to the day's events lay in a house opposite number 54 Berners Street where Samuel Beazley was at that moment shaking hands with Theodore Edward Hook and handing his friend a guinea. The two men had spent many happy hours watching the proceedings in the course of which Hook had undoubtedly won his bet, which was that, within a week, he could transform any house in London into the most talked about in the city. To achieve his aim he had simply sent out around 4,000 orders or requests, to tradesmen, professionals and dignitaries all over town, requiring them to present themselves at Mrs Tottenham's on that day with whatever fanciful order he had decided to ask them for. In the process he had brought a large part of London to a standstill and made 54 Berners Street famous for far longer than a week.

It was said to be the greatest hoax of the era, and one for which, despite the rumours, Hook would never be brought to book. Nor did he ever reveal why he had chosen the hapless Mrs Tottenham as his victim but it is unlikely she shared his good humour about the joke.

Captain Warner's Invisible Shell

Few things attract the interest of the military more than a secret weapon, and few people have strung along generals and politicians alike with the empty promise of one more than Samuel Alfred Warner.

Warner was not a military engineer by trade; indeed, his reputation in Faversham where he grew up was as a smuggler. However, he had gained military experience in the service of the Emperor Dom Pedro of Portugal in 1832, after which he called himself 'captain', although his right to the rank is somewhat debatable. It was also whilst in Portugal that rumours first began to emerge about Warner's secret weapon – the invisible shell – which he tried without success to sell to the Emperor.

Back in London, Warner seemed likely to have more luck. Word of the invisible shell, no doubt put around by the man himself, had reached the ears of the War Office and, through them, had come to the attention of King William IV. He had been told the shell was some sort of mine for sinking ships and, being a naval man himself, took a great interest, ordering the navy to investigate.

A parliamentary select committee was formed to look into Warner's claims but found it difficult to make any sense of them. Warner maintained that he had developed the technology whilst on board his father's ship *Nautilus*, then on covert operations against the French during the Napoleonic Wars. Yet no one could find any evidence of the *Nautilus* even existing, let alone reports of the sinking of two French privateers that Warner attributed to his invention. He argued, of course, that because of the secret nature of these operations the lack of records was hardly surprising.

Further committees of investigation followed, each becoming more exasperated than the last, as Warner refused to demonstrate his device to any critical audience unless he received a promise of £200,000 (which, using average earnings for comparison, would be around £150 million today). More annoyingly still, in between appearances at committee, Warner wrote teasing letters to *The Times*, asking why the government vacillated over this brilliant new technology. Finally in 1841 he was persuaded to make a small demonstration on a lake in Essex. Before an audience of the military and political elite, including Sir Robert Peel, a 23-foot boat packed with timber was floated out on to the water where it promptly exploded. As access to the vessel had been denied beforehand, no one could be quite sure that there hadn't simply been a bomb on board.

Just as the government were about to definitively disentangle themselves, Warner produced his master stroke. He announced in the newspapers that on 17 July 1844, in full view of the public, he would demonstrate the invisible shell off the Brighton coast. Special trains were laid on to bring admirals, politicians and sightseers to the town and the correspondent for *The Illustrated London News* reported that the crowds covered three miles of coastline. Before this throng the ship *John o' Gaunt* was pulled by an Admiralty tug into open water. At a given signal from the shore, the ship exploded and sank. Once again no access was given to the vessel beforehand, or to the device that had allegedly destroyed it, so the politicians returned to London no wiser than when they had arrived. Newspapers reported that the wreckage that washed ashore showed that the timbers had been cut through to pre-weaken the vessel in what was obviously a sham.

The Admiralty were still unable to make a decision about a device they had never seen, so discussions continued. At this point Warner chose to throw another spanner in the works by announcing a new miracle military device – the 'long range'. Again he refused to say what this was and demanded £200,000 in advance to hand over the secret. Not wishing to go through the whole 'invisible shell' process again, the government reluctantly offered £2,000 towards a demonstration.

Expectations must have varied in August 1846 when the military and politicians once again gathered to witness a Warner spectacular. Some believed in him and expected this to be his vindication. Many thought it just another wasted trip. All, however, were surprised. Although the 'long range' was widely reported to be some form of projectile, what actually met their eyes was a balloon. With the great and the good gathered round, it slowly rose into the air and zigzagged off at the mercy of the wind, occasionally dropping shot from its basket on random locations. Entirely out of control this was hardly a weapon of war. The party returned to London thoroughly unimpressed.

Even this setback did not put an end to 'Captain' Warner's fantastical caprice. Seven years later, committees were still sitting in parliament, wrestling with the knotty problem of whether Warner was a cautious genius or a charlatan. Fortunately he saved them the bother of reaching a final decision by dying, suddenly, on 5 December 1853.

Scratching Fanny

The case of Scratching Fanny was one of the most celebrated mysteries of the eighteenth century, drawing into its thrall such luminaries as Horace Walpole and Samuel Johnson.

The strange events in Cock Lane, which lies adjacent to Smithfield Market in London, began in January 1760 with the arrival of two new lodgers, William Kent and Fanny Lynes, at number 33, then the home of Richard Parsons. Although William and Fanny had claimed to be married, they had in fact eloped together after the death of William's first wife who also happened to be Fanny's sister. In the relative anonymity of London they hoped to conceal what was, in law, an incestuous relationship and start afresh.

Parsons was not an easy landlord. A drunk and a gambler, he abused his position to persuade Kent to lend him money but proved very unwilling to pay it back. The couple found his young daughter, Elizabeth, more amiable and on the occasions while Kent was away on business the young Fanny would sleep in her bed 'so as not to feel too alone'. It was on just such a night that she awoke to hear a strange scratching noise coming from behind the wainscoting. Fanny, it seems, believed that this scratching was her dead sister, warning her from beyond the grave of imminent danger. Shortly after, she and Kent left the apparently haunted house for good. Perhaps Fanny's premonitions were right for within a matter of weeks she had died from smallpox.

William Kent did not forget about the debt Parsons owed him and continued to threaten to take him to court if he wouldn't pay. Backed into a corner, Parsons came up with an extraordinary story.

In January 1762 he claimed that the 'scratchings' had started again, but that this time it was Fanny speaking, adding that he could interpret the noises. What Fanny was telling him was that she had died not of smallpox but from having been poisoned with arsenic by Kent. Whilst this tale may originally have been designed simply to keep Kent at arm's length, the story spread like wildfire around London and soon Parsons, never one to miss an opportunity to turn a profit, was charging people admission to the house on Cock Lane at night to hear the ghostly scrapings. Food and drink stalls were soon set up outside. Dignitaries such as Horace

Walpole came to witness the unearthly manifestations of the spirit who had, it was said, formed a special relationship with young Elizabeth Parsons, appearing only when she was in the room.

The 'accusations' of Scratching Fanny soon brought William Kent back to clear his name and his case attracted the attention of a number of more educated and less credulous observers, including Samuel Johnson who, to put it bluntly, thought the whole thing a cheap trick. They interrogated the Parsons family until Richard, now backed into another corner, announced that Fanny would reveal more of the story of how she was murdered by tapping on the lid of her coffin then in St John's church. That night Johnson and the other ghostbusters went to the crypt at 1 a.m. but taking the precaution of excluding Parsons and his daughter. There they waited. By dawn, when no scratching had come from Fanny's coffin, the story was declared a hoax. More thorough investigations were now instituted back at Cock Lane, which revealed that Elizabeth was using a wooden board hidden in the stays of her corset to make the noises. Just how she managed this trick is not recorded.

Richard Parsons was now accused of trying to engineer the death of William Kent to avoid paying his debt. He was pilloried and sent to prison for two years. His wife received a year's imprisonment and their maid six months in the Bridewell prison. Elizabeth Parsons, Fanny's former friend, was excused on the grounds that she was simply obeying her father.

The ghost of Cock Lane went on to become a celebrated and popular cautionary tale, being mentioned in the writings of Herman Melville and Charles Dickens, as well as appearing in two Hogarth engravings, *Credulity, Superstition and Fanaticism* and *The Times*.

The Stock Exchange Fraud

On Monday 21 February 1814, Colonel du Bourg, aide-de-camp to Lord Cathcart, arrived at the Ship Inn in Dover and made the announcement that everyone in the country had been hoping to hear. Napoleon, the scourge of Europe, was dead, killed by a detachment of Cossacks, and the triumphant Allied armies were fast approaching Paris.

Pausing only to ask that the message be transmitted as quickly as possible by semaphore to the Admiralty in London, du Bourg then took the coach for London himself, stopping off to pass round the good news at many of the coaching inns along the way.

By the time du Bourg reached Lambeth where he disembarked, rumours were already flying around the city, although fog had prevented the Admiralty from receiving his semaphore message. A couple of hours later, confirmation of the news seemed to come when three French officers in white Bourbon cockades paraded across Blackfriars bridge and up Lombard Street, announcing the restoration of the Bourbon monarchy. There was delight in the City. On the Stock Exchange, government 'Omnium' stocks began to soar in value as traders looked forward to peace.

It was afternoon by the time the government had official intelligence on the matter and could issue a statement. Regretfully they announced that Napoleon was still very much alive, news that sent stocks slumping back to their earlier levels.

What had actually happened was an elaborate fraud. An investigation by the Stock Exchange soon found that around £1.1 million of government stock, bought in the previous week, had been sold that morning as prices peaked. The buyers had been naval hero Lord Cochrane, his uncle Andrew Cochrane-Johnstone, Richard Butt, Lord Cochrane's financial advisor and three well-known exchange speculators. All were arrested.

It was not long before du Bourg was also taken. He turned out to be one Charles Random de Berenger, a French officer in exile and an undischarged bankrupt who had been employed by Lord Cochrane as a military instructor. Having claimed Napoleon was dead at Dover, he had dashed to London, changed out of his scarlet uniform (which he had no right to wear) and joined the three exchange speculators who had dressed as French officers to spread leaflets through the City. He was eventually traced to Lord Cochrane's house and arrested. In the meantime a killing had been made on the Stock Exchange.

Those in the Cochrane family who seemed to have profited so handsomely from the hoax were all tried and convicted of fraud. Lord Cochrane was sentenced to the pillory although this was remitted as the government feared a riot if it publicly humiliated so prominent an admiral. Indeed, from this point onwards the pillory was never used again. The government was less cautious in striking him off the navy list, fining him £1,000, imprisoning him for a year and expelling him from the Order of the Bath in a ceremony in which his banner was kicked down the steps of Westminster Abbey.

Ironically, Lord Cochrane is now thought to have been entirely innocent, unlike his relatives, and he spent the rest of his life seeking redress for the humiliations and degradations he had suffered. As a radical parliamentary reformer and naval hero, he had many enemies in the government who wished him out of the way, and his familiarity with his uncle and de Berenger had been enough to implicate him. Thus it was that the greatest naval officer in the generation to follow Nelson was brought low by a rumour that his arch-enemy was dead.

The Woman Who Bred Rabbits

One event in 1726 has a unique place in British history, under-lining the incredible naivety of parts of the medical profession, even at the very highest level, whilst also demonstrating the lengths to which the very poor might be driven in the search for money and recognition.

The events that had begun taking place in Godalming and then Guildford, both in Surrey, first reached public notice on 3 December that year with the publication of a small pamphlet entitled 'A Short Narrative of an Extraordinary Delivery of Rabbets, Perform'd by Mr John Howard Surgeon at Guildford'.

This quickly caught the imagination of Londoners used to a diet of 'amazing' stories and hence found its way into periodicals, permeating upwards to the highest level of society.

And it was a truly extraordinary story. The writer of the pamphlet was the very well-respected Nathanael St André, surgeon and anatomist to the Royal Household of George I and hence a man to be trusted, yet his tale seemed incredible. It described how Mary Toft, the illiterate wife of an impoverished clothier, had, that autumn, started giving birth, first to monsters and then to rabbits. The first creature, 'born' on 27 September, had been so hideous that a local surgeon, John Howard, had been called. He had refused to believe the creature to be real until Mary expelled its head, producing what was clearly the mangled head of a rabbit.

To modern eyes this is clearly a fake but medical men of the day were convinced that a woman's thoughts and imaginings could misshape an unborn child. When Mary told Howard that she had been startled by a rabbit when just five weeks pregnant, after which she had craved rabbit meat and dreamt about rabbits, her giving birth to a mutant creature's head seemed quite plausible. To add credence to her claim she was soon in labour again and delivered of a whole rabbit. More were to follow.

Howard was now convinced he was witnessing a real medical event that would make history and, by November, when Mary had produced eight rabbits and looked set to deliver more, he decided to move her to Guildford for closer observation. Sure enough, a ninth dead rabbit was delivered in Guildford just a few days later. By now the rabbits were coming thick and fast, alerting the medical profession. On 15 November, Nathanael St André, the royal surgeon, visited Howard and Mary, just in time to witness the delivery of her fifteenth rabbit. St André examined the pieces of the creature and the other 'monsters', which Howard had thoughtfully preserved in alcohol, and declared the case to be genuine, before rushing back to London to cash in by publishing his pamphlet.

George I now sent Cyriacus Ahlers, surgeon to His Majesty's

German Household, to investigate. He arrived in Guildford just in time to help deliver another partial rabbit but reported to the King that he thought it a hoax. George I, clearly fascinated with the reproductive eccentricities of his new subjects, dispatched another mission, this time consisting of two eminent male midwives, Philippus van Limborch and Sir Richard Manningham, giving St André orders to bring Mary Toft to London.

By now Mary had given birth to seventeen rabbits but the seventeenth would prove her last. Brought to London on 29 November, she was lodged at a boarding house called Lacy's Bagnio in Leicester Fields and kept under a careful watch as well as being publicly displayed, poked, examined and interrogated. More labour pains followed but no rabbits were forthcoming. Finally on 7 December, in the wake of brutal bullying and threats of painful surgical procedures, Mary broke down and confessed.

She had indeed been pregnant that year but had miscarried in August, after which her husband and mother-in-law had concocted a bizarre plan with the hope of raising money. In a scene that can only be described as gothic, they had gutted a cat, pushed the spine of an eel into its intestines and then inserted their monstrous creation into Mary's birth canal. She had duly 'given birth' to this. To make her story credible, she was required to produce a head too. A rabbit's was the first thing to hand and the easiest to procure, so from then on Mary gave birth to rabbits. Those taken in by the deception were furious. The much abused Mary was charged as a 'notorious and vile cheat' and sent to Bridewell to await trial. Fortunately for her, the charges were later dropped and she returned to Godalming.

The great medical men who had been so thoroughly duped were mercilessly parodied in the press and on stage. Alexander Pope used the story as the basis for his *The Dunciad* and two of William Hogarth's most famous engravings – *The Cunicularii, or the Wise Men of Godliman in Consultation* and *Credulity, Superstition and Fanaticism* – make reference to the case. Although many believed St André to be complicit in the fraud, in her confession Mary cleared all her eminent medical attendants of everything – except credulity.

The Cottingley Fairies

Undoubtedly the most charming hoax of the twentieth century, and a secret kept for sixty-three years, lay in the true nature of a handful of photographs taken by two young girls by the Cottingley Beck in 1917.

Frances Griffiths and Elsie Wright were cousins, whose mothers were living together in the village of Cottingley just outside Bradford in West Yorkshire while Frances's father was fighting in the First World War. Elsie's father Arthur, by contrast, was not fighting but still at home and working locally as a mechanic and engineer. And his great hobby was photography.

So it was that on a July day in 1917, Elsie persuaded her father to lend her and her cousin his Butcher Midg quarter-plate camera before running off to play by a little stream near the house. That evening Arthur helped the girls to develop the plate they had taken and noticed strange figures on it. When he made a print of the plate the following day, they turned out to be fairies who seemed to be dancing around Frances. Arthur, a practical man, assumed the fairies were paper cut-outs. When a month later the girls again borrowed his camera, another fairy photograph appeared, this time showing Elsie playing with what appeared to be a gnome.

And so the matter would have been left – no more than two charming keepsakes of a happy summer spent playing by a stream – were it not for a chance remark by Elsie's mother three years later, which was overheard by Edward Gardner at a lecture in Bradford. Gardner was a member of the Theosophical Society, one of whose objectives was to explore unexplained natural phenomena. He asked to see the images. Convinced that they truly were photographs of fairies, he sent the pictures to the leading photographic technician of the day, Harold Snelling, who pronounced that the images were genuine, unfaked, single exposures with no sign of the use of paper cut-outs, painting on the negative or other manipulations. In short, these really were fairies.

Gardner made and exhibited copies of the photographs. In this way they came to the attention of one of the greatest literary names of the day, Sir Arthur Conan Doyle, creator of Sherlock Holmes. He suggested that another expert be called from Kodak's. After examination, this expert refused to certify that the images were 'real' but equally couldn't find any evidence that they were fake. Gardner was then dispatched to Cottingley to interview the girls to see whether they would admit to fraud, but he found them to be cheerful, honest and happy to talk freely about the fairies they had played with. Even Arthur Wright was no longer sure the pictures were a fake, having checked the girls' bedrooms for paper cut-outs and found none. He agreed that Gardner and Doyle could go into print in the *Strand* magazine with the story, provided the children's identities were concealed.

So the Cottingley Fairies came to world attention in 1920 in a sell-out issue of the *Strand* under the headline 'An Epoch-Making Event – Fairies Photographed'. An almighty controversy erupted. For many people, the idea of fairies being real was sheer nonsense, but as amateur photography was still relatively rare, strange things were coming to light all the time. (The girls had also produced another three images of fairies to add to the evidence.) It was the period immediately after the First World War, in which many who had lost loved ones – including Conan Doyle himself, who lost a son and a brother – had turned to spiritualism for comfort. Against this background, magical creatures seemed – indeed, many wanted them to seem – perfectly possible.

Conan Doyle himself went to visit the girls, taking a medium with him to see whether any more apparitions might occur, and he was absolutely convinced of their genuineness. In 1922 these firm beliefs were crystallised in his book *The Coming of the Fairies*, which discussed the background to the case and the implication of the discovery that fairies really did exist.

Frances and Elsie said nothing. In fact, they said nothing or very little for over sixty years, until Elsie confessed in 1981 in the magazine *The Unexplained* that the fairies were indeed paper cutouts, stuck in the ground with hatpins. They had never owned up before, she said, because once such eminent people as Conan Doyle had become involved they didn't want to expose anyone to ridicule.

At this point the story of the Cottingley Fairies should have been laid to rest. Three years later, however, in her last television interview, Frances claimed that there really were fairies in Cottingley and that one of the photographs was, in fact, genuine. So the fairies live on.

The Holy Maid of Leominster

Amongst the people of mediaeval Britain there was an overwhelming belief in God and his power to materially affect life here on earth. Relics of saints were believed to offer miraculous cures and attracted large numbers of paying visitors, as did the presence of 'holy' men and women in a parish. It is therefore perhaps not surprising that there was a degree of fraud amongst some men and women of the cloth.

One of the more brazen cases of fraud came to light with the revealing of the secret of the Holy Maid of Leominster. The affair, and I use the word advisedly, came to light during a council held by the formidable Margaret Beaufort, the mother of King Henry VII, whose court at Collyweston had the power to look into all manner of strange happenings in the East Midlands. A good example might be her investigation into why John Stokesley, later bishop of London, had baptised a cat.

What the court at Collyweston heard about the Holy Maid was that the prior of Leominster in Herefordshire had brought into the church a 'strange wenche' by the name of Elizabeth who, he claimed, had been sent by God. Of course the townsfolk weren't complete idiots and demanded some proof of the Holy Maid's divine blessings. The prior therefore installed her in the rood loft above the chancel and told the congregation that she would live there without food or drink, save for 'Aungels foode' – the communion bread. This was impressive enough, although there was more to come. During the service of Holy Communion it became clear that Elizabeth would not descend from her perch for communion but instead the wafer was seen to fly out of the prior's hands, up and into her mouth. This was a sure sign that she was chosen by God.

A cult soon developed around the miraculous Elizabeth and crowds flocked to the church to seek cures and blessings from the 'Holy Maid'. Margaret's council, less certain that this was a miracle, launched an investigation that led to some startling discoveries. First there was the excrement that the Holy Maid still seemed to produce, despite not really eating much. Not only should this not exist, in their view, but it was reported to have 'no saintly savour'. Then there were the meat bones hidden under her bed – how had they got there? Finally they found that a thin wire stretched from the altar to the rood loft, along which the 'miraculous' communion wafers had actually travelled. It seemed there was more magic than miracle to this performance.

Margaret Beaufort ordered the 'Holy Maid' removed from the priory. When they came for her, she promptly asked for food and drink and shortly after confessed the full, terrible truth. She was actually the (supposedly celibate) prior's lover whom he had, for convenience, installed in his church. To cover his tracks, and to make some money, he had invented the story of her being a Holy Maid. Were it not for the doubting Margaret Beaufort and her court, the prior might have got away with not only having taken a lover but making a small fortune from her. Fortunately for both of them Margaret was merciful and the two were only ordered to perform a public penance.

Piltdown Man

At the beginning of the twentieth century, archaeologists everywhere were looking for evidence of one phenomenon – the

Missing Link. Since the publication in 1859 of Darwin's *The Origin of Species*, his theory of natural selection had suggested to many archaeologists that there must be an intermediate fossil between apelike creatures and man. It would, they suggested, be an animal with the large braincase that we associate with modern humans but with other physical features that were still primitive. Then in 1912, Charles Dawson, a solicitor and amateur fossil hunter, announced at a meeting of the Geological Society of London that he had found that holy grail, the Missing Link.

Dawson claimed that in 1908 a workman from the Piltdown quarry near Uckfield in Sussex had handed him a fragment of a skull. Dawson had subsequently visited the site and found further pieces, which he had shown to the keeper of the geological department at the British Museum, Arthur Smith Woodward. The two men had returned to the site and found there yet more of the skull and half of the lower jaw.

When the pieces were reconstructed at the museum, it was discovered that the skull case, although fragmentary, seemed to be about two-thirds the size of a modern skull although the jaw, despite its human-like molar teeth, was otherwise very similar to that of a chimpanzee or other ape. It was just what the learned members of the Geological Society had been looking for and it had come to light in England. They were delighted.

Not everyone was happy with the discovery. Many of the important diagnostic parts of the skull, such as the articulations between jaw and skull base, were missing, making it difficult to see how such a 'primitive' jaw had attached to such a large skull. Furthermore a reconstruction of the badly damaged skull case by the Royal College of Surgeons produced a skull not two-thirds the capacity of a modern one, but one that was almost indistinguishable from that of an anatomically modern human. Other specialists too, in France and the USA, suggested that the skull was clearly human and the jaw that of an ape, yet no one wanted to listen. Here was the missing link, the vital stepping stone in human evolution, and it had been found here in England, in the home of palaeontology. It couldn't be more perfect.

Dawson entered the scientific literature, as his fossil, *Eoanthropus dawsoni* (Dawson's Dawn Man), was named after him. One scientist enthused that it was the most important discovery ever made in England, if not the greatest ever made anywhere. Nearly half a century passed in which *Eoanthropus* was proudly displayed in London and a memorial to the now dead Dawson was erected at Piltdown itself.

It was 1953 before final proof was published, demonstrating that the find was a forgery. It had been noticed that one of the molar teeth sloped at a different angle from the others and an examination of this under a microscope showed that it had been filed down. Piltdown Man had not been found; he had been created. In fact carbon-14 dating has shown that the jaw was that of a 500-year-old orang-utan from Sarawak on the island of Borneo, the teeth were from a fossil chimpanzee and the skull was a mediaeval human specimen. Where these pieces fitted badly – such as in the teeth, which were a different shape from a human's – they had been filed to fit, while crucial areas that would have easily identified the fraud, such as the jaw articulation, had simply been snapped off. The whole 'fossil' had been stained in iron solution and chromic acid to give it a unified appearance.

Just who created the forgery is still something of a mystery with no one ever claiming responsibility. Charles Dawson is an obvious suspect, as are some of his collaborators. Recent investigations have shown that Dawson 'found' an extraordinary number of artefacts that later turned out to be not quite what they appeared and thirty-eight specimens in his own collections have been shown to be clear frauds. These included *Plagiaulax dawsoni* – a supposed reptile/mammal hybrid – and a host of prehistoric and Roman artefacts.

He is not the only possible candidate. In 1970 a trunk belonging to the palaeontologist Martin Hinton was discovered at the Natural History Museum in London where he had left it in storage. As it contained animal bones filed and stained in a similar manner to the Piltdown remains, the finger has also been pointed at him.

Why the hoax was perpetrated is even less clear. It may simply have started as a practical joke on the establishment but got so far out of hand that no one dared own up. Whatever the reason, it proved for nearly half a century to be the perfect fraud – the thing that everyone was looking for but which, in reality, never existed.

2

Secret Identities

'Who are *you*?' said the Caterpillar. This was not an encouraging opening for a conversation. Alice replied, rather shyly, 'I – I hardly know, sir, just at present – at least I know who I *was* when I got up this morning, but I think I must have been changed several times since then.'

Lewis Carroll, *Alice's Adventures in Wonderland* (1865)

Princess Caraboo

Almondsbury, a small village near Bristol in Gloucestershire, is not now, nor has it ever been, the sort of place to attract bizarre and colourful aristocrats but on 3 April 1817 it briefly stepped into the international press spotlight with the arrival of an extraordinary character.

The woman staggering down the high street that morning was exhausted and apparently on the verge of starvation. In an era when street beggars and vagrants were commonplace, that in itself was not enough to catch the interest of the people of the village. What singled her out was the incomprehensible language she apparently spoke and the outlandish clothes she was wearing, all topped off with a magnificent black turban.

As even mysterious vagrants were not unusual this close to the port of Bristol, the villagers took her to Mr Overton, the overseer of the poor, under the impression that she was perhaps a destitute French woman. Since Mr Overton could no more understand the woman than the villagers, he decided that the local magistrate, Samuel Worrall of Knole Park, should proclaim on the matter and conveyed the woman there. For the rural aristocracy, the arrival of this exotic creature in their humdrum lives was something of an event and Mrs Worrall immediately took to the girl. Her husband was less impressed, particularly when she proved to have no papers other than some forged currency. In the period of the Napoleonic Wars this would in many minds have marked her out as a spy, if a rather obvious one.

After a brief interview Samuel Worrall dispatched the girl back to the village inn with two of his servants who were to arrange board and lodging for her. And that was where things began to get still more unusual. At the inn she began excitedly pointing to a print of a pineapple – then a highly expensive and exotic fruit – suggesting it was something she recognised from home. She then refused dinner, despite her apparent hunger, drinking tea instead, but only after elaborate prayers and always with one hand over her eyes. That night, when shown to her room, she also appeared unaware of the use of a bed and insisted on sleeping on the floor.

By now everyone was becoming rather fond of the stranger, although this did not stop her being taken to Bristol and placed in St Peter's Hospital as a vagrant. Here her fame only grew and the local gentry flocked to see this unusual creature before Mrs Worrall, taking sympathy on her, removed her once more to Knole.

Back at Knole the mystery was soon apparently solved on the arrival of a Portuguese sailor, Mañuel Eynesso, who claimed he could speak their guest's language. The two talked for some time before Eynésso announced that the girl they had thrown in the vagrants' hospital was in fact Caraboo, a tragic princess from the distant island of Javasu, taken from her home by pirates and sold as a slave. She had staggered into Almondsbury having jumped ship to escape her captors as they sailed close by Bristol.

The Worralls were delighted. Very few foreign strangers came to Knole and still fewer tragic princesses. Soon they were advertising her presence around the county, inviting friends to come and witness her incomprehensible language and peculiar habits. Their royal guest's exploits made the newspapers, especially her habit of climbing trees to worship her god 'Allah Tallah' and her fondness for swimming naked in the lake.

Her existence in this little Eden was not to last. Her newspaper appearances brought her to the notice of Mrs Neale, a Bristol boarding house owner, who recognised 'Princess Caraboo' as her former lodger, Mary Baker, the daughter of a cobbler from Witheridge in Devon. She remembered how Baker would entertain her children by talking in a made-up language and how she would wear a turban to improve the effect.

The result of this exposure was ridicule for the Worralls and county society, whom the London papers mercilessly mocked for their credulity. Mary Baker, however, became yet more of a celebrity, fêted as a working-class girl who had duped an old, failing aristocracy. It also soon came out that she had a long and eccentric past, having been expelled from the Magdalen Hospital for Reformed Prostitutes in London when it was discovered that she had never been a prostitute in the first place.

All this proved too much for the Worralls who arranged for their princess's immediate departure for the New World, under the strict supervision of two Moravian sisters. Here she made money for a while, exhibiting herself as 'Princess Caraboo', before returning to England and, in another eccentric change of direction, settling down as a respectable businesswoman, selling leeches to a Bristol infirmary. She died in 1865 aged seventy-three.

King Anthony

Sometimes the most outrageous claims of impostors, regardless of their ludicrous basis, cause enough of a stir to worry the establishment and make us believe that perhaps the whole world has finally gone quite mad. Such was the case with King Anthony.

The most important thing to understand about Anthony William Hall is that he was a former Shropshire policeman, and not a king of England. This was, however, a matter of some contention between the First and Second World Wars. In the late 1920s, Hall had somehow come to believe that he was a direct descendant of Henry VIII, which gave him a claim on the throne. The basis for his claim was a shade haphazard and it regularly changed to suit the situation, but in principle it was as follows.

According to Hall, Henry VIII had had a legitimate (or sometimes illegitimate) son by Anne Boleyn who was hence the full brother of Elizabeth I. For unexplained reasons, possibly through simple carelessness, he had failed to inherit the crown, despite having been made Prince of Wales, contenting himself instead with marrying and having twenty-three children. He finally died in 1618 at the age of ninety. Just to make sure that no one might think the Stuarts had rightfully ruled after Elizabeth, Hall also added for good measure that James I (or 'Goggle-Eyed Jim' as Hall called him) was actually an impostor, a changeling substituted for Mary Queen of Scots' real son who died (or was murdered) in infancy. Of course if Anthony Hall really was a direct descendant of Henry VIII, the true identity of James I hardly mattered, as the Tudor line would have never become extinct.

With a few variations this then formed the basis of the claim to the English throne that 'King Anthony', as he styled himself, started pressing in the early 1930s. He usually made his case through speeches (there were over 2,000 in total) in the Bull Ring in Birmingham but also via his only published document, a single-sheet 'proclamation', which he sent to the Earl Marshal and the archbishop of Westminster (probably mistaking the latter for the archbishop of Canterbury). This rather fine document not only sets out his claim to the throne but makes a number of pledges. Hall promises to write off the national debt; to create full employment, free health care for all and thousands of new police stations; to set up a Ministry of Pleasure (to 'revive the ancient merry times'); and to remove the parliament to Wales – policies that all have something to be said for them.

King Anthony's forceful rhetoric and eccentric claims certainly made him something of a minor celebrity. The 'notice to quit' that he sent to George V and his insistence on referring to King George VI as 'Albert Wettin' brought wry smiles, as did his call for the return of the American 'colonies' to Britain and his issuing of his own banknotes (which he sold for one penny against a face value of a pound, redeemable on his accession). This was very much in the great tradition of the British eccentric.

However, not everyone seems to have been laughing. It is certainly true that in the heat of the moment King Anthony could get a little overexcited, once offering to fight George V through the courts for the throne, the loser to have his head 'lopped off', and regularly being arrested for the use of 'scandalous language'. It seems that neither the government nor the royal family were taking his claims quite so lightly. In a memo of 1931, the King's Private Secretary, Sir Clive Wigram, notes: 'His Majesty quite agrees that a stop should be put to his effusions but feels that it might not look very well for a man who is obviously demented to get six months imprisonment.' He then suggests: 'Would it not be possible to keep him under observation with a view to his final detention in an institution, without actually putting him in prison.'

Any hopes on the part of the royal secretary that King Anthony might be put in a lunatic asylum were dashed by the Home Office's reply, pointing out that whilst 'Mr Hall is eccentric and wrong-headed, he is not so obviously demented or insane that he could be dealt with without recourse to court proceedings'.

An agreement was reached that King Anthony be arrested and charged with 'using quarrelsome and scandalous language'. This would not only give everyone a chance to assess the impostor but might also dissuade him from stating that he wanted to be 'the first policeman to cut off the king's head' or threatening to shoot the poor man 'as I would shoot a dog'. An 'expert in lunacy' was duly called to examine King Anthony, but, to Sir Clive's disappointment, he ruled that the pretender was not insane. Hall was merely fined £10 and bound over to keep the peace.

After one last tirade in the Bull Ring, King Anthony apparently chose to retire, perhaps a little worried that the state was finally taking a real interest in him. He died in 1947. The memos from the King's Private Secretary were classified as secret and only released in 2006.

Mr and Mrs Smith

On 3 March 1848, a poorly dressed couple with no luggage walked into the Bridge Inn in Newhaven, East Sussex, and checked in for the night under the highly unimaginative names of 'Mr and Mrs Smith'. It was probably not the first nor, indeed, the last time that a 'Mr and Mrs Smith' had signed the register at the inn, although it was perhaps the only one when such an assiduously incognito couple were courted by forty or fifty of the local tradesmen, all eager to welcome them – not something most 'Mr and Mrs Smiths' would wish for.

But then this Mr and Mrs Smith were no ordinary couple. Their story had begun some eighteen years earlier when Mr Smith had taken the rather more grand title of Louis-Philippe, king of the French. The intentions of the previous king, Charles X, had been entirely otherwise. When he abdicated following the July Revolution of 1830, he asked Louis-Philippe (who, he knew, was popular with the elected Chamber of Deputies) to tell them that he nominated his ten-year-old grandson Henri, Duke of Bordeaux, as his successor. Louis-Philippe had somehow 'forgotten' to do this and declared himself king instead, leaving Charles X, young Henri and the rest of the erstwhile royal family to shuffle off to England in a sulk.

The following years had been hard for Louis-Philippe, whose nickname was 'the Citizen King'. Despite his early popularity, the rebellious French considered him too conservative and, as the gap between the wealthy and the poor grew ever wider, another revolution became only a matter of time. It finally arrived on 24 February 1848 – a rather civilised affair by the standards of French revolutions – but Louis-Philippe panicked. Nominating his nine-year-old grandson to pick up the shattered pieces of the monarchy, he fled Paris with his wife Marie Amélie, apparently fearing that his former subjects might be considering removing his head, something for which, to be fair, they had previous form.

Forced to leave the capital in haste with no luggage, in an ordinary cab, the couple eventually reached the Channel coast near Le Tréport where they wandered for a while, at times despairing of their predicament and preparing to give themselves up. Eventually a fishing boat was found (probably with the help of the British consul in Le Havre) that could take them offshore to rendezvous with the steamship *Express*, which usually plied the route from Le Havre to Southampton. Once the captain had been informed of the identity of his new passengers, who were under orders from the British to call themselves Mr and Mrs Smith, the *Express* set sail for the nearest British port at Newhaven.

When the *Express* finally docked, news had already reached

the Sussex coast of the celebrity arrivals and a local worthy, William Catt, was sent to welcome them. The King – now resplendent in a blue shirt and jacket that the captain had had to lend the unfortunate monarch – and his wife made their way to the Bridge Inn. Here everyone who was anyone, and many people who weren't, hastened to introduce themselves to the supposedly incognito couple and, according to the London satirists, extravagant oaths were made concerning the protection and restoration of the King. Just what sort of a threat the combined shopkeepers of Newhaven might have presented to the newly installed government of Napoleon III is unknown but was thankfully never tested.

The following day a special train took Mr and Mrs Smith to Croydon where they were met by a coach sent by Queen Victoria to bring them to Buckingham Palace. After a brief reception, Victoria was reminded by Lord Russell that having the French royal couple living on British soil might prove a shade embarrassing. Louis-Philippe and his wife were quickly moved to Claremont, in Surrey, which conveniently belonged to King Leopold of the Belgians, rather than to Victoria. Here Mr Smith died, just two years later, in August 1850.

Cornelius Evans

Cornelius Evans did not have the makings of a convincing impostor. He was a clear head shorter than the man he said he was, had a stoop, unlike his counterpart, and had large rough hands, most unlike the royal hands of Prince Charles Stuart, the future king Charles II. Yet that is who he claimed to be.

Why Evans decided to impersonate Charles isn't really clear. The idea came to him whilst he was sitting in a pub in Deal in 1648 with a group of disaffected sailors from the ship *Providence*. In England at this time the second Civil War had just broken out and Kent in particular was seen as a hotbed of pro-royal sentiment. Evans and his new chums decided, perhaps after a few drinks, to exploit this by claiming that he was King Charles I's son, back from exile on the continent.

While the sailors headed for Sandwich by boat to spread the rumour, Evans went there on foot and, on 17 May, dined there at the Bell tavern. By now word had got out that the prince was in town and soon the mayor, William Mandey, was brought to him, asking why he had come. Evans rather weakly replied that his supposed mother, Queen Henrietta Maria, with whom he was living in France, had tried to poison him so he had fled back to England. The mayor, becoming a shade suspicious, suggested that Evans go to London to prove his identity, at which point Evans changed tack and announced he had come to support the Royalist uprising in Kent.

Oddly, this seemed to do the trick – at least for a time. Evans was now treated as a prince of the blood royal and even held court in Sandwich, making good use of the presents brought to him by citizens and city fathers in the hope of profiting should 'Charles' win back the country. In return Evans made them all vague offers of knighthoods and lordships. Meanwhile it was decided to take down a detailed description of the prince and send it to London, just to be sure. The response soon came back that the man they described was fair haired whilst the real Charles had black hair. In other words, he was an impostor. This intelligence had come a little too late as Sandwich was now full of armed sailors, whose numbers were swelled by former members of the prince's staff, prepared to swear blind that Evans was the prince as, even if they knew he wasn't, he was a good enough figurehead for the struggle that lay ahead.

Evans was also clearly taking to the role. When Sir Thomas Dishington arrived in England from Queen Henrietta's household, he was very surprised to find that Charles was allegedly in Sandwich as he had only just left him in Paris. Rushing to the scene, he accused Evans of being an impostor but was waved away by the now thoroughly haughty masquerader, who demanded the mayor clap the man in chains for treason – which for reasons best known to himself the mayor duly did. When Dishington was eventually released, he again challenged Evans to name people in his household (which Evans couldn't do), only to be stoned in the streets for his pains as he tried to leave the town.

The mayor was in a tricky situation. Dishington had proved beyond doubt that Evans was an impostor but he was surrounded by armed men who claimed he was the real deal. Furthermore, Evans seemed to be slowly convincing himself that he *was* the prince.

Events were about to overtake them all. On Tuesday 23 September, when Kentish Royalist troops entered the town, everyone wondered whether they would 'recognise' the prince. The commanders quickly saw through the fraud but offered Evans a coach out of the town, not wanting to offend people who were, in the end, on the same side. Evans refused and barricaded himself in his house, upon which an extraordinary scene ensued.

With Royalist musketeers at the door, trying to gain entry, the man who claimed to be their 'prince' stood at a first-floor window, demanding that the sailors come to his rescue and throwing money into the gathering crowd. Eventually Evans' supporters smuggled him out of the house and across the water to the Isle of Thanet. Here he finally fell into the hands of the Parliamentarians who had demanded his arrest. He was brought to London and placed in Newgate gaol to await his summons before the House of Lords but somehow, perhaps aided by others whom he duped into believing he was indeed the prince, Evans managed to escape. Having written a letter to the real Prince Charles offering his services (which were declined), he disappeared, never to be seen or heard from again.

(The Other) George Eliot

Joseph Liggins' secret was unusual in that it didn't belong to him and he never seems to have claimed definitively that it did. His story begins with the publication, between November 1857 and

January 1858 in *Blackwood's Edinburgh Magazine*, of three stories entitled 'Scenes of Clerical Life'. The stories, set in the Midlands and enlivened by what were clearly personal reminiscences of people and places, were such a hit that soon readers were clamouring to know more about the author, one George Eliot.

What no one other than *Blackwood's* and a few close friends knew was that George Eliot was in fact Mary Ann Evans, who had two good reasons to keep her real identity secret. First, she was a woman in an age when it was extraordinarily difficult for women to be taken seriously by either publishers or readers; and second, and scandalously for the day, she was living with journalist G.H. Lewes even though Lewes was still married to someone else.

Mary Ann's decision to hide her identity did nothing to prevent speculation; indeed, quite the reverse, which is how Joseph Liggins, perhaps initially quite innocently, appeared on the scene. Liggins, who was well educated but impoverished, after a spell teaching on the Isle of Man had settled back into a life of obscurity in his native Warwickshire, which was, by chance, also George Eliot's home county. Eliot's stories had been particularly popular in this area as they described the people and places around Nuneaton in such detail that it was assumed Eliot must be a local. Thus it first dawned on a reviewer in the *Manx Sun*, remembering having met a gentleman from that region who had worked on the island many years earlier, that perhaps he was the author. The claim that Liggins was Eliot first appeared in print in 1857.

Two years later, following the publication of Eliot's first novel, *Adam Bede*, there was a renewed rush to identify the real author as the fame of the novel spread. The *Manx Sun*, further convinced that they were right, rushed into print to claim Liggins as their man.

At this point Liggins could perhaps have refuted the claim, as he had after the first article, but that had merely seemed to reinforce the 'fact' that Eliot must be him. Now it was also revealed by the newspapers that he lived in poverty and so, it was assumed, his publisher had defrauded him of the royalties that so popular a book must obviously have generated. There was an outcry and several rather self-righteous Midlands dignitaries, including vicars and magistrates, denounced *Blackwood's*. A campaign was started in the letters pages of the popular press for Liggins to be acknowledged as George Eliot and given his just reward. A subscription was even started to alleviate the hardships suffered by this much wronged 'author'.

Initially Eliot responded with her own letters to *The Times*, denying categorically that she was Liggins, and her publisher did likewise, but finally she was forced to act. Liggins had still made no attempt to deny he was Eliot. Not surprisingly, he was happy to let fundraisers believe he was the author, and so in June 1859, braving the scandal they feared would follow, Mary Ann Evans and G.H. Lewes revealed Eliot's true identity. Whilst many readers were stunned, the revelations of Eliot's gender and private life didn't damage her book sales at all.

The same could not be said for Joseph Liggins, however. He died, destitute, in the workhouse in May 1872 in Chilvers Coton – the very same village where George Eliot had been baptised Mary Ann Evans fifty-three years earlier.

The Tichborne Claimant

Roger Charles Doughty-Tichborne should have become 11th Baronet Tichborne on the death of his father in 1862. Indeed, he would have done so, were it not for the fact that he was by then himself already dead. Or was he?

Roger's problems had begun when he fell in love with his cousin Katherine Doughty, a match that prompted huge resistance from both sides of the family, not least because of his reputation as a drunk. So in 1852, with the engagement officially 'postponed', he sold his commission in the 6th Dragoons and decided to travel until the furore died down. Leaving a mysterious 'sealed package' with the steward of the Tichborne estate, he took ship for South America where he toured Chile and crossed the Andes. Then, on 20 April 1854, he boarded the ship *Bella* in Rio de Janeiro that was bound for Kingston, Jamaica. But the *Bella* never arrived and Roger Tichborne was never seen again.

Back in England the news of the loss of the ship was met with resignation by everyone except Roger's French mother, Harriette-Felicité, who refused to believe her son had perished. However, when no further news was received and a longboat from the *Bella* was eventually recovered in mid-ocean, Roger was legally declared dead. Then in 1862 his father died, leaving the title and estate to the infant son of his second child – unless Roger could be found alive. Harriette-Felicité was determined to prove the doom-mongers wrong and in 1863 she began placing adverts in newspapers across the world. Two years later she received a reply to one of these, identifying a butcher by the name of Tomas Castro from Wagga Wagga, Australia, as her long-lost son.

It was at one level an unlikely match. Roger when last seen had been slim, although this was admittedly some years ago, whereas Castro was huge (around twenty-seven stone). Roger also spoke fluent French as he'd been brought up in France until the age of sixteen by his mother, while Castro didn't speak a word. However, both Roger and Castro shared the same, rare genital malformation, and this was perhaps enough to convince a desperate Lady Tichborne. She immediately sent money for him to 'return home' to her.

Castro, known ever after as 'the Claimant', told the story that the *Bella* had indeed been lost but that he'd been rescued by the *Osprey*, which was bound for Australia. In Australia he'd decided to put his illustrious past behind him and worked as a cattle rancher, involving a few brushes with the law, and then, after marrying, he had settled down as a butcher in Wagga Wagga. This was the vaguely unbelievable background against which Lady Tichborne finally met her 'son' on 10 January 1867 in a Paris hotel. Nonetheless, the result was extraordinary. She professed to recognise him instantly, much to the dismay of the rest of the family, and immediately settled on him £1,000 a year.

While Harriette-Felicité was alive there was little anyone could do about 'the Claimant' who, she said, was definitely her son, although her death in 1868 cleared the way for the family to take civil legal action. The resulting case lasted for nearly ten months with over 350 witnesses being called, making it at the time one of the longest cases in legal history.

During this sensational case several strange facts began to emerge. The prosecution noted that on his arrival in the UK the Claimant had first gone to Wapping to ask about the Orton family there. Did this peculiar move have anything to do with the fact that a photograph of the Claimant, shown to a former employee in Australia, was identified as Arthur Orton? Or that a former English sweetheart had identified him as Arthur Orton? And when enquiries were made about 'Tomas Castro' in Chile, why was it that no one had mentioned Sir Roger, yet the name of a young sailor, Arthur Orton, had kept coming up?

The Claimant responded that of course he had known Orton because they had worked together. He also suggested that he and Orton had been involved in some criminal activities, which is why Orton had disappeared and could not now be found.

Then there was the matter of the 'sealed packet'. The Claimant said it contained proof that Katherine Doughty was pregnant with Roger's child when he left for Chile and declared that the package had made provision for her confinement. This shameful secret was why the Claimant had not simply returned home. As the package had since been destroyed this was impossible to prove.

The final nail in the Claimant's case came from Lord Bellew who had been at Stonyhurst School with Sir Roger. He claimed that he had tattooed his friend – a tattoo that was obviously missing from the Claimant's body. At that point the Claimant's defence collapsed.

The way was now open for a criminal trial for perjury. The

Claimant was arrested and subjected to another marathon trial that lasted over ten months; indeed, the judge's summing-up alone took a month. At the end of this Arthur Orton, as he was now said to be, was found guilty and given two seven-year sentences of hard labour to run sequentially. His counsel was also disbarred for making hostile comments about the judge.

The court case proved to have ramifications far beyond the Tichborne estate. Many believed the Claimant was indeed Sir Roger, ruthlessly persecuted by the junior branch of his family that had now seized control of the family fortune. Others saw this as a typical case of the establishment protecting its own and demonstrating the impossibility of ordinary men getting justice in the courts. Indeed the Claimant's cause briefly became the largest popular movement in Britain between the death of Chartism and the rise of the Labour Party.

The Claimant himself bided his time and was finally released after ten years and four months, only to find that his wife had abandoned him. Although he tried to make a living touring the musical halls in the UK and the USA, he was eventually reduced to poverty. He died, rather appropriately, on April Fool's Day, 1898. Before his burial in an unmarked grave, in the presence of 5,000 mourners and with the permission of the Tichborne family, a plaque was attached to his coffin that read: 'Sir Roger Charles Doughty-Tichborne', so in death, if not in life, he finally got what he had claimed.

Princess Olive

The world is full of people claiming to be someone they're not, and probably not a few who really are who they claim to be but everyone thinks they're somebody else altogether. Whilst most are labelled mad or just deluded, a few manage to take their imposture so far that even royalty and governments are forced to take note.

Olivia Wilmot was born on 3 April 1772, the daughter of a

Warwick house painter who had had to make a rather sudden move to London following an unfortunate incident of embezzlement. It was in London that the young Olivia got her first taste of royalty when she took drawing lessons from George III's marine painter, John Serres, whom she married in 1791.

The marriage proved turbulent and, eleven years and two children later, the couple separated, he complaining that she had been repeatedly unfaithful and she protesting that he hadn't settled enough money on her. In the years that followed, the very talented Olivia seemed likely to make a success of herself. Her paintings were highly regarded, being exhibited at the Royal Academy and the British Institution. She published a novel, a collection of poems and an opera, as well as becoming landscape painter to the Prince of Wales in 1806. This further brush with royalty seems to have changed Olivia's game plan and, in 1818, she wrote to the prince, claiming to be the illegitimate daughter of George III's brother, the Duke of Cumberland, by a Mrs Payne, the sister of her uncle.

Initially she met with no success. In 1820, by which time her father, her uncle and George III were all conveniently dead, she decided to up the stakes and make a claim to be a legitimate princess. Calling herself Princess Olive of Cumberland, she had the royal arms painted on her coach and hired footmen in royal livery. Her elaborate story, backed up by numerous documents all lovingly crafted by her own highly skilled hands, was that her uncle Dr Wilmot had secretly married Princess Poniatouski, sister of King Stanislaus of Poland, who had borne him a daughter. This daughter was brought up by Mrs Payne (Dr Wilmot's sister) until, as a young woman, this said daughter came to the attention of the Duke of Cumberland who secretly married her in 1767. Their daughter, Princess Olive, had been placed in the care of Robert Wilmot, Dr Wilmot's brother, whose own child was stillborn. The duke had heartlessly disowned the child.

To say this was a little confusing would be an understatement. Nevertheless, many were persuaded by the now officially rechristened Princess Olive's resemblance to the Duke of Cumberland and the large quantity of supporting evidence (usually 'written' by dead peers who couldn't answer back). As the lifestyle of the self-proclaimed princess was expensive, she was arrested for debt in 1821 but had the chutzpah to try to have the proceedings stayed on the grounds that royalty were exempt from civil arrest. She even issued a poster appeal across London, asking for contributions for 'The Princess of Cumberland in Captivity!'

When this failed, she produced what she claimed was the will of George III in which she was left £15,000. To back her claim she petitioned the court to inspect George III's final will, a request that was refused on the grounds that the court had no jurisdiction – further fuelling the conspiracy theories. Indeed, the identity of Princess Olive was believed genuine enough for Sir Gerald Noel MP to petition parliament in her favour.

The royal family were finally goaded into action, producing Olivia's real birth certificate. Sir Robert Peel went into battle on their behalf in parliament, demonstrating that her documents were forgeries, that George III had not created her 'Duchess of Lancaster' (nor given her the income from the Duchy), and that Princess Poniatouski had never been to England, making her one of the few princesses in Europe who definitely could not have had an affair with the Duke of Cumberland. With a finishing flourish, Peel suggested to the House that as her claim to British royalty had failed, she might care to take up her claims to the Polish throne – preferably in Poland.

Princess Olive did not give up her story, however; indeed, she may well have believed it herself by this point. Without supporters now, Olivia continued to press her claim in between bouts in debtors' prison where she died on 21 November 1835. She was buried under the name 'Olive Cumberland' and left one shilling each to her 'cousins' in the royal house of Guelph that they might 'purchase a prayer for to teach them repentance for their past cruelties and injuries to myself, their legitimate and lawful cousin'. Her own daughter later continued the claim, styling herself

Princess Lavinia of Cumberland and petitioning Queen Victoria for recognition. It was never forthcoming.

Petros I

If there is one thing that can be relied upon among Royalty it is that they will give their children very long names. This must have come as something of a disappointment to Peter Mills but might go some way to explaining why he preferred to be called His Imperial Majesty Petros I, Despot and Autokrator of the Romans, the Prince Paleologus.

Peter Francis Mills was born in 1927, the son of Frank and Robena Mills, and it was through his mother, the daughter of a plumber from Niton on the Isle of Wight, that he claimed his unusual title. Peter's mother's maiden name was Colenutt, a local island name that can be traced back to the eighteenth century and also bears a very cursory resemblance to the name Kolonet, a corruption of the name for the old Byzantine province of Koloneia.

It is at this point that some suspension of disbelief is called for. According to Mr Mills, John Laskaris Palaiologos of Kolnet, heir to the Byzantine empire, died at Viterbo in 1558. He is alleged to have married Maria Colneat Phokas, the daughter of Prince Matthew de Kolonet and his wife, who happened to be the daughter of the Khan of the Turkomans of the White Sheep. One of Maria and John's sons was Richard Komnenos Phokas Palaiologos of Kolonet who married Joanna Dauntsey, daughter of Sir Edward Dauntsey, a cousin of Henry VIII of England. Joanna and Richard, so Mr Mills' genealogy would have it, settled at Combley on the Isle of Wight and had a son, William Colenutt, from whom the claim to the imperial Byzantine throne descended to Peter via his mother, also a Colenutt.

This magnificent pedigree was supported by a large selection of documents that for some reason only Mills had seen. As well as repeatedly publishing his antecedents, Mills also took to wearing faux military uniform or long flowing robes and was often to be seen around Newport on the Isle of Wight, searching the record office for more proofs of his claim to greatness. His second wife, known to him as Her Imperial Highness Patricia Palaeologina, Empress of the Romans, also backed his protestations and he even appointed an Imperial Chancellor, who lived in Dunkineely, in Ireland.

Despite his amazing pretensions, Peter Mills never made a serious attempt to regain the Byzantine throne, a crown that had been swept away by the rise of the Ottoman Empire, contenting himself with filling in the gaps on his largely invented family tree. This is not to say that there might not have been blue blood in Petros I's veins – there is a little of it in just about everyone – but as the last Byzantine emperor did categorically die childless and unmarried, the direct line of descent to this now defunct title is undoubtedly moribund.

His Imperial Highness died in 1988 and, in deference to this splendidly eccentric Englishman's secret history, *The Times* printed his obituary, giving Petros I the full titles he had chosen for himself.

3

Secret Loves

Love ceases to be a pleasure, when it ceases to be a secret.

Aphra Behn, *The Lover's Watch* (1686)

The Spirit of Ecstasy

The Spirit of Ecstasy, that little silver statuette that stands on top of the radiator of every Rolls-Royce, is perhaps the most famous image in motoring, but it is also the keeper of a tragic secret.

When Charles Stewart Rolls and Henry Royce first went into business, there was no standard mascot on the bonnets of their cars. The craze had only recently started of putting small objects there, anything from horses to bulldogs: the choice was very much up to the owner. Indeed, it was one of their friends, the great motoring pioneer John, 2nd Lord Montagu of Beaulieu – a founder member of the RAC and very much with his finger on the motoring pulse as the owner of *Car Illustrated* magazine – who suggested that a standard mascot might help strengthen the Rolls-Royce brand.

But what to put on the bonnet? Lord Montagu suggested that a small statuette might be designed by the chief graphic artist for his magazine, Charles Sykes. Montagu had a particular reason for finding Sykes's work inspiring, for the artist had already undertaken a private commission for him – a silver statuette of a young woman in flowing robes with a finger pressed to her lips, known as *The Whisper*.

The model for this had been Montagu's personal assistant, Eleanor Thornton, known to the family as Thorn. She had a passion for motoring, having gone to work whilst still in her teens for Claude Johnson, then secretary of the Automobile Club and later one of the founding fathers of Rolls-Royce. Here she had met Montagu and a passion of a different kind had developed between the two, although it was a love that, in the eyes of society in general, had to remain secret as Lord Montagu was married. In 1903, Eleanor had given birth to a baby girl who was put out to foster parents to avoid a scandal. In the meantime Johnson, Rolls and Royce had gone into business making cars, Montagu opening their purpose-built Derby factory in 1908 and providing ringing endorsements for their vehicles.

It was in 1910 that he suggested Sykes as just the man to create a mascot for Rolls-Royce, and who better as a model for this than the beautiful Thorn? So, from 1911 onwards Lord Montagu's secret love appeared on the bonnet of every Rolls-Royce, christened 'the Spirit of Ecstasy', although those close to Montagu referred to the lithe figure as 'Miss Thornton in her nightie'.

But the story would not end happily for Thorn or her lover. In 1915, with the First World War raging, Lord Montagu was sent out to India to advise the government on mechanical transport, and Thorn was to travel with him as far as Aden. By now Lord Montagu's wife, although aware of the affair, was apparently resigned to it, and she and Thorn exchanged letters planning the voyage.

The lovers embarked on the P&O liner SS *Persia* on Christmas Day, 1915. Five days later, as they were enjoying lunch in the first-class saloon, the ship was rocked by the impact of a torpedo fired from a German U-boat. Moments later the boiler exploded and the ship began to sink. Lord Montagu and Thorn rushed on deck but the nearest lifeboats had been shattered by the blast. They were still in each other's arms when a wall of water overcame them and swept them off the deck. Thanks to the bespoke inflatable jacket that Lord Montagu was wearing, he surfaced, but Thorn did not. She, along with the majority of passengers and crew, was never seen again, going down with the vessel in one of the deepest parts of the Mediterranean.

After convalescing, Lord Montagu returned home, unable to tell the world of his loss, or of the secret identity of the lady who graced the bonnet of his – and, to this day, every other – Rolls-Royce.

The Secret Vicar

It is debatable whether or not Alexander Keith ever was a real vicar. As with so much of his life, there are two schools of thought – his and just about everybody else's. He certainly claimed to have been ordained by the bishop of Norwich and served as a reader at the Rolls Chapel in Chancery Lane before bowling up at St George's Chapel, Hyde Park Corner, in the early 1730s. This past, like the origins of the MA he claimed to possess, is shrouded in mystery.

If Keith was not perhaps an unblemished cleric, he was at least a good businessman. His sermons proved very popular and, more importantly, he ran a flourishing sideline in clandestine marriages. Dubious unions – usually of couples below the age at which parental consent was needed or whose families (or the local vicar) opposed the match – were problematic for the Church. Rogue vicars operating out of independent chapels had a habit of marrying these people, leaving the authorities with little choice but to recognise the union or strike off the vicar.

Not that Keith found this a problem. In prisons, these marriages had always been common, particularly at the Fleet gaol in London where the parsons would marry just about anyone or anything if the price was right. Keith, however, was operating out of fashionable Hanover Square and attracting a whole new class of runaway. He married Shelley's grandfather Bysshe, Lord George Bentinck, the Duke of Chandos and the 6th Duke of Hamilton amongst others, managing to help 723 illicit couples tie the knot in one year alone. All he asked was a one-guinea fee, to include the five shillings' cost of a stamped licence and certificate – no questions asked.

Of course, the authorities were eventually forced to act, in particular the vicar of Hanover Square who was losing a lot of money from all the marriage services he wasn't now conducting. Keith was excommunicated but responded, with considerable chutzpah, by excommunicating the bishop who had excommunicated him. As a result he was sent to the Fleet prison.

Did that put an end to Keith's career? Certainly not. From a very comfortable room in captivity, Keith continued to run his business, getting Fleet parsons to conduct his marriages and having them send him the marriage certificates for signing. He even advertised his 'Little chapel in May fair' in the newspapers.

There was precious little the Church could do. It couldn't have him arrested – he was already in prison. To make matters worse, he seemed to have generated a lot of sympathy. When his wife died and he was refused permission to leave prison for the funeral, he had her embalmed and announced that she would remain unburied until he was released. Nobody is quite sure what actually happened to the body. In the meantime he married at least another 6,000 couples for good measure.

By this time Keith's activities had even reached the ears of the government, thanks to the howls of outraged aristocrats whose sons and daughters had become attached to wholly unsuitable partners through the good vicar's services. The Lord Chancellor decided to act. In 1753 the Marriage Act was passed, by which only officially endorsed Church marriages, for which banns had been read, were legally binding – and threatening fourteen years' transportation for clerics who ignored it. On the day before the Act came into force in 1754, Keith married sixty-one couples in a final flourish. That, however, put an end to his spree.

Still in prison and having spent most of the money he'd received for all those nuptials, he was reduced to writing angry pamphlets opposing the Marriage Act, claiming rather boldly in one that 'hasty and precipitant marriage . . . is the very foundation of our present happiness and prosperity'. He remained in the Fleet for the rest of his life.

The Other Grey Girl

The story of the rise and tragic fall of Lady Jane Grey and her few days as putative queen of England is hardly a secret, but the story of how her younger sister nearly became queen is far less well known, although it might have changed the history of both England and Scotland at a stroke.

Katherine Grey had survived the plot to put her sister on the throne surprisingly well. The same day that Jane was married to Guildford Dudley as part of Suffolk's plan to put her on the throne and himself in the driving seat, Katherine was married (or perhaps just betrothed) to the son of his ally, William Herbert, 1st Earl of Pembroke. Following the accession of Mary and the triple executions of Guildford, Jane and her father, Katherine's attachment was simply dissolved and she was welcomed, at least cautiously, into the court of Queen Mary.

When Elizabeth came to the throne in 1558, Katherine's prospects looked better still. What had always created a maelstrom of interest around the Grey girls was their royal blood. Katherine was a granddaughter of Mary Tudor (the younger sister of Henry VIII) and hence the great-granddaughter of Henry VII, giving her a good claim to the throne. Furthermore, after the death of her mother in November 1559 she became heir presumptive to the throne under the terms of Henry VIII's will – making her the next in line should Elizabeth have no children.

If it was a time of opportunity, it was also one of danger. Whilst Elizabeth might well be entertaining the idea of Katherine as her Tudor heir, keeping her dynasty on the throne, the Grey girl was also a potential threat. Foreign princes began circling Katherine and marriages into the royal houses of Spain and Scotland were suggested. Katherine would have to tread carefully and, most importantly, keep on the very best terms with Elizabeth, to ensure her own survival as well as her potential accession. Yet this is exactly what she failed to do.

What drove a wedge between Katherine and Elizabeth was Edward Seymour, Earl of Hertford. Katherine and Edward, it seems, were in love. Katherine's mother, who heartily approved of the match, had had no time to promote it at court before her death. This left Katherine in a tricky situation. Elizabeth was loath to give her permission for her ladies to marry, particularly a woman of the blood royal, but failing to ask her was treason under the terms of the 1536 Act of Parliament.

However, this is precisely what Katherine did. Some time in November 1560, at Hertford House on Canon Row in London, Katherine and Edward were secretly married. The following spring

Edward, then twenty-one, was sent abroad to finish his education, leaving Katherine alone and, by this time, pregnant. It placed her in a desperate position. Eventually the pregnancy would show and the secret would be out. She either had to find a way to leave court and have the baby secretly or persuade Elizabeth to forgive her for her secret marriage.

In her anguish she turned to two of Elizabeth's closest friends for advice: Lord Robert Dudley and Elizabeth St Loe. It was a poorly judged move. Dudley – horrified to hear of the betrayal of the Queen and fearful of being considered an accomplice in what might look like a plot against her – immediately went to Elizabeth and told her. The Queen was furious and believed the worst, it not being the first time that Grey marriages had been used in an attempt on the throne.

Katherine was sent to the Tower and Edward summoned from Paris. Both were heavily interrogated and a search was made for the priest who had married them (although he was never found). In September 1561, still in the Tower, Katherine gave birth to her son Edward. The following January an ecclesiastical commission, headed by the archbishop of Canterbury, unable to find any witness to the marriage, declared that it had never taken place and hence the child was illegitimate. Katherine and Edward were to be kept, separately, in the Tower at the Queen's pleasure. Despite this, Edward somehow managed to visit his wife, probably with the connivance of the Lieutenant of the Tower who felt sorry for the young couple, making Katherine pregnant once more, further infuriating Elizabeth.

Indeed, Elizabeth would never again allow Katherine her freedom; from then on, she and her husband came no closer to one another than an exchange of letters. Removed from London during the plague and kept under close house arrest, Katherine continued to petition for a pardon, growing worryingly thin and suicidal, but none came. In London debates still raged about the succession and until these were settled there was no question of Elizabeth setting free a potential heir who had already shown her willingness to disobey her sovereign.

Katherine, the girl who might one day have been queen, died on 27 January 1568, probably from anorexia, and with her died a whole alternative history for England. She was twenty-seven years old. Her husband Edward went on to contract a further two secret marriages.

Find the Lady

It would probably be fair to say that the Earl and Lady Berkeley found their daughter Henrietta a bit of a handful – that's if they could find her at all. The earl's problems began with the marriage of his elder daughter Mary to Ford Grey, Lord Grey of Warke. Lord Grey loved the Berkeleys, so much so that as well as marrying one of them, he also began an affair with the then underage Henrietta, which lasted some fourteen months before her mother found out.

Lady Berkeley was a firm and practical woman and, having forbidden the lovers from meeting again, moved Henrietta and the rest of the family out of London to their Surrey home at Durdans, where no more would be said about it. If Lady Berkeley hoped that a few months in the country would clear the air, she was gravely mistaken. With the Berkeleys came Mary and she, not surprisingly, invited her husband. This put Lady Berkeley in a spot as she had kept the whole affair secret from two people: Lord Berkeley (who might be expected to get rather angry with his son-in-law) and Mary (who might perhaps feel a little betrayed by her new husband). However, with little room for manoeuvre she agreed to Lord Grey coming to the house.

Lady Berkeley did at least have a plan. For the next few days she harangued Lord Grey at every private opportunity, making his stay a misery and finally persuading him to leave. Rather more unexpectedly, Henrietta also fled that same night, aided by two of Lord Grey's staff, and went into hiding. The cat was now out of the bag. Lord Berkeley offered £200 for the return of his daughter who, he announced, was to be sent to a French nunnery.

He also bumped into Lord Grey who admitted he knew where Henrietta was, but refused to say where. Thus the earl was forced to bring one of the more titillating legal cases of the seventeenth century, accusing Lord Grey of the 'unlawful tempting and Inticing' of Henrietta 'to unlawful love . . . with the intent to cause her to live in a scandalous manner'.

At this point Henrietta herself popped up at the trial, clearly intent on maintaining her scandalous manner, although her evidence was dismissed by the judge as unreliable. As the court was breaking up, Earl Berkeley took the opportunity to try to seize his daughter. A fight broke out when she shouted that she was now married to one of Grey's servants. For her own safety she had to be taken to the King's Bench prison. After three days, in which rumour had it she had slept with said servant, she was released.

Despite Grey and his accomplices being found guilty, no punishment was handed down. He and Henrietta continued to live scandalously until he was implicated in the Rye House plot of June 1683 to assassinate King Charles II and his brother James (later James II). Fortunately Grey had got rather good at slipping away and he managed to escape from the Tower of London before fleeing with his lover to a life of exile in the Netherlands.

Lord Grey returned to England, probably with Henrietta, during the Monmouth rebellion, in which he took a less than creditable part, being charged again with high treason and escaping death only by betraying his former friends. Henrietta outlived him by five years, dying at Tonbridge in Kent in 1706.

Arthur Munby's Secret Wife

It is generally agreed that Arthur Munby was a very ordinary chap. On the surface he was a perfectly normal Victorian civil servant and part-time poet, but his diary reveals a very particular interest. Arthur Munby liked to watch and document the lives of Britain's poorest women – the serving classes whose days were filled with hard manual toil. It is, to say the least, uncertain just what he got from this hobby, which he meticulously recorded in his diary and photographic collection. The chief thing is that it brought him into contact with Hannah Cullwick.

Munby often walked the streets of London interviewing working women and that day in 1854, Hannah's twenty-first birthday, was simply another of those. She was one of the 'unbecoming women', as they were known, a maid-of-all-work whose hands and clothes were ingrained with grime from a hard life of physical labour. However, Hannah was different, for, just as he had a fascination with working-class women rather than his own middle-class peers, so she professed a desire to serve middle-class men rather than marry someone of her own background. The two began to meet and Hannah was inspired, perhaps at Munby's behest, to start writing her own diary – a near unique account of the life of a Victorian domestic servant. For nineteen years the two kept in touch until finally, in 1873, they were married.

It was certainly a love match and should therefore have been a very happy one but as Munby, a respected civil servant, was marrying far below his station he insisted the marriage was initially kept quiet. He hoped that, in time, his new wife would slowly 'rise in society' to become the polite middle-class spouse expected for a man in his position. In this he was very much mistaken. Despite the apparent advantages of a genteel existence, free from manual labour, Hannah refused to give up her role as a working woman and became increasingly angry with her husband's refusal to admit to their marriage in public.

The result was an extraordinary household in which the lodgers Munby took in believed they were living with a single man and were looked after by an unusually servile and grimy maid. Indeed, several tenants made passes at Hannah in front of Munby, assuming that this well-bred, middle-class gentleman would be oblivious to what they got up to with a servant. No one ever suspected that the neat civil servant and lowly menial were actually man and wife.

This unusual set-up was not without its strains and after four years the couple separated, Hannah returning to her native Shropshire, apparently with a drink problem. Munby continued to provide for her and the two remained close for the remainder of their lives. They died apart, in 1909 and 1910 respectively, their marriage still an absolute secret.

England's Gretna Green

Runaway marriages will always be associated with Gretna Green on the Scottish borders, a place where couples who could not get parental approval, were too young or for some other reason did not want the banns of their marriage read, might go and secretly be wed. England too once had such a place although it is now almost completely forgotten.

In the Peak District National Park, between Tideswell and Chapel-en-le-Frith, stands the churchyard of Peak Forest and in it the remains of a small chapel. It had originally been privately built on the orders of Christian (sometimes given as Christiana), Countess of Devonshire, who had handed it on to the local minister, making it 'extra-parochial', that is, outside the normal jurisdiction of the Church. As a result the vicar was issued with a seal of office, allowing him to approve wills and issue marriage licences without recourse to anyone else.

Needless to say, this ability to grant what were known as 'foreign marriages' proved a nice little earner and news soon spread amongst runaways looking for a 'quickie' wedding. By 1754 at least two marriages a week were taking place in the tiny village, making the vicar a handsome additional profit of over £100 a year.

Not every story had a happy ending. A local legend tells of one wealthy runaway couple from Scotland, known simply as 'Allan and Clara', who stopped at an inn at Castleton on their way to the chapel in 1758. Here Clara's wealth was spotted by some dastardly local miners who robbed them in Winnat's Pass. Four days later their horses were found wandering and a full ten years passed before their bodies were found down a mine shaft.

As in all good legends, divine retribution plays a major role. Although none of the miners was ever brought to justice for the crime, none of them got away with it scot-free either. One bought horses with his share of the money but they promptly dropped dead; another was tormented all his life by guilt and confessed on his deathbed; one hanged himself; one went mad; one was killed by a stray stone near the crime scene; and another suddenly died when passing the spot. This tied things up nicely.

Nor was there a very happy ending for the vicar of Peak Forest chapel. Whilst the ability to grant marriages ad hoc merely annoyed the Church, it was the government that was vexed by his ability to prove wills and hence falsify the value of the deceased's estate to avoid tax. Whilst an illicit marriage might be inconvenient, it was just a family matter; tax evasion was far more serious. In 1804 an Act of Parliament was passed, specifically revoking his special privileges. Without its runaway brides and thrifty heirs, the chapel fell to ruin and Peak Forest's romantic place in British history slipped into oblivion.

Thomas Cranmer's Hidden Love

Thomas Cranmer, the great architect of the English Reformation, became archbishop of Canterbury at a time when many of the mediaeval requirements of priests remained unchanged. Although much of the ancient Church would soon be dismantled in England by Cranmer's boss, Henry VIII, the King clung doggedly to the ban on clerical marriage. After all, he had no desire to allow his priests to form their own wealthy dynasties, having himself been made rich and powerful by the Dissolution of the Monasteries and the rich pickings still to be had in the clerical arena. So it is all the more extraordinary that the man who engineered this sea change in English religious life, Henry's chief priest, was himself secretly married.

Of course it was hardly unheard of for priests to have affairs, but whilst the taking of a mistress was an ultimately deniable foible – leading to nothing more damaging than perhaps some illegitimate children, who might be hidden or disowned – marriage was simply out of the question. Yet when Cranmer visited Nuremberg in 1532 to win support for his master's divorce, he fell in love with the niece of a leading Lutheran preacher and decided to marry her. For the Lutherans this was perfectly reasonable – Luther had himself been a priest and had married a former nun; for Cranmer, however, it was potentially fatal.

After a brief courtship and marriage, Cranmer was summoned home to become archbishop of Canterbury, but dared not take with him his new wife Margarete or their daughter. Just where Margarete was in these years remains something of a mystery. The Elizabethans told tall tales of Cranmer carrying around a large trunk with holes drilled in it, in which he hid his family, although this seems frankly ludicrous. More likely, Margarete, their daughter Margaret and any other children were smuggled into England and protected in the homes of Cranmer's friends.

The situation was about to get far more dangerous still. Under the old Church laws, only those priests who openly married could be prosecuted, so as Cranmer's marriage was secret he might have believed himself safe. This was changed by the Act of Six Articles, passed on 5 June 1539, which declared that any married priest became a felon, subject to the full weight of the law, unless he admitted his mistake and divorced immediately. Fearing discovery, Margarete and her children were spirited back to Germany before the new edict came into full force. Nevertheless, somehow information about the marriage had leaked and when Henry VIII teased Cranmer about why he had opposed the introduction of the Six Articles, he was forced to confess to his secret marriage. This bold gambit paid off. Pleased with Cranmer's honesty, Henry let the matter pass and Margarete was brought back to England.

It was only following the accession of Edward VI, and the profoundly Protestant regime that it ushered in, that Cranmer recognised his wife in public. The archbishop also now had a son and, finally free to admit this, could begin planning for his family's long-term future. At least, he would have done, had not Edward suddenly died and the Catholic Mary taken the throne. Charged with treason following the plot to make Lady Jane Grey queen, Cranmer was convicted and condemned to death, before being tried again as a heretic for his part in the dismantling of the Catholic Church in England. On 21 March 1556 he was burnt at the stake in Oxford.

But where was Margarete? No contact between Cranmer and his wife is known from his last days, perhaps because he wished to protect her. She stayed in England for a period after her husband's death, then fled to Europe with her son and remarried. After Elizabeth's I's accession in 1558 she returned to England and fragmentary records show she married again, although this time to a man who treated her very badly. She died eleven years later.

Perhaps her best memorial lies not in records of marriages and deaths but in one other document. In 1549, Cranmer was rewriting the marriage service for the Book of Common Prayer when he came to the section on the reasons for marriage, then given rather baldly as for 'the avoidance of sin and the production of children'. To this he added a new reason, in which we perhaps hear Margarete's words, or at least feel her influence, when he writes that marriage was for 'the mutuall societie, helpe and coumfort, that the one oughte to have of thither, both in prosperitie and adversitie' – a tender addition to every public church marriage since, forged in a secret one.

The Naughty Nuns of Higham

Mediaeval nunneries were supposed to be places where women dedicated themselves to God to the exclusion of all other worldly considerations, but not every nun went into the business for the right reasons. Behind some convent doors lay secrets that might make the most liberal patron blush. Nunneries were of course by their nature closed-off and secretive places, so it was not always easy to find out what was happening behind their firmly closed doors. Occasionally, however, an investigation would bring to light some startling truths. One of the more famous was commissioned by the bishop of Rochester in 1513.

Lillechurch priory at Higham in Kent, then under the bishop's care, had been founded by the daughter of King Stephen in 1148. Its nuns quickly established themselves as successful and pious local businesswomen. In 1205 they bought another, larger manor and began moving their foundation there, enlarging and decorating the church. They then successfully petitioned King Henry III to grant them the right to hold a market and took control of the local ferry service across the Thames. To help fund this continued growth, in 1357 they were granted the right to sell a Papal Indulgence, offering forgiveness of sins in return for a series of regular donations to the nunnery over a three-year period – a thoughtful way of letting locals pay for their salvation in instalments.

Perhaps it was this interest in business rather than prayer that began to lead the sisters of Higham somewhat astray. By the time they started a protracted legal dispute with the people of Gravesend over the right to ferry goods across the Thames, rumours were rife that things behind the convent walls were a little 'unusual'.

When these whisperings reached the ears of the bishop of Rochester, who was responsible for the religious foundation, he decided to investigate and in 1513 set out to pay the nuns a surprise visit. Frankly, it was he who was in for a surprise. From speaking to the villagers of Higham he discovered that the revenues of the nunnery were in a dire state, perhaps due to the fact that there were now only three nuns in residence. Not that they could really be considered nuns in any normal sense, nor were they that easy to find. As one of the original depositions states: 'The same priory was situated in a corner out of sight of the public and was much frequented by lewd persons, especially clerks, whereby the nuns there were notorious for the incontinence of their life.'

Worse than that, two of them had given birth to children – both fathered by one Edward Sterope, none other than the vicar of Higham. The bemused bishop was gently introduced to the fact that the Lillechurch nuns, all three of them, were now more famous for 'entertaining' men in holy orders than for piety or even business. At best, Lillechurch was a free-living and free-loving community. At worst, it was simply a brothel. Clearly the order needed 'reforming' but the nuns, who rather enjoyed their lifestyle, proved resistant.

In 1522 the exasperated bishop pre-empted Henry VIII's Dissolution of the Monasteries by suppressing the house and transferring its possessions to the newly founded St John's College, Cambridge.

4

Secret Histories

You would play upon me; you would seem to know my stops; you would pluck out the heart of my mystery; you would sound me from my lowest note to the top of my compass.

William Shakespeare, *Hamlet* (c.1601)

The Fairy Flag of Dunvegan

Whilst there is, to be honest, very little hard evidence for the presence of fairies in Britain, at Dunvegan Castle on Skye is a relic whose supposed fairy origins have, it is said, protected a clan for a thousand years and whose true, secret history may be just as remarkable as the legend.

The fragment of tattered yellow silk known as the Fairy Flag of Dunvegan was said to have been given to the clan MacLeod by the wife of the fourth chief of that clan, Iain. He, as legend has it, was lucky enough to marry the daughter of the fairy king. When the couple returned to this mortal realm after their nuptials to rule the clan, it was only on the understanding that after seven years she would have to return to her own world.

Of course time flew by; when the seven years were up she tearfully bade goodbye to her husband and the baby she had just borne. As the couple parted on the fairy bridge she asked Iain to promise that the child would never be left alone, as the one thing she would be unable to bear was to hear it cry. That night there was a great feast to take the clan chief's mind off a rather depressing day and, being a man, he completely forgot about his promise. So too did the nurse sent to tend the baby, as she had sneaked out of the nursery to hear the singing and pipe playing in the hall.

The lonely baby had duly cried and when Iain spotted the nurse in the hall he suddenly remembered his vow and dashed to the nursery. He was just in time to glimpse his wife who, having heard the cries, was rocking the baby back to sleep and singing what is now known as the Dunvegan lullaby. The moment he entered the room she vanished for ever but on the baby's cot she left a silken blanket.

This fairy flag was said to be able to protect the clan from danger when waved but could be invoked only three times, on the last of which both the flag and its bearer would disappear. Since then the flag has been waved twice but, not surprisingly, no one is too keen to wave it again, although Dame Flora MacLeod of

MacLeod valiantly offered to wave it over the white cliffs of Dover during the Second World War, should an invasion seem imminent. MacLeod pilots in the war were also given fragments of the flag (or pictures of it) to carry with them for protection.

Although all this may seem a shade fanciful, the flag is undoubtedly a mystery. Made of yellow silk spotted with red, it appears to be of Mediterranean origin and is around a thousand years old. One suggestion is that this is the flag known as 'land-waster', once owned by Harald Hardrada, who was defeated by Harold II at Stamford Bridge in 1066, shortly before the Norman invasion. He picked up this 'magical' flag when captain of the Varangian guard in Byzantium and, according to Snorri Sturluson's saga *Heimskringla*, flew it in the battle. Such magical 'raven banners' were often used by Viking warlords, not least against Alfred the Great whose forces are recorded capturing just such a talisman, although in 1066 it seems to have malfunctioned and Hardrada was killed.

Passing to Godred Crovan, later king of the Isle of Man, it may possibly have come down to the MacLeods. That certainly is the view of eminent Scottish historian Sir Iain Moncreiffe. So the fairy flag may have more bloody origins, not as an elfin cot blanket but as a war banner.

Perhaps the last word on the subject should be given to a MacLeod. When Sir Reginald MacLeod had the flag inspected by the Victoria and Albert Museum and was told it might well be the remains of 'land-waster', he politely thanked the curators for their opinion but pointed out that he had it directly from family sources that the flag had been given to them by the fairies.

Testing Mother

It was towards the end of January 1916 that the code word 'puddle-duck' reached the 3rd (Mid Herts) Battalion of the Hertfordshire Volunteer Regiment. On receiving it, they proceeded, as ordered, to Hatfield House where, sworn to secrecy, they joined a naval detachment in the unusual task of digging up the Marquess of Salisbury's private golf course.

No one in the 3rd Battalion or, indeed, the naval detachment had been given much clue as to why they should, in the midst of war, be set to vandalising a sports ground but vandalise it they did, and with great gusto. The small stream that ran across the site was dammed, turning the low-lying areas into a quagmire of thick yellow clay. To either side of this, trench systems were dug, as near as possible to the exact proportions of those then in use by the British and German armies in France. It was hard work in the cold grounds of Hatfield park and to keep their spirits up a band had been brought in, playing rousing tunes like 'Now We Shan't Be Long'. Friends and families of the diggers, watching from the sidelines, had also come to provide some moral support, much to the bemusement of the sentries who had been posted around the 'secret' site.

When the digging was finally finished some last-minute decorations were added to the scene. Barbed-wire entanglements were strung across the 'front' and tree trunks strewn across the marshy lowlands. For the pièce de résistance, one of the officers in charge had, after a long weekend driving around Middlesex and Hertfordshire, managed to find a detachment of Royal Engineers, equipped with explosives, who could pockmark the site with authentic craters in which the texture of the soil would be 'just right'.

Naturally enough, questions were asked as to the purpose of all this. A home counties golf course seemed an unusual place to be setting up a new front, so clearly something was to be tested. Accordingly, a rumour was deliberately put about that the huge tarpaulin-covered machine that stood on the hill overlooking proceedings was a motorised water pump, allowing the diggers to believe they were involved in some sort of drainage exercise. They decided to call the machine 'Big Willie'.

The truth was first revealed – although not to the diggers, who had by then been sent home – on 29 January when the covers came off Her Majesty's Landship Centipede, known to its creators as 'Mother' and known to all succeeding generations as the world's first tank. What the volunteers had laboured so hard on was an assault course designed to prove to the military that the tank was an invention that would change the nature of war. After its preliminary canter that day, the course was re-dressed for the official trial on Wednesday 2 February. There was great nervousness that morning amongst the creators and backers of Mother. If she failed or broke down, the army might walk away – first impressions were everything. Soon the dignitaries began arriving: Lord Kitchener, Balfour, Lloyd George, members of the Admiralty, the War Office and GHQ. The signal was given and Mother lurched from her lair, tearing across the trenches, oblivious to barbed wire and unhindered by craters.

It was a perfect performance and the onlookers were delighted, with a single exception. Lord Kitchener, who had already paid a surprise visit to see Mother that morning, had announced that Mother was no more than 'a pretty mechanical toy'. He now opined that on a battlefield the machine would immediately be knocked out by enemy artillery. Fortunately, as the other dignitaries watched Mother motor easily across the Hatfield no man's land, Kitchener's voice was drowned out by their enthusiasm. Ten days later the Army Council placed an order for 100 tanks and a new era in warfare began.

Peggy's Last Berth

Old country houses hide many secrets although perhaps not as many as episodes of *Scooby Doo* would have us believe. Yet there can be few larger or more surprising finds than the one made at Bridge House on the banks of Castletown Harbour, Isle of Man, in 1935.

Bridge House had been the home in the late eighteenth century of George Quayle, a very distinguished Manx statesman who had been a member of the House of Keys for fifty-one years. Quayle was also very rich, partly thanks to his role in founding the island's first bank but also through less 'conventional' methods, for George Quayle was a smuggler.

Fortunately for George, the requirements of a banker and a smuggler are not dissimilar. Strongrooms and concealed stairways are a must, as the house was also the bank's headquarters. He needed in addition the trappings of wealthy respectability that would ensure people trusted his bank – such as a yacht. In 1789 the Quayle family ordered the construction of the *Peggy*, a schooner-rigged, clinker-built yacht, 26 feet 5 inches in overall length and 7 feet 8 inches in the beam. However, *Peggy* was to be more than just a rich man's plaything; *Peggy* was a working vessel for George's 'other' business.

Nevertheless, *Peggy* was not herself a secret vessel. In 1793 she received an Admiralty licence to pass freely in British ports, which included permission to carry six small swivel guns and six fowling pieces. Her arming was very necessary as Britain was then at war with revolutionary France, and the waters of the Irish Sea were prowled by French privateers. She was also widely exhibited, on one occasion being sailed to mainland Britain and then hauled overland to Lake Windermere to take part in a regatta where her speed and handling (thanks to her revolutionary 'drop keels') were greatly admired.

Of course, if you are in the smuggling game, having a fast, very seaworthy vessel, with drop keels that could be lifted when in shallow creeks and landing places, and armed not only with the six swivel guns of her licence but with eight cannon (three on each side and two sternchasers), proved rather useful. As did her boathouse – an impressive three-storey affair in the grounds of Bridge House from whose boat cellar the *Peggy* could slip out and return little noticed.

The *Peggy*'s greatest secret, her greatest smuggling triumph, is that she smuggled herself from the eighteenth century into the modern world. *Peggy* had originally been named after George Quayle's mother and, shortly after she died, George locked his yacht away, perhaps unhappy with the association between her name and his yacht's nefarious sideline. As the Quayle family's legitimate business prospered, so associations with their smuggling past needed to be hidden. *Peggy* was placed in her boat cellar and its doorway bricked up. The dock beyond, where she had landed so many not entirely legal cargoes, was dried out and turned into a courtyard.

So *Peggy* lay in her boathouse forgotten, or at least unspoken of by the family, until 1935 when, 146 years after she was built and 120 years since she had last been seen, the last Quayle owner of Bridge House was replacing rotten floorboards in the room above where she slept. Shining a light down into the unexpected void beneath the rafters, he saw an amazing sight, a concealed smugglers' den complete with a perfectly preserved, eighteenth-century yacht.

The *Peggy* remains there to this day, a unique survivor from a lost age, whose secret home is now a part of the Manx Nautical Museum.

The Mystery Towers

In June 1918 a detachment of Royal Engineers, all sworn to the utmost secrecy, arrived at Southward Green in Sussex and started building a camp to house the staff for a mysterious project. Not long after, the locals of Shoreham became aware that a huge construction project lay on their doorstep as two gargantuan concrete and steel towers began to rise from the harbourside, laboured on by over 3,000 men, mainly at night.

It being wartime, the nature of the towers was of course secret but their presence could hardly be hidden. Each stood on a hollow concrete base 80 feet thick and the steel column that emerged, 40 feet wide and 90 feet high, was surrounded by a lattice of steel-work. By the autumn of 1918 the enormous structures were visible from as far away as Beachy Head and were known as the 'Shoreham Mystery Towers', prompting speculation in the press as far afield as New York as to their exact purpose.

Back in London, the Admiralty, naturally enough, knew the purpose of the mystery towers but there was still a great deal of speculation even there. The structures were costing over £1 million each (or, using average earnings for comparison, £172 million in modern terms) and eight (some sources say twelve and one sixteen) of them were planned. There was some doubt that the rest could even be afforded.

But what were they for? 'Project M-N', as it was known, had been initiated by Sir Alexander Gibb who was then engineer-in-chief to the Admiralty. With Major John Reith (later Lord Reith, first Director General of the BBC) as his assistant, he had planned to counter the menace of German U-boats in the most dramatic way possible. A chain of twelve huge towers would be placed across the English Channel from Dungeness to Cap Gris Nez, each linked to the next by steel anti-submarine nets, effectively closing off the whole of the world's busiest seaway to U-boats. Furthermore each tower would have a steel superstructure containing gun emplacements and with room for 100 troops to man each lonely outpost. Any U-boat foolish enough to try to enter the Channel would get caught in the nets and be either sunk there or disposed of by the tower crews.

It was undoubtedly one of the most ambitious engineering plans of the war but it was a plan too late. On 11 November 1918, with Tower no. 1 just nearing completion, the war ended and the behemoths became redundant overnight. Tower no. 2 was eventually broken up for scrap in 1924, a task that took nine months – longer than it had taken to build the giant – although surprisingly Tower no. 1 is still visible today because a new use was found for it.

On Sunday 12 September 1920, the 30,000-ton structure was towed out of Shoreham harbour by Admiralty tugs, only just clearing the harbour walls. After a journey of 41 miles, by the Nab Rock, off Bembridge on the Isle of Wight, the tower was tethered and the seacocks in its hollow base opened. Slowly the tower began to sink, coming to rest on a sandbank at a jaunty angle of three degrees from vertical. The new Nab Tower light-house was now in place and its crew of four could begin their first watch on the replacement for the old Nab Rock lightship. Today, now solar powered and unmanned, Tower no. 1 still serves as the Nab light as well as a reminder of what was once the Admiralty's greatest secret.

The Nithsdale Cloak

The story of how Winifred, Countess of Nithsdale, secretly spirited her husband away from the Tower of London is a tale that reflects as well on her as it does badly on the Tower guards.

William Maxwell, 5th Earl of Nithsdale, was an unobtrusive Catholic who generally managed to keep to himself both his religion and his support for the exiled Stuart king James II. In this way he held on to his lands and title in Lowland Scotland after the Glorious Revolution of 1688, which saw James deposed and William of Orange take the throne.

He had met his wife, also a devout Catholic, whilst paying a visit to James II's court in exile at St Germain-en-Laye in France, where her parents were prominent courtiers. The two were soon married and, despite their known sympathies, they returned to Scotland where they might have continued to live peacefully, had it not been for the outbreak of the Jacobite Rebellion of 1715. After initially dithering, Lord Nithsdale, who had always preferred a quiet life, finally threw in his lot with the Jacobites, supporting the son of the exiled James II, James Stuart (known in England as 'the Old Pretender'), in his bid to reclaim the throne. However, after initial successes, the Jacobite forces were surrounded at the battle of Preston and Nithsdale was taken prisoner.

In London, Nithsdale and the other Jacobite prisoners were impeached and tried for treason. Without a leg to stand on, Nithsdale pleaded guilty but begged the King, by then George I, for a pardon, rather unheroically claiming that the other prisoners with whom he stood trial had forced him into it. Not surprisingly,

George I refused and Nithsdale was sent to the Tower to await the execution of the sentence that had been passed on him, of hanging, drawing and quartering.

Fortunately Lady Nithsdale was made of sterner stuff than her husband and when she heard of his plight she instantly took a carriage south. At York she found even the post carriages were not running due to snow but, unwilling to wait, she instead rode to London on horseback. In the city she immediately set about starting a propaganda campaign to get her husband released, asking many of the lords to petition the King in her favour. George I for his part was not amused, refusing either to entertain the petition or to see Lady Nithsdale.

By 22 February 1716, Lady Nithsdale's situation was desperate. Despite petitions to parliament and the court, the King remained unrelenting, which isn't really all that surprising, considering that the man in question was a self-confessed traitor and a Catholic. With the following day set for the execution, Lady Nithsdale's only hope now lay in breaking her husband out of the Tower.

That evening she persuaded her maid Cecilia Evans and two friends, Mrs Morgan and Mrs Mills, to accompany her to the prison for a last visit, railroading them into helping her in her plan on the carriage journey there. Once inside, she arranged an elaborate 'bedroom farce' with maids and ladies coming and going from the condemned man's cell with such regularity, accompanied by a barrage of tearful sorrow and heartfelt pleas, that the guards became too confused to work out what was happening and who was where.

Amid the commotion, Lady Nithsdale had smuggled a spare cloak and some make-up into her husband's room to disguise him as one of the visiting ladies. Despite his still having a beard, she wrapped him in the voluminous cloak and then smuggled him past the guards, who by this time weren't sure who was in the room and who wasn't, before returning to the cell and holding a long conversation with herself to make it appear that she was talking to her husband. When she was sure her husband would be clear of the fortress, she left the cell and told the guards that her husband was praying and shouldn't be disturbed. Feeling rather sorry for the poor woman who had, after all, bought them all a few drinks the previous day, they agreed.

The couple were reunited in a small cottage just opposite the guardhouse where they enjoyed a bottle of wine and a loaf of bread before Lord Nithsdale was taken to the Venetian embassy. Here he was hidden for a few days and then, dressed in Venetian livery, taken to Dover where a boat was procured to take him to France. Lady Nithsdale meanwhile managed to avoid the search parties in London and made her way back to Scotland to secure the family estates and put them in good order before joining her husband in exile on the continent. She died in Rome, thirty-three years later.

The Nithsdale cloak, now sometimes said to have magical powers of concealment, remains in the family's possession to this day.

London's Nazi Memorial

Whilst it is not surprising that there aren't many Nazi memorials in London, there is one, albeit a small and perhaps a reluctant one. Number 9, Carlton House Terrace, now occupied by the Royal Society, was the home of the Prussian legation from 1849 onwards and became the German embassy following German unification in 1871.

By 1932 when the new ambassador Dr Leopold von Hoesch arrived with his Alsatian dog Giro, it was the embassy of the Weimar Republic. Only a year later, with the rise to power of Adolf Hitler, it changed again to become the embassy of the Third Reich. Despite the sudden change of boss and the continual change of his office's name, Leopold von Hoesch managed to keep his job, although his criticism of Hitler might have cut his career short, had not fate intervened when he died at the age of just fifty-five in 1936. This, however, was not before another small tragedy had struck.

In 1934, Hoesch's dog Giro, for reasons unknown, decided to chew on a high-tension electricity cable in the embassy, with predictably tragic results. The grief-stricken Hoesch insisted that the dog should have a proper send-off and so Giro was given a full Nazi burial. Today the small tombstone erected over the animal's grave in that far-off, pre-war year remains remarkably intact, despite later extensive bombing of the area by the Luftwaffe. Its German inscription simply reads 'Giro: Ein Treuer Begleiter' (Giro: A True Companion).

The Lost Church of St Lawrence

During the early 1850s, Canon Jones, vicar of Holy Trinity church, Bradford on Avon, was invited to inspect two stone angels that had been found buried in the walls of a small schoolhouse during work to install a chimney flue. Canon Jones was very much a clergyman of his day, with a keen interest in Church history, and he couldn't help noticing that the clearly ancient carvings bore an unmistakable likeness to images he'd seen in ninth- and tenth-century manuscripts.

Jones was, needless to say, delighted to have found two very rare Anglo-Saxon carvings used, no doubt, in the walls of a later structure. He thought little more of this until he was invited to examine the remains of a chapel on a hill high over the town, prior to a meeting of the Wiltshire Archaeological Society. The chapel was interesting enough but not as interesting as the view Jones enjoyed from this vantage point. In particular his eye was drawn to a tumbling mass of buildings around the schoolhouse where the statues had been found. The area had obviously seen a lot of building over the centuries, with one structure leaning up against its neighbour, but what was most unusual was three lines of roof, all higher than the rest, which looked, to a vicar like Jones, remarkably similar to the nave and chancel of a church.

His companion on that day dismissed the idea as the churches of Bradford were well known and even the ruined chapels, like the one they had been inspecting, had all been located. Still fascinated, Jones examined the site to find not only a school but a private cottage of three storeys, both built in a very unusual way, consisting of massive stone walls into which floors and ceilings (and chimneys) had evidently been inserted later. Here was at least a part of a very old, probably mediaeval building, although he could not date the structure as the outside was partly buried and covered in ivy, masking any tell-tale details. In any case, Bradford already had many mediaeval buildings.

It was only some years later, in 1871, that Canon Jones found himself in the Bodleian Library in Oxford, reading the early twelfth-century *Gesta Pontificum* of the chronicler William of Malmesbury. In this he stumbled upon the following line: 'To this day there is at that place (Bradeford) a little church which Aldhelm is said to have founded and dedicated to the blessed St. Lawrence.'

For Jones this was a revelation. Aldhelm had been a poet, scholar and bishop of Sherborne, in the seventh and early eighth century. Here then was proof that there had once been an Anglo-Saxon church in the town – one not recorded elsewhere. As Jones put it: 'I felt now that I had found the key which unlocked the door of many of our difficulties.'

Jones realised that both the cottage and school he had previously visited were actually parts of an almost untouched Anglo-Saxon church – a unique survival that for a millennium had remained sleeping behind later walls and partitions. The buildings were bought for the nation and declared an ancient monument. The chancel arch, which had been removed to insert the chimney, was replaced and the building made whole again, as it had been over a thousand years before. St Aldhelm's 'little church' was then rededicated to St Lawrence.

The Eardisley Font

At the west end of the church of St Mary Magdalene in Eardisley, Herefordshire, stands an ancient baptismal font, dating from around AD 1150. What has made it famous, other than its great age, are the images carved on its surface, which, over 850 years after it was created, have yet to be fully explained.

The font is the work of a local group of stonemasons and their style, a combination of Celtic, Anglo-Saxon and Norman influences, occurs only in this part of Herefordshire. The main scene depicted is what is known as 'the harrowing of hell'. In this Biblical episode, Christ is said to have descended after death into hell (or perhaps purgatory) and rescued the righteous who, due to clerical errors, found themselves there, perhaps because, having been born before Christ, they couldn't have been saved by him. On the Eardisley font, the harrowing shows a very energetic Christ, with the Holy Spirit (as a dove) sitting parrot-like on his shoulder, hauling a little man, perhaps Adam, out of the tangled knot of hell. Next to this is a large carving of a lion that may represent the power of evil, and a three-quarter-length unidentified figure with a halo, holding a book.

If that sounds confusing, it is actually the other major scene that has aroused so much speculation. This shows a very unreligious image of two Norman knights fighting. One has his sword raised over his head and is about to strike whilst the other has driven his spear through his opponent's leg. The identity of these decidedly unbiblical characters has remained a mystery until recent research into the mediaeval owners of Eardisley suggested a possibility.

From the eleventh to the sixteenth centuries, the manor was owned by the Baskerville family. In the early twelfth century, just before the date of the font, the Baskerville lord, Ralph I, became involved in a land dispute with his new father-in-law, Lord Drogo of Clifford, who had, according to Ralph, not kept his side of the bargain when it came to handing over his daughter Sibil's dowry. Norman lords not being known for their patience or under-standing, this had resulted in Ralph challenging Drogo to a duel at Whitecross at which he managed to kill his father-in-law.

Even in the twelfth century the Church looked unfavourably on the murdering of one's father-in-law and Ralph, suddenly in fear of his immortal soul, was forced to seek penance. This came in the form of making donations of large tracts of land and signing over various rents to the Church. Unlike so many Norman lords who regularly made up for their little murderous excesses by founding a nunnery or two, Ralph seems to have taken his repentance to heart. The font at Eardisley may be part of his penance, a lasting memorial in stone commissioned by him to remind parishioners of his terrible fall from grace and eventual salvation.

For salvation did indeed come. This former Norman bully-boy gave up the secular life altogether, becoming a monk at Gloucester and dying there around 1194 – a very early example of a born-again Christian.

5

Secret Service

Every man is surrounded by a neighbourhood of
voluntary spies . . . where roads and newspapers lay
every thing open.

Jane Austen, *Northanger Abbey* (1818)

Agent Tricycle Shocks America

By 1941, Dusan Popov, known to his MI5 handlers as 'Agent Tricycle', was already a key part of British counter-intelligence. A Yugoslavian by birth, he had been approached in 1940 by the German intelligence service – the Abwehr – as a potential spy against Britain and eagerly agreed to join them. What the Abwehr didn't know was that he had immediately contacted the British Secret Intelligence Service who had suggested he work as a double agent.

As a key part of the 'double-cross' (XX) system, Popov had made three trips to the UK, supposedly to gather information and distribute money for Abwehr agents, but in truth compromising their networks and supplying a torrent of false data to his German handlers. The Germans remained oblivious to this deception and in mid-August 1941, as one of their star agents, or so they thought, he was given the most sensitive mission of all.

Popov was to sail to the USA to rebuild the German spy network there. Crucially, he was also to reconnoitre a number of potential US targets, including some given to the Germans by the Japanese. This list included the home of the US Pacific Fleet at Pearl Harbor, in Oahu, Hawaii, on which the Japanese had specifically requested German intelligence. SIS were delighted to let the plan go ahead but could not work directly with Popov whilst he was in America as the British government had an agreement not to run SIS operations on US soil. So SIS handed their agent over to the FBI.

Popov's arrival proved unsettling, both to the FBI and to the spy himself. The FBI and its chief, the prim J. Edgar Hoover, weren't really prepared for the type of man Popov was. Agent Tricycle, a bon viveur and a playboy, immediately started up a passionate affair with the film actress Simone Simon. He was known to spend hundreds of pounds on meals (paid for out of his Abwehr fees; he refused to charge them to the British SIS) and was said to have favourite rooms in the world's leading hotels where he liked to 'entertain' ladies. Worse still was the (quite unfounded) rumour in intelligence circles that his code name 'Tricycle' was attributed to his penchant for three-in-a-bed romps. Hoover, horrified by this confessed Nazi spy and moral degenerate, put him under heavy-handed surveillance. To make matters more difficult for Popov, he refused him permission to travel to Hawaii as per his German orders and took little notice of his German list of prospective targets, which he considered too generalised.

After repeated requests to the US and British authorities for their intervention, and having failed to persuade the FBI of his true value (whatever his morals), Popov eventually set sail for Brazil where he hoped to acquire a transmitter to open a radio link with his Abwehr handlers in Lisbon. Just over halfway through the voyage to Rio de Janeiro, on 7 December 1941, the Japanese attacked Pearl Harbor.

Sir John Masterman, head of the British XX system, later commented that Agent Tricycle's information, combined with the unusual interest Japan had shown in the recent British aerial torpedo attack on the Italian fleet at Taranto (which Tricycle had also passed on to the FBI), made it 'a fair deduction' that Pearl Harbor would be the first target if Japan should declare war. Hoover's moral compass had sadly pointed him in the opposite direction to that of the Japanese attack.

Garbo Makes It Up

Juan Pujol García had every reason to detest the rise of extremism in the 1930s. During the Spanish Civil War he had been recruited by the fascists as well as by the communists and had suffered at the hands of both, although he later claimed never to have fired a shot for either side. His experience, however, convinced him in January 1941 that he had to do something to prevent the apparently unstoppable rise of Nazi Germany by volunteering to spy for Great Britain, then the only country actively opposing them.

The British response to this offer was, to say the least, dis-appointing. Having approached the British embassy, he was told in no uncertain terms that his services were very much not required – after all, what could a Catalan trained in poultry farming have to offer the British Secret Service? Aware that he needed to increase his value if the British were to take him seriously, Pujol hit upon a new plan. He would offer to spy for the Germans and then, once in their confidence, he would again see whether the British wanted to use him as a conduit for false intelligence.

The Germans seemed considerably more interested in Pujol than the British. He told them he was a committed fascist, having fought for Franco in the Spanish Civil War, and offered to travel to Britain to spy for them. In return they trained him in wireless operation, gave him $3,000 and dispatched him to Portugal with orders to travel to Britain. Except that Pujol didn't go to Britain, mainly because he couldn't get a visa. So, astonishingly, he decided to set up shop in Lisbon and just pretend he was in England. Armed only with a copy of the *Blue Guide to Britain*, a train timetable and some old reference books, he started sending fake reports, claiming he was travelling round Britain and informing the Germans of military installations and troop movements. He then once again offered his services to the British and was again, inexplicably, rejected. His German handlers were, by contrast, delighted with the 'intelligence' he gave them.

Back in Britain there was now some confusion. MI5 were intercepting communications from an unknown German agent code-named Arabel but there was something wrong with them. Arabel claimed to be travelling around the country but his reports were often wildly, and stupidly, inaccurate. On one occasion he had reported back to Germany that there were people in Glasgow who would 'do anything for a litre of wine'.

Eventually, and following further prompting from Pujol, MI5 realised the messages were coming from him and that, amazingly, the Germans believed them. Such were Pujol's extraordinary acting skills that they gave him the code name 'Garbo' after the great silent movie star.

Garbo was now finally allowed to travel to England where he

was teamed up with the brilliant MI5 case officer Tomás Harris. Together they set about creating a network of twenty-six fictional sub-agents, all reporting from different parts of the country and all providing misinformation (while claiming hefty expenses from the Germans). These included a garrulous US Army sergeant and the 'Brothers of the Aryan World Order' – a supposed secret group of fascist Welsh Nationalists in Swansea. Of course not everything could be wrong or Garbo's cover would be blown, so elaborate excuses were made up for fictional agents falling ill (and hence not reporting ship movements) and in one case dying – a fictitious obituary being put in the paper to back this up. On other occasions genuine information was dispatched by letter but sent too late to be of use – the postmark faked to make it appear that the letter was sent earlier and had been somehow delayed.

Meanwhile Garbo's Nazi handlers were more and more impressed, even awarding him the Iron Cross. Indeed, so convinced had the Germans become that he was genuine that the British decided to use his network in one of the greatest deceptions of the war – Operation Fortitude. In the build-up to D-Day, Garbo reported to the Germans that the entirely fictitious 1st US Army Group was mustering on the English east coast for an attack on the Pas de Calais and that the coming invasion on the Normandy beaches (which he tipped them off about) was just a diversionary feint. Four hundred messages were sent by Garbo and Harris, pretending to be various members of Garbo's imaginary network, and the Germans fell for it. After D-Day the Germans kept back two armoured divisions and nineteen infantry divisions in the Pas de Calais, awaiting invasion by an invented army and allowing the D-Day invaders to secure their bridgehead.

After the war, with the Germans still unaware of the deception, Garbo's death was faked to protect his identity and he was relocated to Venezuela. He died in 1988, one of the few men ever to receive an MBE as well as an Iron Cross.

Melita's Silent War

Soviet spying in Britain will always be associated with the names of Burgess, Maclean and Philby but arguably far greater damage was done to Britain's military interests by a quietly spoken secretary who was never even prosecuted.

With the benefit of hindsight it is possible to say that there were clues as to Melita Norwood's political leanings. Her father had been a member of the Marxist British Socialist Party, had translated Lenin's *Collapse of the Second International* and become a firm supporter of Bolshevism before dying in 1918.

By the age of twenty, Melita herself was a member of the Independent Labour Party, living in a house with her future husband and his Russian parents. Both Melita and her future mother-in-law sold the *Daily Worker* outside Golders Green tube station on Saturday mornings and both were members of the Friends of the Soviet Union. In 1935, Melita made her political inclinations absolutely clear by joining the British Communist Party.

By this time she was also working as a secretary at the British Non-Ferrous Metals Research Association (BN-FMRA), a thinly disguised government military research organisation. At the outbreak of the Second World War the BN-FMRA was evacuated to Berkhamsted and Melita went with it, becoming secretary to G.L. Bailey. He was on the advisory board of the even more innocuous-sounding Tube Alloys, but Tube Alloys was not as dull as it appeared, being the cover for Britain's nuclear weapons development directorate. Nor was Melita just the quiet, faithful secretary she appeared to be. In 1934 she had been recruited by Andrew Rothstein into the NKVD, forerunner of the KGB.

Melita's real opportunity to help the Soviet Union came in 1945 when she gained access to documents concerning the behaviour of uranium at high temperatures. This she immediately passed to her Russian handlers who credited her with providing information that allowed the Soviet Union to test a nuclear weapon four years earlier than the British or Americans thought possible – and before Britain had even managed to test its own bomb.

Each night, this apparently guileless secretary, code-named 'Tina' and later 'Hola', would open her boss's safe and photograph the contents with a miniature camera. She would then travel to South London and pass the film to her handler. No one suspected a humble secretary, a woman without official secrets clearance, but with complete access to everything her boss knew. Nor did Melita's work end with spying. In 1967 she also recruited another civil servant, code-named Hunt, who for fourteen years passed on to the Soviets information on British arms sales.

Melita Norwood retired from both the BN-FMRA and the KGB in 1973, having refused a Soviet pension, and busied herself with local politics. Another twenty-six years would pass before Vasili Mitrokhin smuggled out of Russia KGB papers that revealed Hola's true identity. Melita was now eighty-seven years old and it was deemed 'not in the public interest' to prosecute her – or perhaps not in the government's interest to have the whole affair aired in public. She died in 2005, having always refused to financially profit from her spying and maintaining that she would do it again if the circumstances arose. Her only regret following her exposure was, in her own words, 'I thought I'd got away with it.'

Hide-and-Seek

The surrender of Oxford to the Parliamentarians in 1646, during the English Civil War, marked more than the loss of a city to the Royalists. They also lost a member of the royal family – but not for long. Prince James, second son of Charles I and still only twelve years old, became Cromwell's prisoner. As a result his household was dismissed and he was sent to London to be placed under house arrest at St James's Palace. Here he, along with his sister Princess Elizabeth and his younger brother Henry, Duke of Gloucester, was to remain under the watchful eye of the Earl of Northumberland.

Whilst life at St James's was not unpleasant for the three younger children of Charles I (his heir, later Charles II, had already fled to France), it was captivity nonetheless. James determined to escape, a feat he achieved after two abortive attempts, thanks to the subterfuge of a children's game. The man responsible for breaking James out was Colonel Joseph Bampfield, a staunch Royalist who, persuading the Parliamentarians that he was quite the opposite, managed to arrange an audience with the young prince in April 1648.

At this meeting Bampfield suggested an escape plan of childish simplicity. Although the children's home was certainly a prison, it was at least a gilded one in which they were allowed many of the amusements normally enjoyed by royal progeny. Bampfield suggested that James might care to play hide-and-seek with his brother and sister each evening for a week or two, after which his plan would be put into operation.

James agreed and for two weeks the children played this innocent game in the palace garden, James getting a reputation as so excellent a hider that often his siblings searched for him for hours. On the afternoon of 28 April, the day planned for the escape, James told the gardener that he had broken his own key to the garden and asked to borrow the man's, which was duly handed over. After supper he suggested to his brother and sister that they play hide-and-seek as usual.

That night James did not hide. Instead he ran to the garden, locking the door to it behind him, before meeting up with Colonel Bampfield on the edge of the park. Disguising him in a cloak and wig, the colonel hurried the prince into a coach that took him to Salisbury House on the Strand. Whilst the coach carried on into the city as a diversion, the colonel and his charge pretended to head into Salisbury House but instead slipped down Ivy Lane to the river where a boat awaited them. At London Bridge they disembarked and hurried to the house of a surgeon called Loe where Bampfield's fiancée, Anne Murray, was ready with a set of women's clothes especially tailored to fit the young prince. The boy was quickly dressed in this costume and, as she later commented in her autobiography, he 'was very pretty in it'.

Bampfield and his footman now escorted James to Lyon Quay where he took another boat and, after some hard bargaining with a rather suspicious captain, the group were taken downriver, past the Gravesend blockhouse, to Tilbury where a Dutch ship lay at anchor to carry them to Middelburg in the Netherlands.

Meanwhile back at St James's Palace, Elizabeth and Henry had to agree that their brother had hidden so well this time that they were forced to ask the adults for help in finding him. It didn't take long for it to dawn on the latter that they had been duped. When the guard were called out, their progress was hindered by the locked garden door. By the time the message got out to alert the roads and ports, James's ship was already weighing anchor and setting sail for the continent.

The Liar

Thomas Dangerfield certainly lived up to his name, bringing near disaster to those around him, many of whom persisted for years in trying to help him. He was born in 1654 into an era of intrigues and plots. Whilst the 'secrets' that he made a career of peddling all came from his own fevered imagination, their effects proved very real. From an early age there were signs that Thomas Dangerfield could not be trusted, as his contemporary biography *The Matchless Rogue* suggests. Having run away to London three times as a child, he eventually appeared in Spain where he seems to have become a soldier, picking up some more unconventional skills like thieving and counterfeiting en route. It was only a matter of time before his antics were noticed and he was regularly arrested, eventually being saved from the noose only by an English priest, who obtained a pardon for him and sent him back to England with what was then the handsome sum of £30 in his pocket.

Dangerfield, as he would show all his life, was not in the slightest bit grateful for the help and, back in Britain, immediately set about counterfeiting again, being arrested at predictable intervals and twice breaking out of gaol. It was whilst in Newgate that he came to the attention of another well-wisher, Elizabeth Cellier, who worked for the charitable Countess of Powis by befriending Catholic prisoners. Whilst Dangerfield wasn't actually a Catholic, he didn't consider that Elizabeth needed to know that and, professing a devout faith, he persuaded her to pay for his release. Within days, however, he was back to his old tricks and was imprisoned again, this time in the gaol known as the Counter. Here he tried to convince the authorities that he was a valuable informer and had information on the Popish plot, which he didn't, but again Elizabeth came to his rescue, paid his debts and had him set free. To help keep him out of prison, she also got him a job with the Countess of Powis as a messenger and sometime spy.

Dangerfield seems to have taken to his new role, so much so, in fact, that he decided to start manufacturing plots where they didn't exist. The greatest of those that he claimed to have 'uncovered' was the 'Meal Tub Plot', which, he said, was a Presbyterian conspiracy to prevent the Duke of York (later James II) from taking the throne. In an atmosphere of plot and counterplot as Catholics and Protestants manoeuvred for power at court, such a scheme seemed perfectly possible. Dangerfield was introduced to the King and the Duke of York although they seemed to take his 'plot' less seriously than he'd hoped.

What he needed was evidence and, having none, he planted it. Having already accused the whig Colonel Roderick Mansell of being a participant in the conspiracy, he secreted some incriminating documents behind the bedstead in the colonel's bedroom. Other documents were then concealed in a meal tub in the house of Elizabeth Cellier – the woman who had invested so much of her time in helping Dangerfield.

Now ready to reveal the plot, Dangerfield applied for a warrant to search Mansell's rooms but was refused. Initially foiled, he managed to get a customs warrant instead but when he produced the patently fake documents Mansell easily discredited him.

Dangerfield was arrested again, this time for coining, yet miraculously Elizabeth came to his aid once more, standing bail.

Many might think Dangerfield had a lot to thank Elizabeth Cellier for, but he was not amongst them. Worried that his ludicrous 'plot' was unravelling, he told the government that the Presbyterian intrigue was actually a cover for a Catholic plot and for proof he directed them to Elizabeth's house in whose meal tub he had hidden the documents. For good measure he added that he had been offered money to assassinate the King, which he claimed was the very reason Cellier had got him released from prison.

Cellier and her Catholic friends were rounded up and stood trial for treason. Dangerfield, meanwhile, was released with a pardon and a pension. The two met again in court where Cellier had to fight for her life, incriminated by damning testimony given by the very man she had helped over so many years. Fortunately for her, Dangerfield was just about the only witness and, as the plot had been entirely fabricated by him in the first place, his credibility was easily destroyed. Cellier and her friends were freed.

Without the support of the only people ever to have assisted him, who were understandably miffed that their former friend had tried to get them executed for treason, Dangerfield returned to his old tricks. As well as acting as a 'priest catcher', to little effect, he toured the country practising confidence tricks and impersonating the Duke of Monmouth amongst others.

When his pension was cut off, his thieving soon brought him again to the attention of the authorities. He was arrested and condemned to be flogged from Aldgate to Newgate and then, on the following day, from Newgate to Tyburn. On his way back to prison after the second whipping, a scuffle broke out between him and barrister Robert Francis. Dangerfield spat at Francis, who responded by striking Dangerfield with his cane. The tip of the cane seems to have pierced Dangerfield's eye and he died shortly afterwards. As a result, Dangerfield managed to claim one last victim, for the hapless Francis was tried for his murder, convicted and hanged.

The Improbable Life of Alice Wheeldon

Alice Wheeldon's story is one of the stranger episodes from the home front during the First World War and it demonstrates the fine line between capture and entrapment. The Wheeldon family were undoubtedly revolutionary anti-war socialists but their sudden notoriety at the head of what was apparently a fiendish plot worthy of Moriarty himself makes their whole history more unsettling.

Alice had been a suffragette before the war and had passed her firm beliefs on to her children. Her daughter Harriet had also joined the Women's Social and Political Union and was engaged to a member of the Socialist Labour Party, whilst her son William was imprisoned as a conscientious objector. Another daughter, Winifred, may have been less radical, being happily married to Alfred Mason, a lecturer in chemistry in Southampton, and working herself as a teacher.

By December 1916, Alice was also taking in and hiding conscientious objectors on the run from the police and the army, and it was in this capacity that she was approached by Alex Gordon. He claimed to be just such a conscientious objector and asked her for help. In truth he was Francis W. Vivian, a former radical now in the employ of the secret service and working to expose anti-war groups. Unaware of the deception, Alice agreed to hide him overnight, as well as allowing herself to be introduced to his 'friend', whom he called 'Comrade Bert' and described as an army deserter and member of the anarcho-syndicalist organisation, Industrial Workers of the World. He was, of course, another government agent.

Having been accepted into the Wheeldon 'family', Comrade Bert managed to discover that the Wheeldons communicated using a chessboard cipher as they feared their post was being tampered with (as indeed it was). He noted too that the key sentence they used for their code was: 'We will hang Lloyd George from a sour apple tree.' Alice was said to refer often to the Prime Minister in what would then have been viewed as the foulest of terms, calling him 'a bugger'.

If the Wheeldons seemed at first glance rather quaintly 'radical', the case against them redefined them as the most dangerous family in Britain. On 4 January 1917 the secret service intercepted a parcel sent from Winifred to her mother Alice. In it were four small glass phials of the exotic and deadly poison curare. On 29 January, Alice and Harriet – together with another conscientious objector who was unfortunately then at Alice's house – were arrested. Winifred was picked up the next day. They were charged with conspiracy to assassinate Lloyd George and another war cabinet member on a Surrey golf course using a poisoned dart.

The subsequent trial was somewhat chaotic as the only barrister who could be found to represent the Wheeldons was a Persian, Dr Riza, who proposed an archaic trial by ordeal which was, naturally, refused. The prosecution case was led by the Attorney General himself. He suggested that Winifred's husband had obtained the curare from the laboratory where he worked and sent it to Alice with the intention of using it to coat a dart to be fired from an airgun at the Prime Minister. The Wheeldons claimed the poison was for killing dogs guarding camps holding conscientious objectors, thus facilitating their escape. It took just twenty minutes for the jury to return a guilty verdict on them all.

Alice received a ten-year sentence but promptly went on hunger strike and was released after serving just under two. She died only a year later in the post-war influenza epidemic. Alfred and Winifred, who received seven and five years respectively, were released at the end of January 1919.

But did the middle-aged mother and owner of a second-hand clothes shop really plan such an unusual murder? The question has never satisfactorily been answered. As Vivian, aka Alex Gordon, did not appear in court, the exact nature of his and his fellow agent's role in the plot remains a mystery. The quick release of the protagonists after the war indicates that the plot may have been engineered as a pretext to get an undoubtedly radical family out of the way – safely behind bars.

Arthur Ransome – Secret Agent

Arthur Ransome is best known today for his *Swallows and Amazons* books, set in the idyllic countryside of the Lake District to which Ransome himself escaped at every opportunity to relive the happy childhood days he had known before his father's death. But there was another, secret, side to Ransome.

After a disastrous marriage and a bruising legal case, Arthur Ransome decided in 1913 to leave the UK and visit Russia to gather folk stories. Based in St Petersburg, he soon fell in with many of the local intellectuals and radical politicians in the city, taking a job as the correspondent there for the *Daily News* newspaper. And there was plenty of news. Rumblings were growing louder of incipient revolution in Russia and Ransome allied himself with the cause for change espoused by Karl Radek and Vladimir Lenin. The British Foreign Office looked askance, reporting home that Ransome had overly romantic views of the class struggle, but did nothing to prevent his going repeatedly into print in support of radical politics.

With the outbreak of war Ransome remained in Russia to report from the Eastern front and so found himself at the centre of the action when the Russian Revolution erupted in 1917. By this time he was well placed to report on the Bolshevik cause, being close not only to Lenin but also to Trotsky, whose secretary, Yevgeniya Petrovna Shelepina, would later become his second wife.

But Arthur Ransome was not all he appeared to be. Whilst many in authority wondered where his true allegiance lay as Western governments were fighting to turn back the tide of the Russian Revolution, documents released in 2002 reveal a surprise. Ransome, friend of the Communist elite, was also working for the British Secret Intelligence Service, or MI6.

Intelligence files reveal two sides to Ransome's personality. On the one hand there was concern, expressed in MI5 documents, that he shared many of the beliefs of the Bolsheviks and promoted their cause through his articles in the *Manchester Guardian*, which he began writing for in 1919. Its editor C.P. Scott had, after all, called the Russian Revolution 'wonderful and glorious' and his paper stood firmly against foreign intervention in Russia. Convinced that Ransome was a Bolshevik propagandist at the very least, MI5 recommended a close watch be kept on the author; indeed, his name was removed from this list only in 1937.

This, however, was not the Arthur Ransome that MI6 knew. For them he was Asset S76 whose association with the Bolsheviks, they noted, 'was begun, and had been continued throughout, at the direct request of responsible British authorities'. They assisted in smuggling Yevgeniya to Sweden where she too may have become a British agent, as one file describes her as 'a very useful lady'. In 1919, against the wishes of MI5, MI6 helped ensure that Ransome could return to Russia to report for the *Guardian*.

It is still not entirely clear exactly whose side Arthur Ransome was on, but by the early 1920s his thoughts were moving away from radical journalism and towards a different type of writing. Whilst living in Estonia, he had built a 30-ton ketch, the *Racundra*, whose maiden voyage around the Baltic with his MI5 handler Ernest Boyce became the subject of his first great sailing book, *Racundra's First Cruise*. It would mark the beginning of a passion for writing about the simple pleasures of sailing, which would culminate in the series of books that made his name – *Swallows and Amazons*.

Reilly, Ace of Spies

It is probably easier to list what Sidney Reilly was not rather than what he was. He was not the son of an Irish clergyman, nor a sailor, nor a Russian imperial aristocrat, although at various times he claimed to be all three. He did not attend Cambridge or

Heidelberg universities, nor did he study at the Royal School of Mines. He was certainly married four times but, although all his wives outlived him, he was never divorced. The truth, if truth can be found, is that Sidney Reilly was a master of deception and his extraordinary life would later become the model for James Bond.

Reilly first arrived in England in 1895 having been born in 1874 in Russian Poland and thanks to his mastery of Russian, Polish, German, French and English, he received an introduction to the intelligence branch of the War Office. There is also some evidence that he may have been involved in the suspicious death of an elderly and wealthy vicar whose young wife he had seduced. Whether Reilly was an 'official' government spy at this time remains unclear, although in 1899 he certainly took the chance of a commercial posting to Port Arthur in Manchuria to become an industrial spy, trading information on this Russian-held port to both the British and the Japanese in the run-up to the Russo-Japanese War in 1905. From 1906 he transferred his operations to St Petersburg where, in the dangerous years prior to the Russian Revolution, he cultivated contacts in the imperial household as well as on the revolutionary committees. In 1914 he moved to New York where he made his personal fortune as an intermediary in arms sales to Russia.

During the First World War, Reilly did indeed become an agent of the SIS and was involved in perhaps his greatest adventure. In 1918 he led an attempt to overthrow the new Bolshevik Russian government and assassinate Lenin. Perhaps not surprisingly, it is uncertain whether this plan was officially sanctioned in its entirety. It revolved around persuading anti-Bolshevik groups to rise up with the support of the Latvian Riflemen – the most trusted members of the Bolshevik military. Reilly met repeatedly with counter-revolutionary groups and a date for the coup was set for early September that year, during a meeting of the Council of People's Commissars. He also drew up lists of suitable replacements for the Bolshevik officials who would be 'removed' in the coup.

On 30 August events overtook Reilly and his plans when the head of the St Petersburg (then Petrograd) secret police was assassinated and Lenin was wounded by a gunwoman. This provided the excuse for a crackdown on all dissidents in what became known as the 'Red Terror'. It is not known whether the plot had been compromised before this, or, indeed, whether it had even been engineered by the Bolsheviks to catch dissidents. All Reilly's group were rounded up. Reilly himself managed to escape, making the dangerous journey north to Finland, posing as a German diplomat and travelling in a railway car reserved for the German embassy.

Back in London in early November, Reilly found the plot had been headline news in Russia and that, rather alarmingly, he had been sentenced to death in his absence – the sentence to be carried out immediately should he ever be apprehended on Russian soil. Astonishingly, within weeks Reilly was back in Russia, using the cover of a British trade delegation. From 1919 to 1925, from what we can tell, Reilly was working at the periphery of the Soviet sphere with opponents of communism, if not to overthrow the regime, then to at least change it into something more friendly to the West.

In September 1925 his luck finally deserted him when he was identified and lured on to Russian territory by the Ob'edinennoe Gosudarstvennoe Politicheskoe Upravlenie, the Soviet Secret Service, which arrested and interrogated him at their Lubyanka headquarters in Moscow. The sentence handed down to him in 1918 was then carried out and he was shot on 5 November.

Dean Barwick and the Adventurous Women

John Barwick was not born to the life of a royal secret agent. He was the son of a tenant farmer in Witherslack, Westmorland, and it was only his precocious academic talent that removed him from a life on the land to the cloisters of Cambridge University. It was here that he first came to the attention of the King in the years leading up to the English Civil War.

By this time, Barwick was officially a man of the cloth – chaplain to the bishop of Durham – but at the outbreak of hostilities he lost no time in conspiring to support the Royalist movement. In July 1642 he was involved in a scheme to 'liberate' a large quantity of money and silver plate belonging to Cambridge colleges and smuggle them into the King's coffers. Whilst Cambridge was the intellectual home of many of the Parliamentarians, its rich and often conservative colleges also contained enough Royalist supporters to make it a good fund-raising ground for the King, who was then at Nottingham.

Information on the plot seems to have been leaked to Oliver Cromwell and soldiers were posted to intercept the consignment. News of this trap was itself leaked back to Barwick who managed to form a small party of horsemen and, loot in hand, made the dash to Nottingham via the back roads, so avoiding Cromwell's men.

Such behaviour didn't make him overly popular with either the Parliamentarians, naturally enough, or the Cambridge authorities; in 1644 he was ejected from his fellowship of St John's College. Moving to London with his master, the bishop of Durham, Barwick found himself in a still more dangerous position, charged with managing the King's affairs whilst living amongst his enemies, as the King himself was then besieged in Oxford. Never one to avoid a risk, Barwick immediately set about discovering what he could of the Parliamentarians' plans, having received express permission from Charles I to set aside his clerical gown and go amongst the soldiers dressed as one of them. All he had to do was to get the precious intelligence through to Oxford.

Barwick could not go there himself without being noticed so he employed the services of Richard Royston, a bookseller with a unique distribution network for the Royalist pamphlets and propaganda that he produced. These were carried all over the kingdom by so-called 'Adventurous Women', Royalist ladies who would disguise themselves as the lowest of lowly hawkers, women of such insignificance and such unappealing habits that even soldiers would give them a wide berth. Barwick now charged them with transporting between Oxford and London apparently innocuous books whose covers had royal dispatches sewn into them.

After the fall of Oxford and the capture of the King, Barwick continued his work in person, even being allowed to visit the imprisoned monarch, and he arranged for ciphers to be left in Charles's cell at Carisbrooke Castle on the Isle of Wight. After Charles's execution in 1649, Barwick fell ill and his brother Edward had to take charge of getting dispatches from Royalists in London to the King's ministers, then in exile on the continent. Whether Edward was less careful or simply unlucky, his regular trips to the Post Office to collect letters addressed to the fictional Dutch merchant 'James Van Delft' were noticed by a Post Office employee, Mr Bostocke, who reported him to Cromwell.

Having been tipped off that they had been discovered, Barwick had just enough time to burn his letters and ciphers before he was arrested. Edward died a few weeks later and Barwick was committed to the Tower on a charge of high treason. Fortunately, with no material evidence, no charges were ever brought and he was released on bail in August 1652. He remained in London for the rest of Cromwell's rule, still secretly corresponding with the King's ministers and quietly negotiating for the return of the monarchy. He died of consumption on 22 October 1664, secure in the knowledge that by then it had been firmly re-established with the Restoration of Charles II in 1660.

6

Deadly Secrets

It was not until several weeks after he had decided to murder his wife that Dr Bickleigh took any active steps in the matter. Murder is a serious business.

Francis Iles, *Malice Aforethought* (1931)

The Curious Case of Benjamin Bathurst

Benjamin Bathurst was perhaps not the most successful of diplomats. Having secured a job thanks to the intervention of a distant relative in government, he had enjoyed only limited success with European legations. In 1808 he returned home to recover from an unspecified illness and the disappointment of not receiving higher office, but his furlough would be short. Indeed, when he left England within the year, it would be for the last time.

In March 1809 the foreign secretary ordered Bathurst, as envoy extraordinary, to Austria to investigate a possible alliance against Napoleon who was then causing a spot of bother in Europe. Just a month later, what became known as the War of the Fifth Coalition broke out when Austria threw in its lot with Britain and marshalled its forces against France, only to be defeated. At the treaty of Schönbrunn that October, France forced Austria to break off relations with Britain, leaving Bathurst in a tricky position. As he was still in Buda at the time, he was at best worth kidnapping for information and at worst liable to be shot as a spy.

It was certainly time to run. Having decided it was too dangerous to head south to the Mediterranean, Bathurst chose instead to head north through the nominally neutral German states to Hamburg and take ship for England from there. Of course he could hardly travel as a British diplomat so he disguised himself as a German merchant. This was possibly a mistake, for several reasons. First, he spoke nearly no German; second, his lavish dress and coach made him look more like a minor royal than a humble trader; third, he took the pseudonym 'Baron de Koch', not exactly a name designed to deflect attention. Undaunted, and accompanied by a German official and a servant, he set off, reaching the Prussian town of Perleberg on the afternoon of 25 November.

Here he ordered fresh horses before heading to the White Swan Inn to have dinner. He was then shown to a private room where he worked for a few hours, writing letters and apparently burning some private correspondence. It was 9 p.m. by the time the coach

97

was ready once more and Bathurst was called. He is said to have walked out on to the road and then promptly disappeared. No one ever saw Benjamin Bathurst again.

News of the disappearance of the diplomat was brought to London by his travelling companion, who arrived there a month later. No one was particularly surprised, as much of war-torn Europe was infested with bandits and demobbed soldiers, making travelling anywhere perilous. Bathurst's wife, however, remained undaunted and left immediately for Germany to find out the truth. Meanwhile in Perleberg, a town that didn't want to get a reputation for mislaying diplomats, detailed searches had been organised and the river dragged, but to no avail. Two days after he vanished, Bathurst's expensive fur coat was found hidden in an outhouse, and two and a half weeks later his pantaloons were recovered in woods three miles from the city.

It seemed unlikely that the diplomat could have got far without a coat or trousers so when Mrs Bathurst arrived she was warned to expect bad news. Further investigations had also revealed that the coat had been taken by the mother of a man who not only worked at the Swan Inn but had been there on the night when Bathurst was last seen. Had the coat been left behind or had this man murdered Bathurst and stolen it? No one was saying. Thinking money might help, Mrs Bathurst offered a reward of 500 thalers, but this just confused matters further as hundreds of spurious reports came in from locals hoping to claim it. After the entire area had been searched again, the indomitable Mrs Bathurst set off to confront Napoleon himself and see what he knew.

By now the British press was taking an interest in the case, not least because of the redoubtable efforts of Mrs Bathurst. Journalists suggested that the diplomat had been seized and murdered by the French. This was countered by a furious refutation from the French government, accusing the British of being the only civilised nation to regularly employ lunatics in the diplomatic service, such as the clearly unbalanced Bathurst, who had obviously crumpled under pressure and killed himself. To be honest there was a ring of truth to this allegation and, initially at least, Mrs Bathurst herself certainly believed her husband had committed suicide.

What was the truth behind the rumours? There remain several possibilities. Many contemporary sources argue that Bathurst was unhinged by the pressure of his attempted escape and either took his own life or shook off his companions, fearing they would betray him, and was killed as he made his way alone across the German states. On the night of his disappearance he had, strangely, asked for protection from the Prussian military commander but had dismissed his guards two hours before he was due to leave. Was this so he could slip away himself?

More recently it has been suggested that he was betrayed by a British secret organisation working with the Austrians who feared that, in his unsteady state of mind, Bathurst might give away valuable secrets to the French. One French source, a nobleman later exposed as a double agent, claimed that a party of French cavalry had seized Bathurst and imprisoned him at Magdeburg in the hope of recovering Austrian state papers – which Bathurst had probably already burnt.

Such exotic reasons for his disappearance, along with a host of conjectures about ghosts and extraterrestrials, have made Bathurst's unsolved case one of the most talked-about disappearances of the nineteenth century. There is also a more prosaic possibility. Bathurst's manservant reported that he last saw his master sitting by the fire, rather ostentatiously counting money, surrounded by local inn staff. Seeing such wealth in the hands of so nervous a man was a clear temptation to robbery with violence.

Years later, in 1852, the skeleton of a murder victim did indeed come to light in Perleberg. Buried in the cellar of a house once owned by an employee of the White Swan were found the remains of a naked adult male who had suffered a massive blow to the back of the head. It was also noted that after the disappearance the same inn employee who had previously been under suspicion had managed to find large dowries for his daughters, which he couldn't account for. When Bathurst's sister was later shown the skull, she refused to believe it was her brother, but then she hadn't seen him for nearly fifty years. The case therefore remains officially unsolved and Benjamin Bathurst is still listed as missing.

Sir Thomas Overbury's Unholy Ending

The death of Sir Thomas Overbury is a startling demonstration of how the more favoured branches of seventeenth-century aristocracy could literally get away with murder in the most brutal and blatant way.

The train of events leading to Overbury's unusual death began in 1606 with the marriage of Frances Howard, daughter of the powerful 1st Earl of Suffolk, to the 3rd Earl of Essex. A purely political match, it could not initially be consummated due to the very young age of the couple – the earl was only fifteen at the time – but when he returned from his travels three years later it rapidly became clear that it would never be consummated at all. The exact cause of his impotence is uncertain but as the couple's relationship deteriorated he turned to drink while she turned her affections towards Viscount Rochester.

Rochester was certainly not impotent and he was in addition a very good catch, being the favourite of King James I and acting as his unofficial secretary. This was work that required a fine mind – something Rochester certainly didn't possess – but for that he could rely on his old friend, Thomas Overbury. Overbury was initially keen to help Rochester in his love life, dictating the letters to Frances Howard that are said to have won her over. If this was the case, he certainly lived to regret his actions.

In May 1613, Frances petitioned for an annulment to her marriage to Essex in order to marry Rochester. Overbury was alarmed that if the viscount took a powerful Howard wife, he would lose his own influence over Rochester – an influence that had made him a rich man. He therefore began briefing against Frances, hoping to sabotage the match.

It was a foolish move. The Howard family, Rochester, the King and even Essex all agreed the annulment should go ahead. To save face it would be claimed that Essex was impotent only with Frances, not with any other women – a strange idea that almost foiled the plan as it suggested to those hearing the case for the annulment that witchcraft might be at work. Meanwhile it seemed politic to those involved to get the potentially embarrassing Overbury out of the way. The King took the lead, offering him the nominal promotion to ambassador, a job that would of course require him to leave the country. For some reason, possibly as part of an attempt to frame him, Rochester persuaded Overbury to refuse, an act that landed him in the Tower of London for contempt.

Here Overbury's prospects rapidly declined. Whilst Rochester and his new friends tried to persuade him to ally himself with the Howards and hence bring an end to his objections to the union, Frances was planning a more permanent solution. Stung by Overbury's criticism and his attempts to prevent her marriage, according to later trial witnesses she began a campaign to poison him.

Overbury, probably with Rochester's connivance, had been secretly administering emetics to himself to weaken his health in the hope of inducing the King's sympathy. These relatively harmless potions were now laced with arsenic in a bid to kill him, yet somehow he survived. Another attempt was made with mercury but again, after initially weakening, the apparently indestructible Overbury rallied. Perhaps suspecting the truth, he now took the extraordinary step of writing to Rochester, threatening to reveal something (unnamed) in their former relationship that would ruin him. It was probably a fatal step. On 14 September the assistant to the apothecary who served the Tower gave Overbury an enema spiked with mercury sublimate. By the following morning he was dead. Eleven days later Frances Howard's annulment was granted. After three months she was at last able to marry Rochester.

Even at the time the marriage was considered scandalous by some and Frances was portrayed as a harlot, snubbing her rightful husband and entrapping the King's favourite. Eventually the furore died down and at court the couple became the star attraction.

Then, two years later, Sir Gervase Elwes, Lieutenant of the Tower, announced that he knew about the plot to poison Overbury – indeed, he even claimed to have thwarted one attempt. The scandal blew up once more and, under threat of torture, the servants accused of actually administering the poisons pointed the finger of blame at Frances. In January 1616, Frances and Rochester were indicted for murder. Frances confessed before the trial while Rochester furiously maintained his innocence. Both were found guilty and sentenced to death, as were the servants they had employed.

Although this was an astonishing fall from grace for the couple who were now Earl and Countess of Somerset, it would not prove fatal. Whilst their low-born accomplices were hanged at Tyburn, the once-gilded pair were spared and then pardoned by the King. In 1622 they were finally released from the Tower and retired to a quieter life on a handsome royal pension of £4,000 per year.

The Last Walk of Victor Grayson

Albert Victor Grayson was an English socialist politician with a flair for oratory and a knack of upsetting people. Even so, his sudden, unexplained and unsolved disappearance in 1920 remains one of the most surprisingly overlooked secrets of twentieth-century British politics.

Grayson's rise to power had been meteoric but turbulent. A former engineering apprentice once intended for the Unitarian ministry, he had put aside business and religion to join the Independent Labour Party where, despite his stutter, he became famous for his lecture tours. He was particularly well received in the safe Labour seat of Colne Valley near Huddersfield and when a by-election was called there in 1907 he was adopted as a candidate by the local Labour League. Despite having no official support from the national Labour Party, he won an astonishing victory, by just 153 votes, a victory he claimed for 'revolutionary socialism', perhaps hinting at why the national party had declined to back him.

In parliament, Grayson remained just as outspoken, flouting procedure and provoking hostility from Labour members – particularly when he was thrown out of the House twice in two days. In an attempt to discredit him, rumours were soon passing around the lobbies of his love of alcohol and luxury. Shunned by both sides of the House and unwisely offering himself up for re-election as a 'revolutionary socialist' rather than as a Labour candidate, Grayson lost his seat in the 1910 election. Later that year he stood in another by-election, yet polled only 408 votes.

Grayson might have been down but he was very much not out. Working now mainly as a journalist, he continued to give speaking tours, although due to his alcoholism (the one rumour founded on truth) his appearances were less spectacular than they once had been. Slowly he slipped from public view until, after the First World War and the death of his wife, Grayson emerged again, not as an impoverished radical journalist, but living in apparent ease in the West End of London. Where his money came from was never ascertained. Then in the autumn of 1920 he simply vanished.

Exactly what happened to him in the September of that year may never be discovered. No death certificate has ever been issued for Grayson, so he remains officially 'missing'. What is known is that the newly affluent Grayson was by this time acquainted with one of the darkest characters in British politics – Arthur 'Maundy' Gregory, the notorious honours broker, who sold everything from knighthoods to peerages on behalf of Lloyd George's government (knighthoods cost £10,000, baronetcies £40,000).

Perhaps concerned that Gregory was spying on him (the latter claimed to have been employed by Sir Basil Thompson of Special Branch to do precisely this), Grayson began publicly threatening to expose this shabby trade, announcing on one occasion: 'This sale of honours is a national scandal. It can be traced right down to 10 Downing Street, and to a monocled dandy with offices in Whitehall. I know this man, and one day I will name him.'

Such a threat can hardly have seemed that 'veiled' to Maundy Gregory, a monocled dandy with offices in Whitehall, and it may have inspired him, or his friends, to act.

Victor Grayson was last seen alive on the evening of 28 September 1920. While having a drink with a friend, he received a telephone message and announced that he had to go to the Queen's Hotel in Leicester Square but would be back shortly. Some time later the artist George Flemwell, who was working on a painting of the Thames, saw Grayson enter a house near the river, a house that was later shown to belong to Maundy Gregory. Grayson was never seen again.

Whether Maundy Gregory or his friends murdered Grayson remains unproven but it would not be the last time that Gregory would fall under suspicion of murder. In 1932 he persuaded the retired actress Edith Rosse, whom he lived with, to change her will in his favour. Two days later she died, leaving him £18,000. Gregory insisted she be buried in an unsealed coffin just inches below the surface of a riverside cemetery that was known to flood regularly. Not surprisingly, when the police exhumed the body, suspecting Gregory of poisoning her after his fall from grace, the body was already too decayed for any forensic evidence to be recovered.

Gregory did not get away with his every misdeed. After an extraordinary career of bribery, blackmail and corruption, he was eventually arrested in 1933 and prosecuted under the Honours (Prevention of Abuses) Act 1925. With the possibility hanging over him that all the names of those who had bought titles would come out in court (names that to this day are still unidentified), Gregory was persuaded to plead guilty in return for a lenient sentence, and he received the minimum tariff allowed. After his release he retired to Paris on a pension of £2,000 provided by 'well-wishers'.

Here some sort of justice did eventually catch up with Maundy

Gregory. He was captured by the Germans following their invasion of Paris in 1940 and sent to the concentration camp at Drancy. Here he fell ill, dying in the Val de Grâce Hospital on 28 September 1941.

Murder at Bisham Abbey

Bisham Abbey in Berkshire is best known today as one of the five national Sports Centres where athletes and sportsmen and women, including the English football squad, prepare for important competitions. It is also home to a dark and tragic secret.

Bisham Abbey had originally been a priory of Augustinian canons before falling prey to the Dissolution of the Monasteries, only to be refounded as a Benedictine abbey by the ever-fickle Henry VIII who, momentarily, had second thoughts. This institution lasted barely six months before the abbey was definitively suppressed and Abbot John Cordery was expelled. Legend has it that as he was dragged away he cursed all future owners of the site, promising that the sons of its inheritors would be hounded by misfortune. In one particular case, the curse apparently came true.

One of the first of those inheritors was Sir Thomas Hoby, Elizabeth I's ambassador to France, and his wife Elizabeth. Elizabeth was the third of five famously brilliant sisters and the abbey, now rebuilt as a grand Tudor manor, was the home to their young family in the early 1560s. As a humanist scholar, linguist and patron of the arts, Elizabeth determined to supervise the education of her children herself, operating a strict regime with the liberal use of corporal punishment so typical of the day. It was this that would lead to Bisham's secret.

According to the tale, Elizabeth had one young son, William, who was not as gifted as his brothers and sisters. Long after the others had finished their work and gone to play in the garden, he would remain at his desk, struggling to fill the pages of his exercise book without blotting it. Elizabeth was not known for her patience and the child's repeated failure in his lessons drove her to mete out ever more brutal punishments. At the end of one such class the older children had finished their work but William, as always, lagged behind. To punish the boy whom she thought simply lazy, Elizabeth beat him with a ruler and then tied him to his chair in the great tower room, ordering him to finish his work. Having locked the door, she then went riding in the park.

It was whilst she was out riding that she received a summons to the court, which was then at Windsor. As a close friend of the Queen, she went straight there without leaving instructions for the children. At the end of a week at court, she returned home to be met by her children, all save William. When she asked where the boy was, the servants replied that they thought she had taken him with her to Windsor.

Horrified at what this might mean, she hurried to the tower room, unlocked the door, and there, still tied to his chair, was little William, now long dead.

Elizabeth, who lived for more than another forty years, married again, having a second family with John, Lord Russell, but was said to have never got over the tragedy at Bisham. This is how the house has come to gain a reputation as the most haunted in England for it is Lady Hoby, not little William, who is said to walk the dark corridors, ceaselessly trying to wash her son's blood from her hands.

Whether the spectral Lady Elizabeth ever interrupts the preparations of England's sportsmen and women these days is uncertain and the lack of a William in any contemporary Hoby pedigree must cast some doubt on the story in the first place. In 1840, however, there were reports that a Mrs East, who was renting the abbey at the time, had found a child's copybook during building work and that the name inscribed in it was William Hoby. Curiously, the book disappeared before it could be properly examined.

The Strange Death of Kit Marlowe

Christopher Marlowe's great claim to fame is as an Elizabethan playwright but his short life and violent death have always been surrounded by rumours that he led a parallel life as a Tudor spy.

Although there is no conclusive evidence that Marlowe was employed as a government agent, the late sixteenth century was a time when the English secret service was first taking on a recognisable form in the face of what was seen a growing Catholic threat. Queen Elizabeth I, the Protestant ruler of a Protestant country, seemed unlikely now to produce a direct heir and disaffected Catholics who had been persecuted under her rule, along with foreign Catholic powers, posed an increasing danger. In response to this, the government, and in particular Sir Francis Walsingham, had been building up a network of informers to pass on various kinds of intelligence, including Catholic plots, the religious beliefs of senior aristocrats and the activities of the Jesuit priests and foreign agents in the country. This was the world into which the dramatist may have fallen.

The summer of 1587, the year before the Spanish Armada, found Christopher Marlowe at Cambridge University where he had something of a problem. Rumours were rife that he was a secret Catholic and sometimes travelled to Rheims (where there was an English Catholic seminary for training priests). As a result the university authorities considered delaying or even refusing his admission to the degree of Master of Arts. In the climate of the times it was a reasonable fear and the university was right to be on the lookout for potential Catholic agitators.

The response from the government, however, suggests that Marlowe was something else entirely. The Privy Council wrote to the university, commending Marlowe, scotching the rumours and making veiled references to how the young playwright had 'done her Majestie good service'. Exactly what this means is unclear although the rider that he had been employed by the government 'in matters touching the benefit of his country' would have hinted to the university authorities that they could dismiss their fears.

Was Marlowe by then a spy? As with so many spying stories there is no definitive proof, no official record to say one way or the other. At Cambridge he was certainly considered a militant Catholic but the government was keen to suppress this fact. If

Marlowe had at one point been a radical young Catholic, it seemed he was the sort who offered no danger to Walsingham and as such can only have been working for him. If he were indeed a spy infiltrating Catholic circles, that too might explain the next great mystery of his life – his death.

The standard story of Kit Marlowe's death, as it is still often told today, is that he was stabbed in a tavern brawl, yet this is very definitely not what happened. Thanks to the discovery of the inquest, which was located in the Public Record Office in 1925, we now know that four men – Nicholas Skeres, Robert Poley, Ingram Frizer and Christopher Marlowe – met at a house in Deptford belonging to the widow Eleanor Bull at ten o'clock on the morning of Wednesday 30 May 1593. The venue was very much not a tavern. The men had hired a private room at this house where they dined and, later in the afternoon, walked in the garden.

It was six o'clock when they returned indoors to eat again and, after the meal, Marlowe lay down on a bed whilst his friends sat at the table. At this point Frizer and Marlowe got into an argument over the bill and exchanged insults. According to Frizer, Marlowe jumped up, snatched his dagger and struck him twice about the head. At the inquest Frizer obligingly showed the wounds he had received. A fight started, in the course of which Frizer fatally wounded Marlowe over the right eye with the dagger. The coroner's verdict was 'self-defence'.

Nevertheless, if the inquest puts to rest the story of the tavern brawl, it hardly answers every question. In the first place the three surviving witnesses were not exactly above suspicion. Robert Poley was another of Walsingham's spies and had broken the Babington plot. Skeres and Frizer for their part were known swindlers who made their money entrapping rich young gentlemen. Frizer was also a business associate of Thomas Walsingham (Sir Francis's cousin and Marlowe's patron). It is certain that Marlowe died at the hands of a supposed friend, and not at those of a stranger in a brawl, but whether that 'friend' deliberately killed him in the heat of the moment, on the orders of more shadowy figures, still remains as much a mystery as ever.

Lionel Crabb's Last Dive

Few diving stories have attracted more conspiracy theories than the last mission of Lionel 'Buster' Crabb, but then Crabb was no ordinary diver. His first underwater experience could hardly have been more dangerous. Having volunteered for training as a bomb disposal expert, he was sent to the busy port of Gibraltar in 1940 at the height of the Italian attacks on shipping in the harbour.

The Italian tactic was twofold: using divers to attach limpet mines to vessels, and human-guided torpedoes to sink shipping in the busy port. Crabb was tasked with preventing this – attacking enemy assailants and defusing devices that had already been set, as well as undertaking the grim work of recovering dead bodies. It was a baptism of fire but Crabb revelled in the dangers and became an expert naval diver. At the end of the war he received his reward in the form of a George Medal and an OBE.

In peacetime Crabb continued to seek out the more dangerous work his profession offered, diving to two sunken submarines in – sadly fruitless – attempts to rescue the crews. By the time he retired in 1954, aged 45, he had risen to the rank of commander and gained the nickname 'Buster' after the famous US Olympic swimmer and Tarzan actor, Buster Crabbe. At this point his naval career should have come to an end, yet it did nothing of the kind.

Crabb next emerged in Her Majesty's Service on 17 April 1956 when he booked into the Sally Port Hotel in Portsmouth in the company of a man going by the somewhat unconvincing name of 'Bernard Smith'. In fact 'Smith' was a junior member of MI6, which had recently recruited Crabb for a secret mission. The following day the Soviet cruiser *Ordzhonikidze* was due to dock in Portsmouth, bringing with it the General Secretary of the Communist Party of the Soviet Union, Nikita Khrushchev, who was on a diplomatic mission. MI6 wanted Crabb to measure the propellers of the *Ordzhonikidze* to aid in tuning the secret North Atlantic sound surveillance system known as SOSUS, which was designed to locate and identify enemy surface and submarine vessels in the North Atlantic. Obviously the mission had to pass unnoticed by the Russians but it was also imperative that UK politicians, including the Prime Minister, didn't find out as he had warned the intelligence service to stay away from the cruiser.

That evening Crabb and his MI6 minder went to HMS *Vernon*, the Royal Navy diving establishment, where Crabb was fitted with a specialist, closed-circuit, oxygen-breathing system that did not release the tell-tale bubbles of open scuba systems. He was also given a rubber diving suit. The following day the *Ordzhonikidze* and its escort vessel arrived. At 5.30 that evening Crabb entered the waters of Portsmouth harbour at King's Stairs, just 80 metres from where the *Ordzhonikidze* lay alongside, but he got into difficulties and aborted the mission. The following morning he returned to the stairs around 7.30 and tried again, but once more got into difficulties and briefly returned. Minutes later he set off for a third attempt.

The last sighting of Crabb alive probably comes from the lookout of the *Ordzhonikidze*, who reported seeing a frogman in the water at 7.35 a.m. The Russian rear admiral immediately asked for an explanation from his British counterpart who, of course, had no idea what was happening. A diplomatic incident ensued, leaving MI6 in the unenviable situation of having organised the mission without political approval. The Russians were greatly enjoying humiliating the British Prime Minister and the government over the breach of etiquette shown to a visiting dignitary. Far worse still, Crabb never returned.

Attempts were quickly made to cover up the mission. Crabb's possessions were removed from the Sally Port Hotel and the page containing his (and his handler's) name was torn out of the register. The story was put out that Crabb had died in a naval diving accident some 3 miles away. By now the Russian delegation had made it very clear to their hosts and the press that Crabb had been seen near the *Ordzhonikidze*, so the story refused to die. Russian interest eventually waned but Prime Minister Anthony Eden, having been forced to answer questions in parliament, was furious and forced Sir John Sinclair, head of MI6, to retire. What, however, had happened to Crabb?

Searches were made of the harbour as soon as he failed to return but his body was not recovered. It was a year later that a fisherman found a headless and armless (hence unidentifiable) corpse in a rubber frogman's suit, floating off Pilsey Island at the mouth of Chichester harbour. Although this could not be positively identified, the coroner announced that he at least was satisfied it was Crabb.

There is still speculation – and wild speculation at that – about the fate of Lionel Crabb. He had certainly had difficulty with his complex equipment and was also not particularly fit, so it seems highly likely that he developed oxygen or carbon-dioxide poisoning, which may well have killed him underwater.

However, persistent rumours remained, as they do to this day, that he was taken on board the *Ordzhonikidze* through an underwater hatch and either defected or was imprisoned. Various Russian stories have appeared in the press, including a claim from a Soviet diver that he found Crabb near the ship and cut his throat; there is another, competing claim that he became a diving expert for the Soviet navy. One Soviet intelligence officer claimed Crabb was spotted in the water and was shot by a sniper, whilst a British author asserts that Crabb was murdered by an MI5 agent as he was about to defect. According to Harry Houghton, a member of the Portland spy ring, his Russian controller told him that Crabb had been discovered and taken on board the *Ordzhonikidze* in a state of collapse due to oxygen poisoning. He had later died in the cruiser's sickbay.

None of these stories is provable, at least until the full records are released, which will not take place until 2057. Indeed, all that is really known is that as Lionel Crabb entered the water on 19 April 1956, he walked out of history and into conspiracy-theory legend.

The Darnley Mystery

Henry Stewart, Duke of Albany, should have a glorious place in British history as the direct male ancestor of every ruler of England, Ireland and Scotland since the accession of James I in 1603. Instead he remains a murky figure at the centre of an unsolved conundrum.

Henry Stewart was almost always known by his father's subsidiary title, Lord Darnley, and he became the second husband of Mary Queen of Scots. In terms of family he should have been an ideal match, being a descendant of James II of Scotland and Margaret Tudor (Henry VIII's sister), yet the marriage proved disastrous. Darnley was younger than his wife by three years but his immaturity made him seem younger still. He was violent, had a drink problem and desperately coveted the 'crown matrimonial' – a right that would have given him the crown of Scotland outright on his wife's death and made him much more than the consort he actually was.

Perhaps not surprisingly, Mary refused to give her husband any real power, knowing both his unpopularity with the nobility and his unstable temperament. In return Darnley developed a deep jealousy of those with apparent power, focusing his hatred in particular on musician David Riccio, the secretary responsible for his wife's French correspondence. Riccio was a Catholic at a time when the Protestant faction were growing in power in Scotland, and he was widely believed to be a papal agent, although it was his closeness to Mary and his boasting about it that would prove his downfall.

Having formed a bond with other disaffected nobles, the turbulent Darnley, with an audaciousness matched only by his foolhardiness, arranged for the murder of Riccio in the Queen's presence – perhaps in the hope of causing her to miscarry the son she was then bearing. If so, the plan succeeded only in part. Riccio died terribly in a fury of dagger blows but Mary and her child survived. A month later there were already rumours that Mary was petitioning the Pope for a divorce.

Darnley responded by playing the good husband, apparently returning to the Catholic faith (he changed his religious allegiance frequently) and waiting dutifully on his wife. However, with the birth of their son (the future James VI of Scotland and I of England) in June 1566, he could no longer bear his perceived loss of status and began conspiring to undermine his wife's authority. In the late autumn of that year Mary and her council met at Craigmillar to discuss what to do with Darnley – on the one hand a jealous fool threatening the throne, yet on the other the father of the future king. The result was the Craigmillar Bond, a now-lost document.

Whilst it is not known what exactly was in the bond, events began to unfold that suggest it was no less than a death warrant for Darnley. Darnley had refused to attend his son's baptism, retiring instead to his father's house in Glasgow where he had fallen ill with what was announced as smallpox but more probably was syphilis, contracted during one of his many forays into the seamier side of Edinburgh life. Appearing sympathetic, Mary had Darnley brought back to Edinburgh, nominally to nurse him, and explaining the decision to keep him at the Old Provost's Lodging at Kirk o'Field (not the royal palace of Holyrood where the Queen and her son were staying) as being for his health's sake.

Here Darnley made a good recovery, writing to his father to say that Mary seemed again to be a 'loving wife'. It would be amongst his last letters. As his health was improving, the date of 10 February 1567 was decided upon as that of his return to Holyrood to be fully reunited with his family. The reunion never took place. During the night of 9 February a huge explosion completely destroyed the Old Provost's Lodging.

The following day the bodies of Darnley, still dressed in his nightshirt, and that of a servant, were found in the garden some distance away from the house. Next to their bodies were a dagger, a chair, a coat and a cloak. Initially it was assumed that the bodies had been blown there by the force of the explosion but an examination showed no marks from blast, shot or dagger. It seems they had escaped the initial impact, only to be caught and probably suffocated as they fled. One contemporary report from a neighbour claimed they heard Darnley begging for his life in the garden.

The death created a scandal that would help undermine Mary's government further, particularly as the main suspect seemed to be the Earl of Bothwell, a man who would later marry Mary. Bothwell faced a sham trial but was acquitted, further damaging the Queen's reputation as it was widely assumed she at least knew about, and probably approved, the plot. Having lost the support of the nobles and the people of Scotland, Mary was set on a path that would lead to her exile and, ultimately, her execution in England. Darnley's son would go on to rule both countries.

The Atonement of Charles Peace

The life of the now largely and, some would say, thankfully forgotten Charles Peace was so full of secret liaisons, clandestine loves, multiple aliases and narrow escapes that it is remarkable that even he knew who he was. *The Dictionary of National Biography*, that seminal tome in which all the great and the good (and a few of the bad) of this nation are recorded, has less trouble pinning him down and simply calls him a 'burglar and murderer'.

Charles Frederick Peace did not really have the looks for a life of crime. In a job where anonymity is a useful attribute, Peace, who was born in 1832, was described as 'thick-featured', 'monkey-faced' and 'bandy-legged', missing three fingers on one hand and walking with a permanent limp (following an accident in a steel-rolling mill). None of these characteristics would seem to mark him out as the ideal cat burglar, yet that is what he became.

To be fair to Peace, he had on occasion made a stab at legitimate work. He was famed for having taught himself the violin, although his instrument had only one string, and he was billed in the pubs of his native Sheffield as 'the modern Paganini'. Nevertheless, burglary was what Peace mostly did and, initially at least, he did it very badly. By the time he was twenty-two he had already clocked up gaol sentences of twenty years although remission greatly reduced the time he actually served.

In just five years he was out of prison and able to marry Hannah Ward, who already had a young son, and he moved with her to Sheffield in 1872 after another spell inside, finally setting up shop as a legitimate picture framer. A secret liaison would soon be his downfall. In 1876 this most unpromising-looking Lothario began an affair with Katherine Dyson, the wife of a local civil engineer. Peace had an unusual way of wooing women, which involved threatening them with his gun, and on one such occasion he was seen doing this by witnesses, leading to the issuing of a warrant for his arrest. Keen to evade justice, Peace fled to Manchester where, despite his disguise, he was cornered by the unfortunately named PC Cock. More unfortunately still, Peace again wielded his pistol and shot the constable dead.

Amazingly, the police managed to lose Peace at this point, arresting instead two local lads, John and William Hebron, for the murder. Peace, now convinced he was a genius at disguise, even attended the trial at which William Hebron, then only eighteen and absolutely innocent, was convicted and sentenced to death.

While Hebron awaited his fate, Peace dashed back to Sheffield where an argument flared between him and Mr Dyson, who was now well aware of Peace's unhealthy influence on his wife. Peace again resolved this situation with his trusty pistol, shooting Dyson dead. It was time for a new disguise and a more permanent move so, with his wife and stepson, he headed south, reaching London via Nottingham. Here he managed to pick up yet another mistress, Susan Grey, who, surprisingly, came to live with the family in Peckham.

Using the new name 'Mr and Mrs Thompson', Peace and his recently acquired mistress enjoyed a bizarre quasi-gentility in a small villa, with his wife Hannah living in the basement and pretending to be their housekeeper. At night the money to fund this strange ménage would be found through burglary.

Charles Peace's one-man crime wave continued until 1878 when he was cornered by two policemen as he broke into a house in Blackheath. Despite the ample use of his pistol he was overpowered and arrested, later being given a life sentence for shooting with intent to murder.

Extraordinarily, the police still didn't actually know whom they had caught – indeed, it must have been difficult for Peace himself to keep track – but luckily for them there is no honour amongst thieves. At this point Susan Grey shopped him in the hope of claiming the £100 reward.

However, Peace's story was not quite over. On the train north to stand trial he managed to escape from his two guards and leap on to the track, although he knocked himself unconscious in the process and was soon picked up. At the Leeds assizes it took the jury just ten minutes to find him guilty of the murder of Dyson for which he was sentenced to death. Finally admitting exactly who he was, he offered one last act of atonement. Sending for the governor of the gaol where William Hebron languished following the commutation of his sentence from death to life imprisonment, Peace confessed to the murder of PC Cock, drawing a diagram of the scene to prove he had been there. He then went to his death having composed his own memorial cards, which read:

In
Memory
of
Charles Peace
Who was executed in
Armley Prison
Tuesday February 25, 1879
Aged 47
For that I don but never
Intended.

7

Secret Stashes

There comes a time in every rightly constructed boy's life when he has a raging desire to go somewhere and dig for hidden treasure.

Mark Twain, *The Adventures of Tom Sawyer* (1876)

The Great Concealer

Christopher William Clayton Hutton, known as 'Clutty' to his friends, was probably responsible for more prison breakouts than any other man in history, and all with the blessing of the British government.

Clutty had always had an interest in concealment, ever since he had bet the great Houdini £100 that he could not escape from a wooden box built by one of the workmen in his uncle's timber yard. Houdini had accepted the challenge and then simply bribed the workman, making his usual spectacular escape and winning the £100. It was a lesson that Clutty would never forget.

It was also a story that came to the attention of Norman Crockatt many years later in 1940, when he was setting up the British intelligence operation MI9, whose job it was to train fighting men to evade capture or escape from the enemy. Since the signing of the Geneva Convention in 1929, minimum standards had been set down for the treatment of prisoners of war, including the requirement that the maximum punishment for attempted escape could be nothing worse than a period in solitary confinement. The British High Command now considered that it was a POW's duty to try to escape as this would return valuable fighting men to the battle, help relieve the boredom of camp life and improve morale when escapes were successful. Clutty, with his interest in the magic of concealment, was asked to provide the secret tools to enable captured servicemen to do just this.

Interviews with Johnny Evans, one of the few men to escape from a German POW camp in the First World War, suggested three essentials for the escaper – a map, a compass and food. All these items would, of course, have to be concealed so that, when escapees were captured, the Germans did not find them. Clutty first set to work on locating suitable maps. Sadly, with typical bureaucratic dogmatism, the War Office refused to give him maps of Germany as these were 'classified'. Undaunted, Clutty hopped on a train and went to Bartholomew's, Edinburgh's most famous mapmakers, where he bought hiking maps of Germany, France, Poland and other suitable places, which, apparently unknown to the War Office, were still readily available. Having heard what use would be made of them, Bartholomew's agreed to waive all its reproduction fees.

However, maps were bulky and rustled when opened, both of which made them unsuitable for an escapee. So Clutty hit upon printing them on parachute silk, which could be folded up very small, yet without rustling or creasing. Initial attempts to print on silk failed as the inks ran, until Clutty suggested mixing them with pectin. The results were perfect, which just goes to show that a little knowledge of jam making is never a bad thing. By the end of the war over 400,000 of these maps had been printed.

A compass was next. Clutty approached the instrument makers Blunt Brothers, who came up with a number of tiny compasses so small that he realised he could place one in the back of a button. Henceforth every uniform contained one unscrewable button with a compass inside. When the Germans cottoned on to this, Clutty simply reversed the screw thread so that guards trying to unscrew buttons actually tightened them instead. When this was discovered in turn, other versions were invented, including the simplest of all – the magnetised razor blade. If it was hung on a thread, the G of 'Gillette' always pointed north. From that point on all razor blades were magnetised.

All these devices were packed in special escape kits, consisting of a small cigarette tin stuffed with razor blades, maps, condensed food, water-purifying tablets and a rubber water bottle. By 1941 no aircrew left the ground without one of Clutty's escape kits. A later addition was the escape boot – an apparently normal flying boot that could easily be cut down to a (less recognisable and more comfortable) walking boot, while the top sections when put together made a warm waistcoat. Flexible saw blades were threaded through the laces and the heel contained a secret compartment holding a compass, maps and a file.

There was the further problem of getting escape equipment to men already in captivity. The Red Cross could not be used for smuggling as it might compromise their whole operation if found out.

So, through a series of bogus charities, MI9 arranged for concealed escape equipment to be sent in its own parcels to the prisoners. Silk maps were pressed into gramophone records or hidden in the thick boards used for Monopoly and Ludo; German currency was tightly rolled in the handles of awls used for tightening the lacing on footballs; whole packs of playing cards peeled apart when dropped in water to reveal a fifty-two-part map of the German frontier. Even escape clothing was provided. Blankets were sent that, when wet, revealed the outline of an overcoat, which could then be cut out and stitched together. Fountain pens with multiple concealed dyes in the ink sacs were used to dye the blanket coats a suitable colour.

Not all of Clutty's inventions proved quite so useful. His fountain pen airgun, which fired gramophone needles, was not considered sporting (although the Free French made good use of them) and his self-heating soup tin exploded during a demonstration before the top brass. Nevertheless, by the end of the war 35,000 prisoners of war had Clutty to thank for the help he had given them to get back to Blighty.

The Hidden Duchess

In 1876 the London fine art dealers Messrs Agnew boasted a fabulous new attraction for their gallery at 39 Old Bond Street. At a very lively auction at Christie's they had purchased the most famous painting of the moment, the recently rediscovered portrait of Georgiana Cavendish, Duchess of Devonshire, by Thomas Gainsborough. It had cost Agnew's a small fortune – 10,500 guineas – making it the most expensive portrait ever purchased at that time. However, they had every hope of making another fortune from it themselves. They had commissioned an engraver to make copies of the picture to sell at 25 guineas each and 12,000 guineas had already been taken in advance orders. Then there was the painting itself, which many considered Gainsborough's masterpiece; that would surely sell for thousands more. In short, Agnew's gallery was the talk of the town.

Then, on the night of 16 May, aided by two accomplices, Adam Worth slipped through an upstairs window of the gallery, which unaccountably had been left unlocked. Taking a knife from his pocket, he cut the duchess from her frame, leaving one small triangle in the corner to help prove he had the rest when negotiations were opened for its return, rolled her up under his arm and made good his escape.

This was perhaps the high point of Adam Worth's criminal career. Born in Prussia, he had moved to America as a child and begun his life of crime as a 'bounty jumper' in the US Civil War, signing up for regiments, receiving his pay and then absconding (preferably without having to fight). From this he had moved on to far more lucrative bank robberies, in the process coming to the attention of Pinkerton's Detective Agency but avoiding capture.

With a move to England, his underworld empire grew further, leading Scotland Yard to refer to him as 'The Napoleon of Crime'. In London he led a highly lavish and very public lifestyle, masquerading as a wealthy American oil tycoon, owning yachts, race horses and grand houses. All this was actually funded by his crimes although he was always careful to avoid direct contact with his associates, making the police suspicious but providing them with no actual evidence. Furthermore he assiduously avoided any violence in his crimes, marking himself out as a different class of criminal – a real-life Raffles and a gentleman thief.

Now he was in possession of the most famous painting of the day, but what did he intend to do with it? He had in fact stolen it in the hope of using it to bargain for the release of an associate then in Newgate gaol, a plan that had fallen through. Whilst the portrait would be too difficult to sell, it could always be ransomed back to Agnew's, who were offering a substantial reward for its return. This Worth refused to do, angering his accomplices who threatened to betray him to the police and Pinkerton's agents if he didn't turn the painting into cash. Yet Worth would not relent. Instead of making a fortune from this most audacious of robberies, he had a special airtight trunk made with a false bottom, in which he placed his duchess, perfectly packed, hidden and safe. From then on she would travel everywhere with him. This time, Worth didn't want the money; he was in love with his painted lady and wanted to keep her.

No criminal spree on Worth's scale can go on for ever and in 1892 he was briefly arrested and imprisoned in France after a botched raid on a money delivery cart. Although Worth still denied his true identity, men from Scotland Yard and Pinkerton's identified him. Both organisations were getting information from his accomplices, who were more than ready to incriminate Worth in return for lighter sentences.

On his release from prison, he was a hunted and a haunted man, now nearly destitute and perhaps finally tired of his life of crime. Back in the USA he made contact with his old adversary, William Pinkerton, and announced his intention to 'return the lady', on condition that he received the reward so that he could provide for his family and was himself given immunity from prosecution. After protracted negotiations with the owners, Morland Agnew arrived in Chicago with the $25,000 reward money. In a hotel lobby he was approached by an unusually elderly bellboy (almost certainly Worth himself) who left a trunk with him and took the cash. In the false bottom of the trunk was the painting, still in perfect condition. Within hours Agnew's had sold the picture to the US millionaire J. Pierpont Morgan for $225,000. Agnew's then took the portrait back to London to be restored to its frame. Irresistibly drawn after his lost love, Worth followed.

On 4 January 1902, Agnew's handed over the Gainsborough to Morgan. Four days later, Adam Worth died and his unusual love story came to an end. His own story would live on, however, thanks to the author Sir Arthur Conan Doyle, who was already using Worth as the model for the nemesis of his hero Sherlock Holmes: Professor Moriarty.

The Secret Drawer of Dr Dee

Dr John Dee was one of the great figures of the Elizabethan age. His extensive library and collection of scientific instruments made him one of our first true scientists, responsible for the navigational manual *General and Rare Memorials pertayning to the Perfect Arte of Navigation* that helped send Britons across the world. His was also a devout age that was simultaneously riddled with superstition, and his scientific enquiries included using astrology to predict the most auspicious day for Elizabeth's coronation as well as, more peculiarly, attempts to converse with angels.

Dee's interest in the occult would prove his undoing. When he was accused of being a wizard, his library at Mortlake was burnt to the ground by an angry mob, whilst his patrons, including the Queen herself, kept the man at arm's length for fear that his dark reputation would taint them. In 1608, the great magus ended his days, living in poverty and selling penny horoscopes, his reputation apparently gone – at least, temporarily.

In 1659, Méric Casaubon published an astonishing book titled *A True & Faithful Relation of What passed for many Yeers between Dr. John Dee (A Mathematician of Great Fame in Q. Eliz. and King James their Reignes) and some spirits.* Casaubon had been handed a series of Dee's manuscripts by the antiquarian Robert Cotton who had found them buried in the grounds of Dee's old home in Mortlake – perhaps to hide them from the mob. These included a series of conversations that Dee believed he had with angels from 28 May 1583 onwards. The idea of this Elizabethan magus talking to spirits (although Casaubon believed they were actually evil spirits) caused a sensation and threw Dee's memory back into the spotlight. At the same time how he had come to converse with angels, how he had learned to do it and what he had been doing before this date remained a mystery.

It was three years later, in 1662, when Mr Wale, a yeoman warder at the Tower of London, married the former Mrs Jones, widow of the late lamented confectioner John Jones of the Plow, Lombard Street. She brought to the marriage a small dower – some pieces of furniture, keepsakes and a few treasures from her former married life – which were delivered by cart to the couple's new lodgings opposite the Tower. Amongst them was a fine chest that she and

Mr Jones had bought many years before, when they were still courting, from one of the 'joyners of Adle Street'. She had immediately been taken by the piece as it had, as she put it, a 'very good lock and hinges of extraordinary neat work'. The joiner had told them that the piece had previously belonged to Mr John Woodall, a surgeon and the father of Thomas Woodall, surgeon to King Charles II. He had bought the chest at the sorry sale of the remaining effects of John Dee in 1609, the year after the magician's death.

The chest had then sat in the Jones' house, largely unremarked upon, for twenty years. But on being emptied and moved, the new Mrs Wale noticed it rattle. As this was an unusual quality for an empty chest, her husband decided to investigate. He pried up the base and found beneath 'a large secret drawer stuffed full of papers, and a rosary of olivewood beads with a cross that had caused the rattle'.

The papers, though an exciting discovery, made little sense to Mr Wale. Some were in Latin, some in a cramped handwriting and some in what looked like an entirely foreign language. Thinking they might be worth something, he took them to the antiquarian Elias Ashmole, founder of the Ashmolean Museum in Oxford. He was well known in the city as a buyer of old manuscripts, and he arranged to barter the strange papers for a copy of his book on the Order of the Garter, to which Mr Wale had rather taken a fancy.

It would be fair to say that Ashmole did very well from the deal. He could see, as the warder could not, that this concealed trove contained many of the lost early works of John Dee, some so secret (and in his lifetime so dangerous) that he had hidden them far from prying eyes. They included transcripts of the conversations Dee believed he had had with angels before 28 May 1583 and several of his secret books concerning the origins of and methods behind these conversations, including the *48 Claves Angelicae* (the 'Angelic Keys') containing forty-eight angelic prophesies, *De Heptarchia Mystica* (a sort of angelic encyclopedia) and the *Liber Scientiae Auxiliis et Victoriae Terrestris* – the 'Book of Knowledge, Help and Earthly Victory'. Together they provide a unique insight into one of the greatest minds of the Tudor era, an exotic mix of science, then in its infancy, and the arcane magic of the mediaeval world. These works were considered so lethal at the time they were compiled that, were it not for the good taste and good hearing of a yeoman warder's new wife, they might have been lost to the world for ever.

Gentle Johnny

There is something very exciting about stashes found locked away in a safe and Johnny Ramensky spent more time than most attempting to get his hands on such secrets. Unfortunately, Johnny was anything but discreet in his safe-breaking, spending over forty of his sixty-seven years in prison. It is therefore ironic that the one occasion when he worked heroically for King and Country was quietly erased from the records.

Ramensky – known as 'Gentle Johnny' for his refusal to use violence in any of his raids, prison escapes or recaptures – was an arch recidivist. If ever there was a career criminal, he was one and, whilst it would be wrong to condone a life of safe-breaking, his story definitely belongs in the more gallant camp of villains.

Gentle Johnny had learnt to use dynamite in 1919 whilst working in a Scottish mine aged just fourteen, before moving with his family to one of the most deprived areas of Glasgow. Here he drifted into petty crime, spending time in borstal where he met more hardened criminals. His explosive skills seemed to point him towards a career as a 'peterman' or safe-breaker.

Johnny was undoubtedly good at breaking safes but he seldom got away with it. His technique was very distinctive and his escape plans were not overly rigorous, so he soon found himself back inside. Whilst he was serving a term for blowing a safe in a bakery in 1934, his wife died, which led directly to the start of his other career as a serial escapee. When the authorities brutally refused to allow him to attend the funeral, he promptly escaped, humiliating the staff at Peterhead prison where there had never previously been an escape. He was picked up just a few miles away and returned. Again with quite unjustified brutality, he was then shackled to his cell. His chains were released only with the intervention of an MP, who in the process ensured that shackling was never used again in Scottish prisons.

On his release Gentle Johnny went straight back to his trade and was almost instantly caught again, this time receiving a five-year sentence. By 1942, however, some in authority were taking an interest in his particular gifts. He could blow safes and escape from heavily guarded institutions, both of which might prove useful in wartime. So, just before his release date, Johnny Ramensky was taken to the War Office and asked to enlist in the army for 'special operations'. Having trained as a commando, he was promoted to sergeant and given his mission. From now on Gentle Johnny would parachute into enemy territory, locate headquarters buildings, break in, blow the safe and recover Germany's secret military plans.

It was a scheme of breathtaking audacity and near-suicidal risks, but it was highly effective. We know that Johnny worked with the Eighth Army in North Africa, successfully blowing Rommel's safe before moving on to the invasion of Italy where, in one day, he and his team managed to crack fourteen safes in foreign embassies in Rome. As the Allies rolled across Europe, so did Ramensky, famously opening the safes and strongrooms at Goering's headquarters in the Schorfheide forest.

This extraordinary story was, for once, one that Johnny could be proud of, yet the full details of exactly what he did and what he found in those Nazi safes will probably now never be known. In 1945, Ramensky, now calling himself Ramsay, was given the Military Medal (although it's uncertain whether he accepted this) and demobilised. He almost immediately went back to his life of crime, being caught breaking into a jeweller's in York within days of returning to civvy street. After five years in prison he was released but arrested yet again after just seven days for cracking a post office safe, receiving another five years' sentence.

With a lot more time on his hands, he decided to record his war memoirs, despite the fact that his signing the Official Secrets

Act barred him from doing so. Having written his book, Gentle Johnny started to look for a publisher. Being hampered by the fact that he was in prison, in his inimitable way he escaped, only to be recaptured at the very same place he had been found after his first prison break. The authorities now impounded the manuscript and destroyed it, so the only part of Ramensky's life that he wished to be made public will now forever remain secret, whilst the vast majority of his nefarious life, which he wished to keep quiet, is today public information.

Gentle Johnny never rewrote his memoirs. On his release he lost no time in robbing a bank and went down for another ten years, being sent back to Peterhead prison, from which he made another three escapes in a single year. Four more stretches in prison followed until he collapsed in Perth prison, dying in the Perth Royal Infirmary on 4 November 1972.

A career criminal, he had also served heroically in the war and his gentle methods made him a local hero, a latter-day Robin Hood. He was famed for writing get-well cards for the detectives whose careers often focused on chasing – and catching – him and for warning safe-owners of charges he had placed in their safes but had now blown. His epitaph is perhaps best left to his long-suffering lawyer, Nicholas Fairbairn QC, who described his life as a quest 'to break into whatever he was out of and out of whatever he was inside'.

Agent Pickle Cleans Up

On 30 April 1746 two ships, the *Mars* and the *Bellona*, dropped anchor at Loch nan Uamh, Arisaig, in the Scottish Highlands. From the hold they unloaded seven casks of gold coins, once intended to fund Bonnie Prince Charlie's attempt to regain the English and Scottish thrones. Now, two weeks after the prince's comprehensive defeat at Culloden, the money was to be used instead to spirit the remaining Jacobites (and the prince himself) out of the country.

Things got off to a bad start when one of the casks was stolen, although the rest were safely brought to Loch Arkaig and buried.

The secret of the location of the treasure then passed through several hands, starting with Donald Cameron of Locheil, chief of the Clan Cameron, and ending up with Macpherson of Cluny. Playing a deadly game of hide-and-seek with the British, he was holed up in a cave known as 'the cage' where he stayed for an impressive eight years.

Bonnie Prince Charlie had meanwhile escaped to France and was understandably keen to be reunited with his cash, even suggesting later that Cluny had embezzled it. This seemed unlikely behaviour in a fervent Jacobite who was forced to live in a cave. Two possibilities remained: either someone else had stolen the money or it was still buried. Wanting to know which, in 1752 Charles dispatched Dr Archibald Cameron, brother of the first keeper of the treasure's location, to find it. Cameron was a loyal Jacobite whose unstinting belief in the return of the Stuart monarchy rarely did him much good. Back in Scotland many of his clan despaired at his continued support for what was clearly a lost cause whilst his involvement in hare-brained schemes – including one to kidnap and murder George II, in what was known as the Elibank plot – put his and other lives in danger although, ironically, not that of George II.

Having arrived in Scotland, Cameron set to work trying to locate the money and further the Elibank plot. It was through the latter that he came into contact with Alasdair Ruadh MacDonnell of Glengarry. Glengarry had also suffered the vicissitudes of being a staunch Jacobite. He had fought for Bonnie Prince Charlie and tried to warn him against the invasion of 1745 but had arrived on the scene only after the prince had already embarked on the ill-fated invasion that culminated in the Culloden defeat. Glengarry had been captured by the English and imprisoned in the Tower. Destitute, he had endured conditions in Paris and London of dire poverty, yet in return for his loyalty the Jacobite leadership had offered him nothing. This was a mistake.

What neither Bonnie Prince Charlie nor Archibald Cameron knew was that Glengarry was also known in England by another name – Agent Pickle. Now, having worked his way into the lunatic Elibank plot, he promptly gave the location of Cameron's hiding place to the English authorities. Cameron was arrested at Glenbucket and sent to London for trial. Not wanting to depress the markets by announcing that there had been a plot against the royal family, and keen to protect Agent Pickle's identity, the government had Cameron tried for his role in the 1745 uprising instead of his involvement in the Elibank plot.

Unsurprisingly, he was found guilty and sentenced to a traitor's death – hanging, drawing and quartering. Even in 1753 this was considered somewhat barbarous and furious attempts were made to at least commute the punishment to a less brutal death. The King refused, however, and on 7 June 1753 Cameron was hanged, cut down alive, disembowelled and beheaded. He was the last Jacobite ever to be executed.

Pickle got away with his deceit. Glengarry was revealed as the spy only in 1897 when the historian Andrew Laing noticed that the two men shared the same handwriting and the same habit of spelling the word 'who' as 'how'.

In the meantime, what about the Loch Arkaig gold? Thankfully that was safe: safe in the hands of Agent Pickle. Perhaps those involved with Glengarry in the Elibank plot wondered how a man who was penniless in 1749 had become wealthy just a few months later. In fact Pickle had by then successfully forged the signature of the Old Pretender, James (father of Bonnie Prince Charlie), and the last custodian of the secret hiding place had handed over to him the gold in the belief that it was on its way to help the Stuart cause. It was actually on its way into Pickle's bank account – a reward he felt he was owed for his years as a committed Jacobite.

Tutankhamun's Last Secret

Highclere Castle in Berkshire is the home of the Earls of Carnarvon, a family forever associated with the discovery of the Egyptian tomb of Tutankhamun – perhaps Egypt's greatest secret. However, the castle is itself home to a secret hidden within the walls, telling one final chapter in the memorable story of the 5th Earl of Carnarvon and his Egyptian odyssey.

Highclere is not the sort of stately home usually associated with hidden panels and priest holes, having been built in 1842, long after such things became obsolete, to a design of Sir Charles Barry, architect of the Houses of Parliament. However, in July 1987 when Henry, 7th Earl of Carnavon, was preparing an inventory of the items in the house prior to a film being made there, that is exactly what he found. When the valuers had finished their work, the earl casually asked his retired butler, Robert Taylor, who had started work at the house in 1936, whether that was 'the lot'. The reply some-what surprised him: 'Yes, my lord, all except for the Egyptian stuff.'

The 5th Earl's interest in Egyptology was, of course, very well known. In 1907 he had travelled to Egypt to convalesce after a serious accident. There he had met Howard Carter and come under the spell of Egyptian archaeology. For years Carnarvon had funded Carter's expeditions, until finally they had struck the jackpot in 1922 – the almost undisturbed tomb of Tutankhamun. The following year the earl died.

Shortly after, much of his private collection of Egyptian artefacts – from all those years of excavation before the discovery of Tutankhamun, along with some other judicious purchases – was put on the market. In November 1924 these items were labelled by Carter at Highclere and packed off to the Bank of England, prior to being sold to the Metropolitan Museum of Art in New York. It was only some time after the sale that academics noted that the Metropolitan collection didn't seem to account for all the items Carnarvon had received as his part of the fifty-fifty deal struck with the Egyptian authorities, but it was assumed these had been dispersed in private sales.

Although the connection between Highclere and Egypt was then supposedly cut, in the Smoking Room in 1987 one last concealed Egyptian treasure was about to come to light. Robert Taylor showed to the 7th Earl a disused doorway leading to the drawing room. In the thickness of the walls, between two doors, were two hidden panels opened by a tiny key that Taylor remembered seeing there when the house was opened up again after the Second World War. Behind them were rows of old cigarette tins neatly stacked in pigeon-holes, and carefully wrapped in these was the missing part of the Earl of Carvarnvon's Egyptian collection. The butler had looked in one of these when he first discovered the cache but had then closed it up again, assuming the current earl was aware of it and viewing it as 'none of my business'. In fact behind the panels lay 300 ancient items, hidden for over half a century, the last part of the collection of one of the most famous names in Egyptology.

The House that Time Forgot

By 1985 the great mansion of Calke Abbey near Ticknall in Derbyshire was falling into serious disrepair. The cost of running this rambling house and its grounds, plus the imposition of extensive death duties, had left the owners with little choice but to offer to the nation the place that had been their family home for 300 years, donating it to the National Trust.

What the Trust discovered when they took possession of their new property, however, was like no other bequest. Calke Abbey was an entirely secret world, a time-warped stately home, cut off from reality, where the nineteenth century had never ended.

The Harpur-Crewe family had risen to prominence in the Tudor period and the Calke estate, built on the remains of a cell of nearby Repton priory, came into their hands in 1622. Early family members were keen to establish themselves amongst the aristocracy by doing the usual things: purchasing a baronetcy, serving in parliament and, of course, buying and improving a stately mansion as the 'family seat'.

In 1789, Sir Henry Harpur-Crewe inherited the estate, at which point the history of Calke began to diverge from that of all other country homes. Henry had been on the Grand Tour and developed a love of collecting, but he was also the first family member to show the profound sociopathy that would characterise many of his heirs and lead to his being known as 'the isolated baronet'. Shunning local and national society, he avoided London and society venues, rarely leaving his estate. To compound this 'social' crime in the eyes of his peers, he also took a lowly lady's maid, Nanette Hawkins, as his mistress and later his wife.

Henry filled his spare time at Calke, of which he had a great deal, with taxidermy. As the years passed, so Calke Abbey became crammed with case after case of stuffed animals that were seen only by his immediate family and staff as few visitors were ever invited. His grandson shared this passion as well as his social antipathy. One of the telling survivals at the house from his time is a mid-Victorian visitors' book. Most great houses of the era would have whole shelves of these, crowded with the names of all the great men and women of the day, the politicians, generals, society hostesses and academics who visited. The Calke Abbey visitors' book is 'as new' and empty.

Henry's great-grandson, Sir Vauncey Harpur-Crewe, proved even more eccentric. Very benevolent towards his staff and the tenants on his estate, he was far less tolerant of his own family. Even though they lived under the same roof, he would often communicate with them solely via notes sent with his footman or even by post.

He also began taking the family love of collecting to new extremes. The taxidermy cases started to take over whole wings of the house, complemented by new collections of geological specimens, butterflies, insects and orchids. Meanwhile, another form of collection was also growing. As well as bringing hundreds of new wildlife specimens into the house, the Harpur-Crewes never threw anything away. On the death of most aristocrats, their possessions would be sorted; some would be kept, others sold, or given in bequests. In this way, a house would gain a new complexion as it passed on to the next generation. At Calke this process stopped at some point during the nineteenth century.

When Sir Vauncey moved from his bachelor room to his married suite in the house, the old room was not cleared but simply sealed up. It remains today as it was the day he left it. Through every period of life and at the end of every life, the belongings of the era were simply shut away. This was the secret that the National Trust uncovered when they took possession of the house in 1985.

The black-bordered writing paper on which notices of Sir Vauncey's death had been written continued to lie on the table; ancient artefacts from the time of the early Georgian Harpur-Crewes had been labelled, wrapped in tissue and stored. In the kitchen there were trunks stuffed with nineteenth-century children's clothes, whilst the schoolroom, still resplendent with Victorian rocking horse and doll's house, contained battalions of perfectly preserved lead soldiers still in their cases and china dolls in unopened boxes. Perhaps most extraordinarily of all, in the linen closet was found an early eighteenth-century state four-poster bed, complete with Chinese silk hangings, still in the packing cases in which it had been delivered to the house – the remnant perhaps of an idea that Calke might one day welcome royal visitors and, if so, an idea the Harpur-Crewes had quickly thought better of.

Today Calke is kept much as it was found. A few main rooms have been cleared but most are still packed with the flotsam and jetsam of hundreds of years of country life. The stables contain the carriages that the family once used, for they almost entirely avoided motor vehicles, whilst the state rooms remain as they were on the very day Sir Vauncey died. At Calke the last of the era of great country houses has been secretly preserved, not with an eye to the future but from a profound reluctance to ever leave the past.

Doll Philips' Hidden Gold

The seventeenth century was the great era of the 'true crime' pamphlet, often scurrilous tales that told of the feats and fortunes of highwaymen, robbers and confidence tricksters. The forerunner of these occurs at the very end of the Elizabethan period and concerns a con-woman whose 'discoveries' of other people's hidden treasure left only herself any the richer.

What we know of Judith Philips, known in her day as 'Doll

Philips', comes from a handful of such pamphlets but also from the more sober records of the Secretary of State, Sir Robert Cecil. Doll Philips had originally been married to a man called Pope. Disliking the dull, penurious existence that was the best he could offer, she ran away to live with 'Egyptians', or gypsies. While travelling around southern England she decided to make her fortune as a confidence trickster, letting gullible folk into her supposed 'secret powers' as a seer and friend of the Queen of the Fairies, able to find hidden treasure.

Of the two cases we know about in detail, one concerns the tricking of a Mrs Mascall, the widow of a wealthy London tripe-seller. Rich widows were a real prize for the men who could marry them and Doll seems to have fallen in with a man called Peters who had precisely this intention. Managing to get into Mrs Mascall's confidence, Doll persuaded her that she was possessed of magical powers and could advise the widow on whom to marry – this, not surprisingly, being Peters. For this fortune-telling act she even induced the poor woman to hand over a lock of her pubic hair, which she said was essential for the work.

Indeed, so easily fooled was Mrs Mascall that Doll decided to go further. She told her that there was gold buried in the house and that she could find it for her. To do this, Mrs Mascall would have to gather together all the gold she already had and put it in one place, which would act to 'draw the hidden gold out'. The credulous widow duly obeyed and, when she wasn't looking, Doll switched the valuables and made her escape. Greed getting the better of her, she later returned to try for more, by which time the switch had been noticed and she was arrested. The theft came out when Doll was interrogated in Newgate prison, for which she was whipped through the city.

However, Doll's most famous con occurred outside London, as recounted in the pamphlet 'The Bridling, Sadling and Ryding of a Rich Churle in Hampshire'. In the village of Upsborne she found a mark in the form of a local farmer. Burying a small quantity of gold on his land, she knocked on the farmhouse door and introduced herself as a fortune-teller blessed with magical gifts. The farmer and his wife were understandably suspicious but Doll had done her homework. In the village she had made enquiries about the farmer and found out some personal details, including the fact that he was involved in a legal case. She recounted to him some of the specifics. The farmer and his wife were intrigued. How did she know so much about them? Then to clinch the deal, she told them that she knew where gold was buried on their land. They followed her to the place where she had buried the coins and, sure enough, there was the money. Now they knew she must have magical powers – why would anyone deliberately bury their own gold on someone else's land and then tell them?

With the couple well and truly hooked, Doll reeled them in. She told them that she was a friend of the Fairy Queen, who had given her amazing powers, and that she could arrange for the Queen to visit them if they would trust her implicitly. Needless to say, a visit from the Fairy Queen would leave them both rich and happy. Doll told the couple to prepare for the visit by getting out the very best of everything they had in the house.

Then, for a bit of fun, she told the farmer to get on all fours whilst she saddled and bridled him. She then rode him round the garden three times while his bemused wife looked on at what she was told was a vital part of the ritual. Finally she announced that the Fairy Queen was coming and that they must both lie on the ground with their eyes closed until she arrived. With this, she slipped back into the house and, with the aid of two accomplices, stole the farmer's goods. As her skills in setting up a con were not matched by those needed for escaping afterwards, she was eventually arrested and imprisoned.

Whilst Doll never greatly profited from her crimes, being often caught and sent to gaol, the pamphlets about her life made her famous. Indeed, both William Shakespeare in *The Merry Wives of Windsor* and Ben Jonson in *The Alchemist* create scenes with fake Fairy Queens that are very similar to Doll Philips' original con, so perhaps her crimes have made her immortal after all.

8

Secret Lives

What are little boys made of?
What are little boys made of?
Frogs and snails
And puppy-dogs' tails,
That's what little boys are made of.
What are little girls made of?
What are little girls made of?
Sugar and spice
And all that's nice,
That's what little girls are made of.

J.O. Halliwell, *Nursery Rhymes* (1844)

A Girl Called Tommy

Dorothy Lawrence was eighteen when the First World War broke out and was living in Paris looking for work as a newspaper journalist. In the early days of the war it was almost impossible for newspapers to get accurate information from the front lines as all civilians were barred from the area, so when Dorothy wrote to editors, suggesting that she might become a war reporter for them, the universal response was ridicule. If they couldn't get male reporters to the front, what hope did a mere woman have and why would they want to send such a delicate creature there in the first place? Only one editor gave her a straw to clutch at, writing: 'Of course, if you could get to the front . . .'

That's exactly what Dorothy decided to do or, as she put it in her autobiography, 'I'll see what an ordinary English girl, without credentials or money can accomplish. If war correspondents can't get out there, I'll see whether I can't go one better than those big men with their cars, credentials and money.'

Dorothy's initial attempts to get sent to the lines – volunteering for a first-aid posting – were rebuffed and it soon became clear that as a woman she would never be allowed near the actual fighting. So if Dorothy couldn't go to the front as herself, she determined to adopt the disguise of a man. Befriending two English soldiers in a Parisian café, she persuaded them to smuggle to her a British uniform, which they delivered to her flat in small parcels, claiming she was doing their laundry. With the uniform padded in places and strapped in others, she could just pass for a soldier at a distance. Her new friends were then set to work, training her in basic drill so that she could act like one of them. She managed to convince two Scottish military policemen to give her a 'regulation' haircut and, to finish off the look, she dyed her face with furniture polish to make it appear tanned and weathered.

Now looking the part, she forged her own papers, based on a real identity disc that she was given in the name of Private Denis Smith, 1st Leicestershire Regiment, before getting a safe-conduct pass from the mayor. Without further ado, she bicycled to the front.

Some way behind the front lines, at Albert, she was befriended by Tom Dunn, a Lancashire coalminer. He, like many of his trade, had found work as a sapper in the British Expeditionary Force tunnelling company whose job it was to lay mines under enemy positions. He found Dorothy a position in the company and a place to stay in an abandoned cottage in the Senlis forest.

Life at the front proved extremely hard: Dorothy was under constant fire, carrying out work that was physically hugely demanding as well as dangerous. With the danger came the realisation that were she to be injured or killed, her identity would be revealed and those who had helped her might be held to account. So, after ten days' active service she announced to her commanding officer that she was not Private Smith, but Miss Lawrence. The commanding officer was a shade surprised, to say the least, and had Dorothy placed under military arrest.

She was taken to the British Expeditionary Force headquarters, where no one was quite sure what to make of this eighteen-year-old female sapper who claimed to be a war reporter. Dorothy was therefore quickly dispatched to Calais. Here six generals and twenty other officers took turns in interrogating her to find out who she really was. It might have helped if she had not escaped soon after her arrest and had to be captured again – this led some to assume she was a spy. Others were convinced that only one sort of woman goes to the front: a prostitute, or, as they euphemistically put it, a 'camp follower'. Because Dorothy didn't know what the term meant and they didn't tell her, they talked for hours at cross-purposes.

In truth, the army was seriously embarrassed. They were terrified that people could apparently come and go as they pleased to the British lines – even women – and worried that it might encourage other females to seek adventure at the front. Dorothy was thrown into a cell at St Omer and re-examined, before being placed in the Convent de Bon Pasteur where she was forced to sign an affadavit, promising not to write of her experiences in the newspapers. Finally shipped back to Britain, she was further made to agree to reveal to the press nothing of her adventures until given written permission. Needless to say, no such permission ever came from a discomfited High Command, so the story Dorothy had gone to such great lengths to procure never made it into the newspapers.

Having been released by Scotland Yard, where she was detailed on her arrival back home, she spent the rest of the war in obscurity. In 1919 she did finally publish her autobiography although it was heavily censored. Nor did her treatment improve at the hands of a male-dominated world. Having moved to Canonbury in London, she claimed to the police that she had been raped by her church guardian. Declared insane, she was sent to Colney Hatch Lunatic Asylum where she died in 1964.

William de Longchamps' Drag Race

William de Longchamps was a mediaeval chancellor of England, chief justiciar and bishop of Ely, none of which was likely to endear him to everyone, particularly as he was active during the turbulent reigns of two monarchs, Richard I and John. We might therefore expect some of the chroniclers of the day to be rather hard on him, so the story of his hapless attempt to flee the country may owe at least a little to wishful thinking. It was, however, widely reported and there is undoubtedly a kernel of truth to this, one of a serious period's more slapstick moments.

William de Longchamps had many complicated reasons for wanting to run away but, in short, they boiled down to the fact that he was left in charge of running England by Richard I whilst the King went on the Third Crusade. This made him a touch unpopular, not least with Richard's brother John and his illegitimate half-brother Geoffrey, archbishop of York. Nor was William, a native of Normandy, especially familiar with English customs; indeed, he couldn't speak a word of the language and this, combined with his unquestionably lavish lifestyle, made him none too well-liked by many English people.

Things came to a head in 1191. Longchamps tried to arrest Geoffrey when he landed at Dover in an attempt to seize his arch-bishopric. Geoffrey fled to St Martin's priory and claimed sanctuary but was besieged there and eventually dragged out. As this reminded everyone rather too much of what had only recently happened to Thomas Becket at Canterbury, the popular mood turned against William. His enemies held a 'trial', which Longchamps didn't attend, but which declared him deposed nonetheless. He was then excommunicated for good measure. In a last bid to hold on to power, Longchamps tried to take control of the Tower of London although he was forced to relinquish this when it became clear that the people of London would not support him. It was time for him and his few remaining friends to run away.

The main source for what happened next is an open letter from Hugh de Nonant, the bishop of Coventry and a vociferous critic of Longchamps, so it may be a little embroidered. Nevertheless, the scene it describes is so wonderful that it was picked up by nearly every mediaeval chronicler. According to Nonant, Longchamps elected to make his escape in disguise, dressing himself as a female cloth-seller, but evidently going over the top: 'in a woman's green gown of enormous length instead of the priest's gown of azure colour having on a cape of the same colour, with unsightly long sleeves, instead of a chasuble, a hood on his head instead of a mitre'.

When he reached the beach at Dover, where he hoped to find a boat to take him across the Channel, he was in for a shock. A local fisherman, seeing this odd-looking 'woman' hanging around, not unnaturally assumed she was a prostitute and made a move: 'he ran up to this wretch, and embracing his neck with the left arm, with his right began pulling him about, upon which he almost immediately discovered that he was a man. At this lie he was greatly surprised, and, starting back, in a fit of amazement, shouted out with a loud voice, "Come all of you and see a wonder; I have found a woman who is a man!"'

Longchamps' friends managed to defuse the situation and the party continued waiting for the boat. Another disaster, however, was about to strike. A woman passing by saw the chancellor and took him for a cloth-seller – which is, after all, what he had intended – and so asked the bemused cleric the price of his cloth. 'He, however, made no answer, as he was utterly unacquainted with the English language; on which she pressed the more; and shortly after another woman came up, who urgently made the same enquiry, and pressed him very hard to let her know the price at which he would sell it.' His inability to reply made the women suspicious, so they pulled back his hood to reveal not a female cloth-seller but a man. This they took rather badly, shouting: 'Come, let us stone this monster, who is a disgrace to either sex.'

William Longchamps, the most powerful man in England, was pelted with stones and dragged off to a local cellar where he was imprisoned. After a great deal of explanation he was finally allowed to leave and departed for France. It was the last time he would try to escape in drag.

Isabel's Surprise

Just why Isabel Fubister wanted to go to Canada is still not really known. Some claim that she had heard stories of wild adventure from her brother George who was employed by the Hudson Bay Company; others that she needed money as she was too disfigured by smallpox to hope for a husband; the more romantic say she was searching for a long-lost lover. Whatever the truth, Isabel Fubister left behind her life on the Scottish Orkney islands in June 1806 and signed up with the Hudson Bay Company (HBC) for a three-year contract at £8 per annum.

Now before you think that employing a woman for a dangerous role in the early nineteenth century was far-sighted of the HBC, it's worth noting that Isabel didn't sign up under her own name, but as 'John Fubister', and as far as David Geddes, their agent at Stromness, could tell, she was a 'he'. So on 29 June, 'John' set sail on the *Prince of Wales*, carrying a cargo of chickens, geese, eggs and Orkney pioneers, on a six-week journey across the North Atlantic to Rupert's Land.

'John' did extremely well in the service of the HBC and the surviving records, such as they are, show that she 'worked at anything and well like the rest of the men'. This is a testament to her strength as her fellows were chosen for their extreme hardiness, having to live off the land in poorly explored territories and often in harsh weather conditions, supporting the fur-trapping business. Arriving at the settlement of Moose Factory, she was taken first by shallop to Fort Albany and thence into the interior to bring timber downriver for boat-building. In June 1807 she joined a larger brigade heading upriver on an epic 1,800-mile canoe journey to Martin Falls, continuing on to Pembina in North Dakota to supply various company outposts. Throughout this time no one suspected 'John' of being anything other than a well-built, strong and hard-working man, but at this remote settlement in North Dakota this would all suddenly change.

Pembina, on the Red river, was an outpost of the North West Company. As the winter of 1807 closed in, it also became the base of the HBC brigade, whose daily lives there were documented in the diary of the post's manager, Alexander Henry. He recorded that on the night of 29 December he heard a banging on his door and, answering, found 'John' Fubister in some distress and in need of shelter. Being a kindly soul, he invited him in, sat him by the fire and then retired to bed. A little while later he was awoken by terrible screams and ran to the fireplace where he found 'John'

> extended out upon the hearth, uttering most dreadful lamentations; he stretched out his hand towards me and in a pitiful tone of voice begg'd my assistance, and requested I would take pity upon a poor helpless abandoned wretch, who was not of the sex I had every reason to suppose. But was an unfortunate Orkney Girl pregnant and actually in childbirth.

This was rather a lot for Alexander Henry to take in but 'John' proved the point when she 'opened her jacket and display'd to my view a pair of beautiful round white Breasts'.

Moments later Isabel gave birth to a son, James, and from then on her life would be changed for ever. First, there was the matter of the father of the child. She claimed that she had been raped by one John Scarth, an HBC employee who had been on many of the expeditions with her and who had come over from Orkney with her on the same boat. Had he recognised her and black-mailed her? Scarth was certainly listed as the father yet Isabel later inexplicably changed her surname to Gunn.

Of greater concern for Isabel than paternity issues was her immediate future. As the HBC did not employ white women abroad, she was sent to work as a washerwoman at Fort Albany, a job she hated. On 20 September 1809 she was put back aboard the *Prince of Wales* with her son and shipped home, dismissed from the service.

Very little is known of her later life other than that she was a pauper. She was recorded at her death on 7 November 1861, aged eighty-one, as being a stocking and mitten maker. No one saw fit to note that she was also the first European woman ever to travel to Rupert's Land – a female pioneer of the New World.

The Rise and Fall of a Breeches Player

Charlotte Charke should have had every advantage in life. Born in 1713, the youngest child of Poet Laureate and theatrical impresario Colley Cibber (1671–1757), she enjoyed an unusually liberal education for a woman of the era, being taught Latin, geography and Italian as well as the more traditional dancing and singing. At home the spirited Charlotte as also taught herself how to race horses and shoot a gun. Aged just thirteen she set herself up as a doctor, her medical career coming to an end only when her father received a large bill for all the medicines she had been prescribing.

By now it was clear that Charlotte didn't want to accept the traditional role of a woman in seventeenth-century society and so, with the help of her father's connections, she decided on a life in acting. As the conventions of the age required, she married Richard Charke, one of her father's actors and composers, in 1730. Charlotte did not take to married life, believing her serially unfaithful husband had married her solely in the hope of improving his business prospects – which was probably true. The couple did have a child, Catherine, in the same year of their nuptials, when Charlotte was still only seventeen years old.

Nor was her relationship with her father much better. After an argument with Cibber, Charke and Charlotte set up their own rival company. By this time Charlotte was usually dressing as a man and taking on more and more male roles, becoming one of the most famous of what were known as 'breeches players', although she was already developing a reputation for walking out on productions.

In 1737 she made the extraordinary decision to appear in Henry Fielding's satirical play *Pasquin*, in which she was cast in the role of her own father. Worse still, it was a production in which Cibber was lampooned for his sycophantic attitude towards Walpole's government and his lack of poetic ability. Cibber never forgave his daughter. Nor was the government happy. Walpole immediately rushed through the Stage Licensing Act, which prevented theatres from operating without a royal patent and ensured that every play had to be passed by government censors. Unable to work and deeply in debt, Richard Charke ran away to Jamaica, abandoning Charlotte to bring up their daughter alone.

Ever practical, Charlotte set upon a new enterprise, receiving a licence to run Punch's Theatre on the old tennis courts in St James's. As this was a puppet theatre, with no human actors, it was exempt from the Stage Licensing Act. Here Charlotte began what was perhaps the forerunner of *Spitting Image*, producing a series of plays caricaturing politicians and celebrities without fear of prosecution. After a short tour, however, she fell into debt and had to sell the theatre.

By now she was considered an eccentric character about town, not least because she nearly always dressed as a man. When her family refused to help her out of debt, she was arrested, being saved from debtors' prison only by the generosity of the coffee-house owners and prostitutes of Covent Garden who took up a collection to pay her bail. Using her male disguise, Charlotte escaped her creditors and was employed in a number of unusual male roles, first as valet to the rakish Richard Annesley, 6th Earl of Anglesey, and then as a sausage-maker.

Evidently the footlights beckoned because, by 1742, Charlotte was back on stage, acting in her own play, *Tit for Tat*, and opening a pub on Drury Lane, which proved to be another financial disaster. More male acting roles followed before she was forced to flee London yet again to escape her creditors, living as a male strolling player, and accompanied by her daughter and a companion whom she called 'Mrs Brown'. A series of yet more unusual jobs followed, as a pastry-cook, a farmer, a proof-reader on a newspaper and a prompter in a Bath theatre.

In 1754, Charlotte finally returned to London, penniless once more but determined to make her living as a writer. Although her novel was sold for just 10 guineas (she had asked 30), her poignant narrative of her own history proved a great success, being seri-alised in the *Gentleman's Magazine*. The story of a woman who had lived the life of a man proved massively popular, being consid-ered utterly scandalous and irresistibly titillating. The one thing Charlotte hoped its gently self-deprecating tone might do was reconcile her to her father but the letter she sent him, begging forgiveness, he returned unopened. When he died a hugely wealthy man, three years later, he left her nothing.

Despite her struggling on for another three years, acting in minor roles, her fame as the woman who had lived as a man brought her little financial success. She died destitute in her lodgings in Haymarket on 6 April 1760, still only forty-seven years old.

The Knight in White Satin

Amongst the foreign ambassadors, legates and attachés at the court of St James in London, there have always been suspicions as to what kind of men haunt the palace halls: are they honest politicians or thinly disguised spies? The advent of the Chevalier D'Éon in London prompted an entirely different question, as what everyone wanted to know was simply whether he was a man at all.

Charles Geneviève Louis Auguste André Timothée D'Éon de Beaumont was a child of the French nobility, as his name would suggest. A brilliant student, he obtained several degrees and was a lawyer at the French *parlement* by the time he was nineteen. Not long after, he was recruited into King Louis XV's private diplomatic spying system, known as the *secret du roi*, and sent to Russia.

By the time D'Éon arrived in London in 1763 he was well known both as a brave soldier (he fought briefly in the Seven Years War) and as an expert diplomat. He was also known to enjoy dressing as a woman, having boasted that he had done so for a ball at Versailles and been hotly pursued by the King. He further claimed to have revealed his true identity to Madame de Pompadour within hours of his conquest of the King and enjoyed her too. This made him perhaps the only man ever to seduce both members of a French royal couple, in the same evening at least.

D'Éon's role in London was to help with negotiations for the end of the Seven Years War. He performed well in a very difficult situation, as France had precious little to bargain with. For his efforts he received the Royal and Military Order of St Louis, being known from then on as the 'Chevalier D'Éon'.

The Chevalier was put to use, gathering information in London for a vengeful Louis XV who, humiliated in the Seven Years War, was planning an invasion of England. D'Éon found himself caught between the orders of the government and the French royal faction represented by the *secret du roi*. The one told him to spy on the

English, the other to spy on the new French ambassador whom the King didn't trust.

When a rightly wary French ambassador arrived in London, the Chevalier, who until then had himself been acting ambassador, claimed that the incoming diplomat had invited him to the official residence in Soho Square where an attempt was made to poison and kidnap him. Whilst his government demanded his immediate recall to explain this extraordinary allegation, the King privately sent word that he should go into hiding and dispose of the letters from the *secret du roi* that he was carrying.

The English, delighted with all this infighting, gleefully refused to extradite the Chevalier. The French state stopped his pension, which he needed to maintain his lavish lifestyle, and when the King refused to help, D'Éon scandalously published his correspondence with the French authorities (although keeping some back for later use). The British government could now barely contain their amusement as an irate French spy went about publishing secret letters that exposed not only his country's intelligence-gathering on foreign powers but also the huge rifts between the French government and the crown itself. Louis XV was forced to arrange a secret pension for D'Éon just to shut him up.

To make matters worse, the French ambassador sued D'Éon for libel in London. Unable to defend himself, D'Éon fled, disguised as a woman, and lodging in the home of an opposition MP in Byfleet, Surrey. From here he organised a countersuit, claiming that the ambassador had incited one Tressac de Vergy to kill him. Once again Louis XV was prevailed upon to offer money to the Chevalier (who was still providing him with useful information). In return D'Éon handed back some papers whilst threatening to sell the rest to William Pitt, Earl of Chatham, if further funds weren't forthcoming. Chatham for his part couldn't have been happier; if the British government wished to know what the French secret service was up to, all they needed to do was sit in the public gallery of their own courts.

It was around this time that other rumours began circulating about the Chevalier. A fellow member of the *secret du roi* claimed that D'Éon had told him he was really a woman. This chimed with what had been widely noted in London – that D'Éon was always very clean-shaven and quite 'pretty'. To be fair, he was also living as a woman in Surrey and had previously claimed that he had been born a girl but raised as a boy, so that he could inherit from his father under France's strict inheritance laws. In London the gentlemen of the City were intrigued and a betting pool was started on the London Stock Exchange regarding his true gender.

Those same gentlemen may have thought they had their answer on the death of Louis XV. With the *secret* disbanded, D'Éon was desperately in need of help with his debts as the King had promised much but, typically, delivered little. He begged the French government to be allowed to come home and an agreement was reached – although with conditions. D'Éon could return but only if he spent the rest of his life as a woman, something that was hoped might make the turbulent spy a tad more controllable. Surprisingly, D'Éon agreed, provided the government would pay for a new wardrobe for him and that he could still wear his cross of the Order of St Louis.

D'Éon arrived at Versailles in August 1777 and presented himself at court, but dressed in military uniform. He was ordered to change at once into a woman's gown and was given the services of Marie Antoinette's personal maid. Evidently unhappy to be seen wandering around Versailles in a frock, he soon returned to his family estates where he was arrested for again wearing male uniform and thrown in prison. When he was released he was finally granted permission to return to London where he eventually pitched up, still in full female garb. This shocked some commentators, including James Boswell, who noted: 'She appears to me a man in woman's clothes.'

By now sixty-five and impoverished, D'Éon took to making money by demonstrating his fencing skills as 'Madame D'Éon', a female sword-fighting act that was something of a novelty, cut short, however, by a serious wound. He died in penury on 21 May

1810, when at last the gentlemen of the Stock Exchange could resolve their bet. Several surgeons were called to inspect the body and all proclaimed the Chevalier to have been in every way a man. On hearing the news, the lady who for the last seventeen years had been living with him as his companion fainted clean away.

The Dangerous Life of Marcy Clay

The short life of Marcy Clay is perhaps typical of the small but celebrated band of highwaywomen who operated in the seventeenth century. The exact details of her life are sketchy as our only account of her life comes in one anonymous pamphlet. Nevertheless it gives what is probably a typical outline for the careers of that elusive band of female criminals whom society liked to believe didn't exist but whose regular appearances in court and at the gallows suggest otherwise.

According to the pamphlet, Marcy came to London aged fifteen and fell in with a gang of thieves who taught her to shoplift. Marcy became so successful at working the shops of central London that she eventually needed to lie low for a while, so she returned to her native Dorset where she made a living pick-pocketing and thieving at country fairs and markets. It was a hard and dangerous living, offering precious little return for the risk, so in time she turned to the more lucrative profession of highway-woman, dressing as a man to intercept the mail coaches. In the South-West she seems to have rapidly gained something of a repu-tation and a rather favourable one at that, mainly thanks to her personal courage (then considered unusual in a woman), her ability to wield both pistol and sword together in a fight and also for her wry sense of humour. Amongst the many whom she robbed in male disguise was her own husband.

Marcy later returned to London and resumed her life of shoplifting, perhaps thinking the heat was now off and evading capture four times. On the fifth, however, she was taken for trial and the full dangers of her profession became apparent when she was sentenced to hang at Tyburn on 12 April 1665. However, Marcy, always a slippery character, would cheat the hangman. On the morning before her execution she managed to get four papers of white mercury smuggled to her in Newgate prison. With these she poisoned herself, taking twelve hours to die, surrounded by hundreds of ghoulish visitors who came to watch her death throes. She was buried at Tyburn on 14 April with a stake driven through her heart, as was traditional for suicides.

The Female Drummer Boy

The story of Mary Anne Talbot demonstrates how it was possible to fall into a 'secret' life without any initial intention of deceiving anyone. Mary was born on 2 February 1778, the youngest of sixteen children. It was an unfortunate start as she was illegitimate (her father was probably William Talbot, 1st Earl of Talbot) and her mother died in childbirth. She was apparently provided for and received a reasonable education, if a lonely one, up to the age of fourteen. During this time she also inherited a large sum of money from her deceased older sister, the Honourable Miss Dyer, who left her a fortune of £30,000, yielding a very respectable yearly income of £1,500.

Here Mary Anne's life took another unexpected turn. As Mary was still legally a child, her sister had chosen a guardian for her, and she had chosen badly. Mr Sucker squandered her fortune on himself and put Mary under the care of Captain Essex Bowen, a soldier in the 82nd Regiment of Foot. He promised Mr Sucker he would send Mary to school but instead raped her and forced her to become his mistress. It was at this point that Bowen received orders for the West Indies and conceived the plan that would affect the rest of Mary's life. Rather than leave her behind, he had a suit of men's clothes made for her so that he could take her along as his personal servant or 'foot boy' and continue to 'enjoy' her company.

The crossing to the West Indies was rough and something of

a baptism of fire for Mary who was forced to help with the running of the ship, learning skills that would later serve her well. Having survived the crossing, the two arrived in Port-au-Prince in June 1792, only to find that Bowen had received orders to return immediately to join the Duke of York's forces, then in France. Not wishing to be without his Mary, he offered her the options of signing on as drummer boy or being sold into slavery. Not surprisingly, she chose the former.

So the daughter of an aristocrat re-crossed the ocean from the West Indies to Europe, no longer a 'male' foot boy but now a soldier. In Flanders she was reported to have fought bravely and was wounded in action before finally getting a chance to escape her tormentor when Bowen was killed during the capture of Valenciennes. Deserting from her regiment, she dressed in sailor's clothing and travelled to the French coast, sleeping rough along the way.

Here another misfortune befell her as she signed on as a sailor with Captain Le Sage, unaware that his ship was a privateer, preying on the English. Four months into her voyage, she was captured by Lord Howe during a battle with an English squadron and taken aboard the *Queen Charlotte* for interrogation. Still maintaining she was a man, she told Howe she was a British sailor duped into fighting on a French privateer. Astonishingly, he believed her and recommended her as a powder monkey for the 74-gun *Brunswick*. Whilst serving on the *Brunswick*, Mary again came face to face with the French, this time fighting against them. In the engagement, grapeshot shattered her ankle, forcing her to spend four months at a Royal Naval Hospital while she recovered.

Now perhaps inured to the life of a sailor, she returned to service, signing on with the bomb ship *Vesuvius* as a midshipman. Captured again by the French whilst cruising off the coast, she was sent to a prison in Dunkirk for a year and a half. Having fought with and been captured by both sides in the war, she decided to try sailing under a different flag and, on her release, signed on with Captain John Field of the American ship *Ariel*.

She travelled to New York and back with the *Ariel*, yet further bad luck befell her when, as she was drinking with her sailor friends at Wapping, she was press-ganged.

By this time thoroughly sick of the British (and French) navies, she chose to reveal her sex to avoid another spell at sea. Her captors, although somewhat taken aback, duly apologised and she was discharged.

Although she had finally been released from naval service, Mary's troubles were not over, however. The wound she had received from the French whilst on the *Brunswick* continued to trouble her, not helped by her frequent drinking bouts with her old naval comrades – as she freely admitted. She was also very poor and was forced to go into battle with the navy pay office to receive the pension, which, although not the man they had thought her to be, she had so richly deserved. When this was finally granted, with the aid of donations from Queen Caroline amongst others, she secured a position as a domestic servant in the house of the publisher Robert S. Kirby, who recorded her extraordinary tale in his book *The Life and Surprising Adventures of Mary Anne Talbot*. It was published in 1809, the year after Mary died, never having completely recovered from her wounds. She was just thirty.

9

Secret Societies

In countries where associations are free, secret societies are unknown.

Alexis de Tocqueville, *Democracy in America* (1835)

The Ferguson Gang

From the late 1920s until 1940 a notorious gang operated in England whose members, although all now dead, have, with one exception, managed to retain their anonymity. Their exploits were legendary and their every adventure was written up with gusto in their own minute book, known as 'the Boo'. The gang member known as 'Red Biddy' recorded one such exploit there:

> I goes up to the door and says to the man at the door – Ear's my card – please give it to the Secretary of the National Trust – Well e looks at me suspicious like and sez 'Av yer got an appointment?' – I sez 'No, but the Secretary will see me when e sees my card' – Well off he gose hesitating like & back he comes, & the Secretary, a dear old man, sez 'Come this way please'. So im and I goes into a Private Room like & he sez 'Sit down please, we are always pleased to see the gang.'

The Ferguson gang always operated under pseudonyms, which included The Right Bludy Lord Beershop of the Gladstone Islands and Mercator's Projection, Red Biddy, Bill Stickers, Sister Agatha, Erb the Smasher, Kate O'Brien, Silent O' Moyle, See Me Run, Gerry Boham and Black Maria. They invariably wore masks and communicated in mock cockney.

This gang, however, were neither terrorists nor criminals but a group of young, wealthy women with an eccentric sense of humour and a single shared passion. Having read Clough William-Ellis's book *England and the Octopus,* which warned that ugly urban sprawl was ruining the country, they determined to do something about it. So the gang was born.

Their first major operation was Shalford Mill, an eighteenth-century watermill in Surrey that had fallen into disrepair after the First World War. At the time the potential loss of such buildings, which today would be considered national treasures, was considered very much the business of the landowner, and old buildings that were no longer useful were fair game for demolition. Not, however, if the gang heard about it. They promptly bought the mill and restored it before handing it over anonymously to the National Trust for safe keeping.

Indeed, the National Trust would be the beneficiary of most of their 'raids', which ranged from the outright purchase of buildings and land to the delivery of money to the bemused Trust's secretary in a variety of forms under a multiplicity of disguises. On one occasion a cash donation was delivered sewn into the carcass of a goose; on another banknotes were wrapped around miniature liqueurs. During the 1933 'raid' by Red Biddy, described above, a sackful of Victorian coins worth £100 was dumped on the secretary's desk, with specific instructions for how it should be used. Red Biddy then 'escaped' in a taxi that 'The Nark' had positioned outside the building ready for the getaway.

The Ferguson gang also liked to visit the places they had rescued, always in disguise and, being rather well off, usually chauffeur driven. Lord Beershop is described at one meeting arriving in 'diadem, tunic, cape, liturgical boots and running shorts'. For their formal, secret meetings the National Trust even allowed them to create a hideaway at Shalford Mill, designed by the architect John Macgregor, who was known to the gang as 'The Artichoke'. These meetings were said, by those who overheard them, to be riotous all-night affairs in which they chanted in Latin, danced and shouted battle-cries, all to the accompaniment of the very best food and drink, provided by Fortnum & Mason, whose delivery van could invariably be seen parked outside when the gang were in residence.

By the time the gang disbanded in 1940 they had raised the modern equivalent of well over £500,000 for the National Trust, saved Shalford Mill, the Old Town Hall at Newton on the Isle of Wight, and Priory Cottages at Steventon in Oxfordshire, as well as purchasing the miles of Cornish coast that are today one of the country's top holiday destinations but which stood, at the time, in danger of being lost to the public for ever.

Only one member of the Ferguson gang was ever officially

'outed'. In 1996 the obituary of Margaret Steuart Pollard, the Cambridge Sanskrit scholar and Cornish bard, who had just died aged ninety-three, revealed that she had been 'Bill Stickers'. No other member has ever been officially identified.

The Secret Army

Our image of the home front in the Second World War is dominated by *Dad's Army*, a fond but hardly fearsome portrayal of the Home Guard. Yet had Britain ever been invaded, as looked so likely in the autumn of 1940, the Home Guard would not have stood alone against the Nazis. Another, far more secret and more deadly 'welcome' had been arranged for any Germans who crossed the Channel.

Since before the war the British government had been making secret contingency plans for a possible invasion and, in particular, ways in which an effective resistance force might be structured. In 1938 the job of organising this had been given to the secret General Staff (Research) department at the Foreign Office, usually known simply as 'Section D', which on the outbreak of war became a part of Military Intelligence, known as MI(R).

By the spring of 1940, when German forces began building on the French coast ready to invade, MI(R) had moved to the centre of operations and Churchill ordered that resistance units should be put in place. The man given the job of planning Britain's last-ditch defence was Colonel Colin Gubbins, an expert in guerrilla warfare recently returned from Norway where he had headed the Independent Companies, predecessors of the Commandos.

Using the cover of the Home Guard, men were approached to join the deliberately innocuous-sounding but top-secret 'Auxiliary Units'. The whole country was to be divided up into small patrols of these, each covering a radius of 15 miles, recruited into two sections. The Special Duty Sections consisted nationally of 4,000 observers who were to be trained in identifying military installations, weapons and top-ranking officers, and who would work as signals officers. Through a network of 200 secret radio transmitters and thousands of dead-letter drops, they would provide intelligence for the second section. These were the Operational Patrols, individually selected from the best recruits to the Home Guard, vetted by senior police officers and made to sign the Official Secrets Act.

Each patrol of four to eight men of the Operational Patrols had a secret underground base, built for them usually by the Royal Engineers, in which they would take cover as soon as word of the invasion reached them. Some of these bases consisted of scratch-built underground shelters, lined with cork to prevent condensation and fitted with a camouflaged entrance hatch – often attached to a log or tree stump. Others were adapted from what was available, including reusing ice houses, mine shafts and natural caves.

Here was stored surprisingly sophisticated weaponry including plastic explosives, silenced pistols and commando knives. There were also sleeping bunks, a chemical toilet, an escape hatch should their base be discovered and enough food and water for two weeks. After that the patrol would have to live off the land, although the assumption was that they would probably not last that long. Some units also had secret observation posts near by.

As soon as the initial invasion fighting had died down, these units were to become operational, working autonomously with the Special Duty Sections to identify military targets for sabotage and senior German officers for assassination. Once in position, they were not to return home to their families whom, it was assumed, they would never see again. Most were expected to be caught and, as they operated wearing uniform and were allocated only to unregistered 'fake' Home Guard battalions (201st, 202nd and 203rd), it was assumed they would be shot if captured.

In all, 3,500 recruits were trained in covert warfare at Coleshill House in Wiltshire in preparation for the invasion, priority being given to those counties in the South that would be attacked first. Fortunately the assault never came and they were never forced to become operational.

With the end of the war it was decided that the Auxiliary Units would remain secret. The Royal Engineers were instructed to remove the operation bases, of which around 500 had been built, and which today can often only be identified as a depression in the ground surrounded by fragments of corrugated-iron sheeting. Most former patrol members, as signatories to the Official Secrets Act, kept their silence too, and information on the Auxiliary Units didn't emerge until 1968. The organisation was only officially admitted to in the 1990s.

The Paper Congregation

The story of the vicar of Warleggan is as sad as it is strange. Warleggan was, until the arrival of a road in 1953, known as the most remote village in Cornwall, and even today the settlement of barely a dozen houses and a church perched on the edge of Bodmin Moor is more out of the way than many would care to venture. Although undoubtedly an isolated spot, it proved more lonely than most for its last incumbent rector.

The Reverend Frederick Densham arrived in Warleggan in 1931 and was very soon raising eyebrows amongst the hundred or so people who made up the congregation in St Bartholomew's church. To begin with, his decision to paint the interior in bright red, yellow and blue was undoubtedly eccentric, whilst his insistence on allowing his dogs to roam free over the moors where his parishioners grazed their sheep was hardly likely to endear him to them. As his relationship with his human flock (and their ovine ones) deteriorated, his actions became ever more extreme. Having closed the Sunday school, he surrounded the rectory with barbed wire and began placing increasingly elaborate locks and bolts on the church doors. The organist was driven away and none dared to replace him, the one contender being locked up overnight by the rector before fleeing the next morning. Densham then told the remaining congregation that he intended to sell the organ.

After two years the situation had become bad enough for the parishioners to apply to the bishop of Truro for the apparently unstable Densham to be replaced. Quixotically, the bishop refused. In response the entire church council resigned and it was agreed to boycott St Bartholomew's until a new rector was appointed. Both the bishop of Truro and Densham himself proved stubborn. With his congregation now numbering precisely zero, Densham simply made a series of cut-out figures, each named after a previous rector of Warleggan, sat them in the pews and preached to them each Sunday – a misanthropic cleric delivering his sermons to a cardboard congregation.

Regardless of the inanimate nature of his new flock, Densham continued as though nothing had changed, preaching each Sunday and dutifully filling in the church register, one entry famously reading, 'No fog. No wind. No rain. No Congregation.'

And so he continued, all alone, for another twenty years, an absolute recluse, if an increasingly celebrated one. Daphne du Maurier is said to have based the mad vicar in *Jamaica Inn* on Densham, but whether he was 'mad' is still a great matter of contention in the area. He was certainly highly reclusive and apparently antisocial, but also extremely contradictory. He shut the Sunday school, yet built a children's playground, although no child ever came to play there.

In 1953, twenty-two years after first arriving at Warleggan, Frederick Densham died aged eighty-three, barricaded in his rectory. His body was found at the bottom of the stairs but no one knew how long it had been there. The theme for his last Christmas Day sermon to his cut-out parishioners, as recorded in the church register for Christmas 1952, was 'God is Love'.

The Mystery Runners

On each New Year's Eve a celebrity 'mystery runner' lays a wreath on the grave of Guto Nyth Bran in the churchyard of St Gwynno's, Llanwonno, before lighting a flaming torch and running with it to the village of Mountain Ash where races are then held to see in the coming year. They trace their origins to an extraordinary man whose story goes back almost 300 years.

Guto Nyth Bran was born Griffith Morgan in the Rhondda Valley in 1700. As the son of a sheep farmer he spent much of his childhood on the hills where his athletic abilities were soon noticed. Fabulous tales began spreading through the villages that the boy had caught a hare whilst rounding up the sheep, or that he had plucked a bird from the air. One had it that he had run from his home to the shop in Pontypridd (a journey of over 7 miles) to buy tea, returning home again in the time it took his mother to boil the kettle.

Whilst these stories might be a shade fanciful he was certainly fast enough to gain the attention of local shop owner and gambling entrepreneur Sian, known as Sian-o'r-Shop (Sian the Shop) for obvious reasons. She began training Guto and arranging races, pitting him against local runners. His first race, over a 4-mile course, was against a local English army captain stationed in Carmarthen, whom he beat with ease, making Sian £400 in the process. In her day this would have bought the modern equivalent of over £50,000 of goods in her shop. Such was his success, however, that finding willing opponents became progressively harder. After a relatively short running career, Guto retired and Sian revealed herself as not only his manager but also his lover.

Their story would have a tragic end. In 1737, Sian found one more contender willing to race against Guto – an English soldier named Prince in the barracks at Monmouth. Despite now being thirty-seven, Guto was persuaded to run against the man for a prize purse of 1,000 guineas over a 12-mile course from St Woolos church in Newport to St Barrwg's church in Bedwas.

The race began badly for Guto with Prince taking an early lead but in the closing stages he produced a sudden burst of speed up a steep hill and took the prize in the astonishing time of fifty-three minutes. Sian, who was waiting at the finish line, rushed forward and slapped Guto on the back in celebration. The shock apparently proved too much for the exhausted runner, who collapsed and died in her arms.

His headstone in St Gwynno's churchyard is carved with a heart to symbolise their love. It is in memory of this poignant story that the 'mystery runner', usually a famous athlete, runs to the village of Mountain Ash each New Year's Eve to mark the start of the memorial races.

The Hawkhurst Gang

Smuggling was one of the great open secrets along England's south and west coasts in the eighteenth century. With high tariffs imposed on tea, coffee and spirits, there was every temptation to slip goods into the country without the customs man knowing. Whole communities were complicit, or at least turned a blind eye, to a trade that made them all a little richer.

However, even smugglers couldn't always rely on the silence of their neighbours, as one violent ring discovered. The downfall of the Hawkhurst gang, a large and well-organised smuggling group, began in September 1747. Their ship *The Three Brothers*, carrying 2 tons of tea, thirty-nine casks of brandy and rum and a small packet of coffee, had been intercepted by the customs cutter *Swift* after a short chase. The crew had managed to escape in a small boat but the ship was impounded and its valuable cargo placed in the Customs House in Poole, Dorset.

You might expect them to have written this off as a loss – an occupational hazard of the smuggling trade – but such was the power and confidence of the gang that they decided on a daring raid. Meeting in Charlton Forest, the group planned to ride to Poole, break into the Customs House and take back their cargo. The next day they set out from the village of Rowlands Castle, arriving on the outskirts of Poole around eleven that night. One of the leaders, Thomas Kingsmill, went ahead to reconnoitre the scene and noticed that a sloop of war was in the harbour with its guns trained on the Customs House. Fortunately, as the tide ebbed, so the line of sight from sloop to Customs House was lost. When the guns no longer bore down on the building, Kingsmill and his thirty heavily armed men attacked. Unchallenged, they broke open the door, recovered their property and rode off.

The following day the smugglers, flushed with their success, could be found riding openly through the countryside with their cargo, down streets lined with people, apparently believing themselves immune from danger. At Fordingbridge one of these smugglers, Jack Diamond, made a mistake. He gave a bag of tea to a poor shoemaker, Daniel Chater, a man with whom he had worked at harvest time and who, later, accidentally let slip that he had recognised Diamond. Such gossip soon got around the villages, eventually reaching the Customs House where a furious Revenue service was offering a large reward for the capture of the gang.

On Sunday 14 February, a riding officer of the Revenue, William Galley, arrived at Daniel Chater's home to escort him to a Justice of the Peace where his evidence, identifying one of the gang members, would be taken down. Neither man would arrive at his destination alive. That evening they stopped at the White Hart Inn in Rowlands Castle, apparently unaware that the place was regularly used by the smuggling ring. Here the landlady overheard them talking and sent for two gang members, Jackson and Carter. They proceeded to ply Galley and Chater with drink, in the process finding out the story of their mission.

Having been put to bed drunk, Galley and Chater were woken a few hours later by Jackson digging his spurs into their throats. Dragged from bed and whipped, they were tied to a horse and carried off, being beaten and abused as they went. At the Red Lion at Rake, Jackson and Carter stopped for a drink and here they decided to kill their charges. William Galley, already unconscious, was buried alive, as the later exhumation of his body showed. Chater was kept chained to a post for another two days whilst other gang members were summoned, still being regularly beaten and, on one occasion, having his face mutilated with a clasp knife. None of the gang wanted to take responsibility for his actual murder, however, so eventually he was simply thrown into a well. When that didn't kill him and his screams could still be heard, rocks were thrown down until silence descended at last.

The gang began terrorising the neighbourhood, revelling in their violent reputations but secure in the belief that the local people would still support them or at least be too intimidated to act. In this they were quite wrong. The people of Kent might have supported a little smuggling, but a murderous mob was quite another thing. The Hawkhurst gang had already got a reputation for shocking violence, having whipped to death a farm labourer they accused of stealing from them at the Dog and Partridge Inn at Slindon, and the subsequent death of Chater began to loosen tongues. One by one, the gang members involved in the two deaths were betrayed to the authorities. The people of Goudhurst even banded together to form a militia to keep the smugglers out of a town that had once welcomed them, goading Thomas Kingsmill to threaten to burn the place down. Without the quiet support of the locals, however, he was impotent. When the gang did attack Goudhurst, the militia drove them back, killing three of their number in the process.

Public opinion had now turned completely against the Hawkhurst gang. The names of members were readily given up by terrified locals and published in the *London Gazette*, with a warning that they had forty days to surrender or face an automatic death sentence. One escaped to France but most of them were captured, tried and executed. Kingsmill and his men were hanged and their bodies suspended in chains as a warning, both to other smugglers and to anyone who might in future threaten the rural peace of Kent.

The Circuit Maker

Henri Peulevé was in many ways an ideal recruit for the Special Operations Executive (SOE). Having been born in England during the First World War where his mother was a refugee from the German invasion of France, he had grown up in both England and France, was fluent in both languages and had a technical interest in broadcasting, becoming one of the first television cameramen at the BBC before the war.

On the outbreak of the Second World War, Henri found work in radar development before becoming one of the first batch of agents recruited to SOE, a paramilitary organisation founded to organise and support guerrilla warfare in occupied territories. After extensive training at the SOE special training schools, Henri was parachuted into the Pyrenees area on the night of 30 July 1942 to help found the 'Scientist' circuit of agents. Almost immediately, disaster struck when the plane carrying him flew too low and on landing he broke his leg. Despite this he found a safe house and recuperated enough to cross the Pyrenees into Spain on crutches. Here he was immediately arrested as he had no papers, but he managed to escape to the British embassy in Madrid during a hospital visit and hence made his way back to England.

This experience might have put off a lesser man, but not Henri. His second mission began on the night of 17 September 1943 when he was successfully landed in France, in order to set up the new 'Author' circuit of agents. Operating in the Corrèze area, he soon managed to recruit numerous members of the Armée Secrète and communist resistance groups, arranging for RAF drops of equipment and further agents to support his growing sabotage operations. By the time of his inevitable capture he had recruited over 3,000 fighters. Acting as his own radio operator, he remained entirely undiscovered by the Gestapo until, through simple bad luck, he was wrongly identified as a black marketeer. When the Gestapo arrived suddenly to arrest him on suspicion of this, on 21 March 1944, they found him operating his radio.

As a potential spy Henri was subjected to torture and the ever-present threat of summary execution, yet he refused to talk. After nearly a year in solitary confinement at Fresnes prison, he attempted to escape but was shot in the leg and recaptured. Refused any medical assistance, he was forced to remove the bullet himself, without anaesthetic, using just a spoon.

When he had recovered, Henri and thirty-six other agents were sent to the notorious concentration camp at Buchenwald where members of SOE, or those thought to be members of SOE, were routinely executed. Shortly after their arrival, the first sixteen agents were hanged in the crematorium basement, and less than a month later a further eleven were shot.

On the day before Henri was due to face the firing squad, his luck suddenly changed. Resistance and escape operations in the camp were organised by another SOE officer, Wing Commander Yeo-Thomas, codenamed 'White Rabbit', who selected him for a daring escape attempt. Changing identities with Marcel Seigneur, a Frenchman in the camp who was dying of typhus, Henri avoided execution and was instead sent to work in a forced-labour group. As this regularly worked outside the camp, there was now much more of an opportunity to escape.

On 11 April 1945 he made his bid. As he was digging anti-tank traps near Barby on the river Elbe, he made a dash for freedom. When he was within sight of the advancing US forces he was stopped by two Belgian SS officers. Without papers, all looked lost for Henri but he tried one last, brilliant bluff. Telling them he was a French collaborator running away from the advancing Allies, he suggested that they, like him, might want to change out of uniform to avoid capture. They agreed. As they were changing he grabbed one of their pistols and declared them his prisoners. He then marched across the battle lines and handed them over to the 83rd US Infantry Division. For them, and indeed for Henri, the war was finally over.

The Whiteway Colony

The Cotswolds is not the sort of place you would expect to find an anarchist colony, yet tucked away in 40 acres near Stroud in Gloucestershire the successor of just such a community still survives.

The founders of the Whiteway colony were Tolstoyan anarchists, members of a group who followed the religious views of Russian novelist Leo Tolstoy, refusing to acknowledge the authority of anyone or anything other than God. In 1898 they had left their home – in the also rather un-anarchic Surrey – and bought the land at Whiteway, immediately burning the deeds on the completion of the purchase to demonstrate that they didn't believe in property rights. In case the law didn't agree with them, they went to court to prove the land now had no legal owner.

Initially it was decided that the whole community would live together in one house, all tending the land and determined not to live off the work of others. Some also declined to pay taxes as they claimed they neither received nor needed anything from the state. The state begged to differ, as we might expect, and sent them to prison.

Other radical beliefs (or at least radical for the time) were also experimented with at Whiteway, including the replacing of marriage with 'free union', vegetarianism, the rejection of money, and equal rights for women. Such high ideals proved difficult to live by in the confines of one house. After the first year it was agreed that different households could choose a plot of land and build their own home on it, abiding by their own rules, provided they never made a claim to the land and relinquished it as soon as they no longer worked it.

In this form the colony thrived, attracting political anarchists, conscientious objectors and war refugees, in an eclectic mix that led to the group becoming known locally as 'the queer folk'. Actually it proved a very successful assortment and the community was soon joined by other less driven individuals who simply wished to live off the land, including the son of a baronet and a former Scottish bank manager.

With the influx of new people, the complexion of the colony changed. In 1924 the group clubbed together to build a communal hall, whilst the luxury of piped water was added in 1949. Mains electricity finally arrived in 1954 and a swimming pool was built in 1969. Today the Whiteway colony – still run by a general meeting of its residents but no longer overtly anarchist in outlook – survives, a Tolstoyan secret in the English hills.

The Happiest Memorial

During his tours of the country in the 1930s, writer Arthur Mee, who was then compiling a series of guides to post-First World War Britain, noted that thirty-two of the villages he visited seemed mysteriously to be missing something. In an era when virtually every family had been touched by loss on the battlefield, why did these villages not have war memorials?

Since the end of the war, such memorials had become focal points in 16,000 towns and villages that lost their men or women but, strangely, not in this particular group. Initially this appeared to have been perhaps a terrible oversight or a sign of callous indifference on the part of local authorities, but when Mee made further enquiries he discovered it was for a much happier reason. The 'Thankful Villages', as he christened them, had no memorial because everyone who had gone away to war had come safe home again.

Since Mee's survey a further eighteen (some sources claim ten) Thankful Villages have been recorded, accounting for just 0.3 per cent of all such places. In France the percentage was even lower. There, only one village, Thierville, can claim to be thankful, doubly so because it lost no one in the Second World War either.

There is a strange postscript to the story as there are now technically three fewer Thankful Villages than there were just a few years ago. So central has the war memorial become to village life that some Thankful Villages have felt somewhat left out, having no focal point for Remembrance Day at which they could at least remember their good fortune. In the villages of Rodney Stoke, Aisholt and Stocklinch, Somerset County Council have now put this right, erecting plaques that read: 'For those who served in World Wars I and II and returned home safely.' They are the only English villages with a memorial to those who didn't die in the war.

10

Secret Truths

Plots, true or false, are necessary things,
To raise up commonwealths and ruin kings.

John Dryden, *Absalom and Achitophel* (1681)

The Bisley Boy

There have been many explanations given of some of the peculiarities of the reign of Elizabeth I. Her failure to marry, her early baldness and her strict instructions that no post mortem should be carried out on her body have all attracted their fair share of conspiracy theories. Few, however, are as colourful as the tale of the Bisley Boy.

Bisley in Gloucestershire is the site of Over Court, which in 1542 was a royal hunting lodge and, briefly, the home of Henry VIII's youngest daughter, Princess Elizabeth, whilst her father hunted at the nearby Berkeley castle. According to the legend of the Bisley Boy, there ensued one of the nation's greatest royal disasters. The young Elizabeth suddenly developed a fever and died, leaving the courtiers at Over Court and the villagers of Bisley in something of a quandary – how were they to tell Henry VIII?

To say court affairs were volatile at the time would be an understatement. On 13 February of that year, Henry's fifth wife, Catherine Howard, had been beheaded for adultery, an event that had greatly upset the nine-year-old Elizabeth. Not only had Catherine been kind to her, but she was the cousin of Elizabeth's own mother, Anne Boleyn, who had also suffered execution at Henry's hands. Telling Henry of the death of his daughter would stir all this up again and so they decided not to tell him at all.

Now Henry's relationship with Elizabeth varied; sometimes he would be fatherly; at others he would declare her illegitimate and disinherit her. If they were to get away with the deceit, they would definitely need a proxy. While the body of Elizabeth was being secretly buried in Over Court, the village of Bisley was being searched for a replacement. One was indeed found, of the right age and stature and with the necessary red hair. The only problem was that the replacement was male. Nevertheless the 'Bisley Boy' was duly dressed up as a Tudor princess and went on to become one of England's greatest monarchs as Elizabeth I, always carefully eschewing marriage and any other means by which 'her' true sex might be found out. Or so the story has it.

One final flourish to this unlikely tale was given in the late nineteenth century by the usually dour vicar of Bisley, the Reverend Thomas Keble. He told his family that during building work at Over Court in 1870 he came across a stone coffin containing the remains of a young girl in Tudor dress. Perhaps with a wry and rare smile from this famously serious man, he added that he had secretly reburied the child when he realised who it must be, so as to ensure the house did not become a melancholic shrine.

The Secret Life of Lady Grange

Rachel Erskine, Lady Grange, came from a tragic Scottish family. Her father had shot dead the Lord President of the Court of Sessions in revenge for agreeing to his wife's alimony claim, for which he had been tortured, executed and hung in chains whilst Rachel was still just ten. Her own tragedy began in 1707 when this renowned beauty married James Erskine, himself, ironically, a Lord of Sessions.

The couple, who lived in Edinburgh, had eight children but the marriage was not a happy one, it being claimed that Erskine had seduced her and agreed to marry her only because she had threatened to expose him. Rachel also, according to the rather pro-Erskine sources, had a fiery temper, which she put to good use when he left her in favour of his long-term mistress. Although Erskine had shipped his now inconvenient family out of Edinburgh, Rachel regularly returned to the city and would stand beneath his window, shouting obscenities – a lively performance that certainly did the trick of embarrassing him. It was only when she threatened to reveal her husband's role in the Jacobite rising of 1715, however, that things began to go badly wrong for Rachel.

James Erskine might put up with being sworn at but suggestions that he was involved with his brother's rebellion were too dangerous and probably too true to pass without action and so he turned to the old family method for dealing with difficult wives – kidnap.

James had previously been involved in the abduction of his brother's wife Lady Mar, who was mentally ill, and hence was already a dab hand at these things. With the help of the Jacobites Lord Lovat and Norman MacLeod of Dunvegan, at 11 p.m. on the night of 22 April 1732, Rachel 'disappeared' from her Edinburgh lodgings.

Bound and gagged, she was taken by horse to Linlithgow and then to Polmaise. As there was still a danger she might return, she was moved from there to the tiny island of Hesker off North Uist in the Outer Hebrides, where she was kept for two years. When her secret captor there, Sir Alexander MacDonald, told Erskine he could no longer afford to keep her, she was moved again in 1734 to the most remote spot he could think of – the St Kilda islands, 42 miles off Uist. Here on the tiny islet of Hirta she was kept for eight years in a small hut, surrounded only by Gaelic speakers.

So remote, indeed, was Rachel that James Erskine felt safe in announcing in Edinburgh that his wife was sadly dead, even going so far as to hold a mock funeral for her. Rachel, however, had not given up. Eventually she managed to befriend the local minister's daughter and persuaded her to smuggle out a letter in a ball of wool, addressed to her cousin the Lord Advocate. When the Lord Advocate heard, he was understandably cross and sent a gunboat. This arrived to find Rachel long gone and no one on St Kilda willing to admit she had ever existed there. In fact, Norman MacLeod had been tipped off, conveying Rachel to Assynt in Sutherland and then to Skye, where she was effectively abandoned to her fate.

Here she was reported to be living in a cave and it was here, at Idrigal, that she finally died, three years later, in 1745. The conspirators arranged for her quiet burial in the isolated churchyard at Trumpan on the Waternish peninsula. Back in Edinburgh, and to their eternal shame, the secret abduction and death of Lady Grange went apparently unnoticed and unmourned by her friends, her children (now grown) or her husband.

The Dalrymple Mystery

Any marriage might be considered something of a risk but there have been few as risky as Janet Dalrymple's in the latter half of the seventeenth century. Janet was the daughter of James Dalrymple, 1st Lord Stair, a whiggish lawyer and politician with an eye to securing the further rise of his ambitious family. His daughter, meanwhile, had her eye on the penniless Archibald, 3rd Lord Rutherford, a man of exactly opposite political opinions (being a firm Jacobite) and declining fortunes.

Janet and Archibald had sworn to marry by the time her parents found out about it, and swore that she wouldn't. In the meantime Lord Stair found a far more suitable bridegroom for his daughter in the form of a puce-faced young man with an unhealthy interest in farming, David Dunbar of Baldoon. When he asked for her hand, Janet, embarrassingly, was forced to admit that she had already offered it to Rutherford. Lady Stair, when she heard about this, immediately wrote to Rutherford, telling him in no uncertain terms that the engagement was off, but he refused to accept the rather terse missive, demanding an interview with his beloved and her mother in the hope of changing her mind. However, he hadn't counted on the barrack-room legal skills of Lady Stair who rather neatly showed, using extensive Biblical quotations, that a betrothal vow made by a daughter when still under the care of her father was null and void if the father disagreed with it.

To cap this legal flourish, an apparently overawed and humbled Janet returned her half of a gold coin (Archibald had the other half) that they had split as a sign of their vow. Decisively out-manoeuvred, he swept out of the room, hissing at Janet: 'For you, madam, you will be a world's wonder.' This was not as nice a thing to say as it sounds today, actually implying that something terrible would befall her, as indeed it duly did. Archibald then left the country, never to marry nor return.

So on 24 August (some sources say 12 August) 1669, Janet Dalrymple and David Dunbar were married at the Kirk of Old

Luce two miles from Carscreugh castle, the Dalrymple family seat. Later folklorists claim that her brothers who accompanied her to the church said her skin was as cold as ice and that she showed no emotion at all. A reception at Carscreugh ensued, after which the usual tradition was followed of locking the bride and groom in the bridal suite for the night. One of the groomsmen was given the key with strict instructions to keep the door locked so that no tricks could be played on the couple.

What took place behind that locked door is a matter of conjecture, save to say that some time later wild screaming was heard from the other side. After the groomsman had finally been persuaded that this wasn't a joke in itself, the door was opened to reveal David Dunbar seriously wounded and bathed in blood. His bride sat some distance away, crouched near the fire, 'dabbled in gore' as one account rather vividly puts it. She had apparently gone quite insane and would only shout, 'Tak' up your bonny bridegroom.' She died just nineteen days later on 12 September.

What led to this scene is still a mystery. The wounded David Dunbar survived and remarried, eventually dying from a fall from his horse on 28 March 1682. He, however, refused to ever mention the night of his wedding to Janet Dalrymple and took the secret with him to his grave. Whether she attacked him, he attacked (and fatally wounded) her or whether the insanely jealous Lord Rutherford secretly stole into the room and attacked his rival remains unknown to this day. One person at least did well from this tragic tale as the story later formed the basis for Sir Walter Scott's hugely successful novel, *The Bride of Lammermoor*.

John the Painter

The strange and sad case of John the Painter throws light on the secret life of Britain's first real terrorist, an unlikely figure whose motives have yet to be fully untangled.

Although James Aitken was not born a revolutionary, events may have conspired to make him one. He had received a relatively good education for his background, thanks to the charitable George Heriot's Hospital School in Edinburgh, where he gained a place following the early death of his blacksmith father. Here he developed a love of books, which could have fired his later radical ideas, but his stammer also held him back academically. He left at fifteen to apprentice himself to a local painter. He later travelled to London to set up in business, except that James, alias John, never did become the painter that his nickname suggests. Instead, and for unknown reasons, John took to a life of petty crime, punctuated by an unsuccessful attempt to start a new life in Virginia.

It is unclear what happened to John in the American colonies but by 1775 he was back in England where, in a pub in Oxford, he overheard a conversation about the war raging across the Atlantic. This fired his imagination and by the following summer he had devised a plan to bring the American revolutionary cause to the Mother Country. John had invented some sort of device for igniting incendiary charges with a delay, which he intended to plant at government installations, escaping undetected before the fires broke out. And the scope of his plan was enormous: to set fire to and destroy all six Royal Naval dockyards, crippling Britain as a naval power.

Before putting his sabotage scheme into operation, John first travelled to France to inform the American commissioner, Silas Deane, of it. Deane was not wholly convinced of the practicality of the plan nor of the reliability of John, and he certainly didn't want to be openly associated with a proposition that at the time would be considered an absolute outrage. He did, however, give John some money to buy materials.

Back in England, John approached a tinsmith in Canterbury who, without realising their purpose, was commissioned to make the incendiary devices. John then headed for Portsmouth where, on 7 December 1776, he managed to gain access to the hemp house in the dockyard and lay a device. When this failed to ignite, he returned and simply set fire to the building, managing somehow to slip away unnoticed.

John travelled back to London, news reaching him there that

the hemp house had burnt to the ground. He reported the success of his actions to Dr Edward Bancroft, a contact that Silas Deane had given him and who had previously spied for Benjamin Franklin. What neither Silas nor John knew was that Bancroft was actually a double agent.

John headed for Plymouth but, having failed to gain access to the docks there, moved on to Bristol where on two nights he set fires on the waterfront before leaving for Hampshire. By now there was some panic at the Admiralty and the Navy Board. Although the hemp house at Portsmouth was immediately rebuilt, rumours were spreading of French or Spanish agents at work in the docks and King George III himself had asked for daily updates on progress. For good measure the America High Treason Act was rushed through, suspending the habeas corpus laws for American revolutionaries, and allowing suspects to be detained without trial.

By Christmas, news had reached the authorities, perhaps from Bancroft, that a man known only as 'John the Painter' had been seen loitering near the hemp house in Portsmouth on the night of the fire. Soon descriptions of John were circulating in the local press and rewards totalling £2,735 were offered for his capture.

His final arrest came about purely by chance. On 27 January 1777, James Lowe, a Wiltshire shopkeeper who was tracking a man he believed to have burgled his shop, and John Dalby, the keeper of the Andover Bridewell, captured a man at Hook in Hampshire whom they took to Odiham gaol, where he was, much to their surprise, identified as the notorious saboteur John the Painter.

John was taken to London for questioning but would not talk until a fellow painter was sent to befriend him. This simple tactic led to John opening his heart to his new 'friend' who of course reported his confession back to the authorities. John was indicted at the assizes, held in the Great Hall in Winchester, and appeared there on 6 March. Refusing to take expert advice, he decided to represent himself in a seven-hour trial, in which the prosecution called twenty witnesses to testify against him while he called none to defend himself. He was still maintaining his innocence. His only hope was to have the testimony of his fellow painter struck from the records, but the judge refused this and John was found guilty. Sentence was passed that he would hang on 10 March, the judge adding that he was at a loss to explain John's terrible deeds. Hoping, according to a friend, to avoid having his body displayed on a gibbet, John later confessed.

As he had tried to bring war to the peaceful streets of England, John's execution was to be a major event. The mainmast of the fifth-rate frigate HMS *Arethusa* was unstepped and taken to Portsmouth Common, making the highest gallows ever seen in England. Twenty thousand people gathered to watch him die. After the execution, and against his last wishes, his body was hung in a gibbet over the gate to Portsmouth harbour where it remained for years. It should surprise no one that Silas Deane denied all knowledge of the man.

The Lady Vanishes

Elizabeth Canning should have led a very anonymous life, yet her mysterious history became one of the great causes célèbres of the eighteenth century, involving famous novelists, politicians and whole political factions. This might be considered quite good going for the daughter of a humble sawyer.

Elizabeth's tale began normally enough. Born in 1734 into a poor London family, she received precious little formal education and from around the age of fifteen was sent to work as a maid-servant. From October 1752 she took a position with Edward Lyon, a carpenter in Aldermanbury in the City, where she was said to be a good and diligent worker. On 1 January 1753 she disappeared.

Twenty-eight days later Elizabeth stumbled through the door of her mother's house, partially naked and emaciated, telling an extraordinary story. She said she had been walking in Moorfields when she was abducted by two thugs who tore her clothes and knocked her out before dragging her off to a house on the Hert-ford Road, Enfield. Here she had been imprisoned and was given only bread and water, supplemented by a small mince pie she happened to have in her pocket. Whilst she was in captivity, a woman in the house had cut off the stays of her corset and invited her to become a prostitute. When Elizabeth refused she had been locked in a small attic room. It was from this room that she had escaped and staggered back to her mother's house.

It was a time when stories of abductions and white slavery were rife in London. Having heard the tale, one of her friends suggested she might have been taken to a notorious brothel in Enfield Wash (today in the North London borough of Enfield), owned by Susannah (Mother) Wells. Elizabeth Canning repeated this allegation to an alderman and a warrant was issued for the arrest of Mother Wells. Elizabeth, her mother and some City officials meanwhile went to Enfield Wash, where Elizabeth identified the house as indeed being the place where she had been imprisoned. Her descriptions were noted as not being entirely accurate but in such a dire situation what else would one expect? At the house she also identified a gypsy, Mary Squires, as the woman who had cut off her stays. Mary was arrested for stealing the stays as theft was then a potentially capital offence, with Mother Wells indicted as an accessory.

At this point the novelist Henry Fielding entered the fray in his role as a Justice of the Peace. Convinced of Elizabeth's tale, he issued warrants for the arrest of the whole of Mother Wells's household. The subsequent trial was chaotic, with witnesses for both sides being threatened, ignored and misrepresented, amid a fevered atmosphere electric with stories of forced prostitution and sexual slavery. One of the girls in the house claimed that Elizabeth had been there, but Mary Squires produced three witnesses to prove she was in Dorset at the time of the alleged abduction and couldn't have been involved. Other witnesses who came to appear for Mary were prevented from entering the courthouse by the mob outside.

Not surprisingly, Mary and Mother Wells were both found guilty. Wells was sentenced to branding on the thumb and six months in prison. For Mary Squires the situation was far worse. Found guilty of theft (of the stays), she was sentenced to hang.

The trial had left a number of questions – indeed, most of the questions – unanswered and the Lord Mayor, Sir Crisp Gascoyne, decided to step in. Not only did Canning's testimony seem full of holes but the girl who had claimed to have seen her in the house had now withdrawn her statement. Clearly something was wrong. The Lord Mayor successfully petitioned the King for a stay of execution for Mary, followed by a full pardon.

With more and more evidence apparently supporting the gypsy Mary Squires, it was Elizabeth who was now indicted, for perjury, leading to an utter media frenzy. On the one side, the Canningites stood by Elizabeth – an innocent girl, as they saw it, roughly man-handled and pressed into a life of depravation and sin. Henry Fielding and others rushed into print with supportive pamphlets. Just as eager, however, were the 'Egyptians' – supporters of Mary Squires. They believed a poor gypsy woman was being framed as a cover-up for the fact that a London maid had engineered her own disappearance, probably because she was pregnant and was either running away to have the baby or seeking an abortion. Pamphlet and counter-pamphlet flew back and forth as the new trial approached.

When the case opened at the Old Bailey on 29 April 1754, thirty-seven witnesses swore that Mary Squires was in Dorset at the time of the 'crime', whilst twenty-two others swore they had seen her around Enfield Wash. Witnesses lined up to state cate-gorically that Elizabeth was in the house and just as many that she was not. In the end the jury was so confused that they sent down the extraordinary verdict of 'guilty but not wilfully so'. This the judge refused to accept. Eventually they settled for guilty but recommended clemency, although two jurors later claimed that they had been forced into this. The sentencing proved even more confusing but with a 9–8 majority the judge settled for a month in prison followed by seven years' transportation.

Outside the court, the press were still a little hot under the collar. The Lord Mayor went into print supporting the Egyptians, and had his coach pelted with rocks for his efforts. The Canningites responded with four separate refutations of the trial, whilst Henry

Fielding, now rather wishing he had kept out of the case, let it be known that he was no longer sure one way or the other.

Elizabeth Canning meanwhile served her time and was transported, although not in a convict ship, as powerful supporters in the East India Company had arranged a more civilised passage to her new home in Wethersfield, Connecticut. Here she married and had children, and here she remained for the rest of her life. She made no further comment on what had happened that January in 1753 and no evidence has ever been found to indicate where she might have been, if not at Enfield Wash. The case is a mystery to this day.

The Cato Street Conspiracy

Britain has a surprisingly good record of not assassinating its politicians – with the odd exception – but the Cato Street conspiracy, had it succeeded, would have changed that overnight by wiping out the entire cabinet.

The beginning of the nineteenth century was a time of social unrest in much of England. The end of the Napoleonic Wars in 1815 had coincided with a period of famine and unemployment, and resentment was growing at the lack of representation in government for most working people. At St Peter's Fields in 1819, that government had responded to a large public demonstration with a cavalry charge, leading to what became known as the Peterloo massacre. The consequence was the introduction by Lord Sidmouth's government of the 'Six Acts', which made any radical gathering 'an overt act of treasonable conspiracy'. This simply fanned the flames.

Many people sought parliamentary reform but some had more sweeping ideas. Arthur Thistlewood – a member of a group known as the Spencean Philanthropists, after the radical speaker Thomas Spence – was one of these. When the death of George III in 1820 caused a constitutional crisis, Thistlewood saw the chance for a French-style revolution in England. Having read in the newspapers that the cabinet was dining at the home of the Lord President of the Council on 23 February, he planned to attack the dinner venue with pistols and grenades, thus decapitating the state at a single blow.

At least, that is what the government wished him to believe. In fact there was no cabinet dinner and one of Thistlewood's closest allies, George Edwards, was an agent provocateur for the authorities. Edwards had come into contact with the Spenceans through his work – he made plaster busts for a living, including one of the unpopular headmaster of Eton, which the boys often bought for target practice – and had been commissioned to make one of Spence. Having joined the group, Edwards began passing information to the Home Office about the conspiracy.

On the night of the supposed dinner, Thistlewood and twelve other conspirators were preparing for the attack from the loft of a house in Cato Street that one of their number had rented. What they didn't know was that, in the pub opposite, a Bow Street magistrate and another police informer were watching, along with a dozen officers of the Bow Street Runners (the forerunner of the Metropolitan Police). At 7.30 the trap was sprung and the authorities rushed into the house. In the resulting brawl, Thistlewood killed one of the officers with a sword before escaping but was apprehended just a few days later.

In total, eleven men were charged with the plot, two having turned King's evidence, and all were found guilty. Thistlewood and four others were convicted of treason and murder, and were sentenced to the mediaeval punishment of hanging, drawing and quartering. This was later commuted to simple hanging, after which their bodies were decapitated and buried in quicklime in Newgate gaol.

The spies in their midst were spirited away and George Edwards, the government agent responsible more than anyone for engineering the plot, did not even appear in court to testify. This heavy-handed government entrapment did not go unnoticed, however, and a campaign was started to find and prosecute the mysterious Edwards. Shortly afterwards, he disappeared, probably dying in 1843 in Cape Town, South Africa.

The Baccarat Scandal

Sir William Gordon-Cumming was a man of his era – a late nineteenth-century playboy with royal connections and a love of gambling and womanising. He had stalked tigers in India, fought the Mahdi in the Sudan and been shipwrecked off southern Africa. He also had a habit of swearing loudly although, thankfully for the delicate ears of his aristocratic friends, this was usually in Hindustani.

In England he became a firm favourite with the 'in' set, including Albert, Prince of Wales, later Edward VII. In September 1890, Gordon-Cumming was invited to join the prince at a house party at Tranby Croft near Doncaster, where the prince had been attending the St Leger race meeting. So it was that on the first evening, and at the request of the prince, the group sat down to play baccarat, a gambling game for which, these being wealthy people, the stakes were high. It was only after the game had finished that the son of the host told his mother, friend and brother-in-law that he thought he had seen Gordon-Cumming cheating.

It was an astonishing accusation. The four decided to closely watch Gordon-Cumming the following evening when more baccarat was scheduled. Again he apparently cheated. The indignant group decided to confide in the senior courtiers present, starting something of a panic in the process. It was one thing to find that someone had cheated your prince, but quite another when he was being cheated at a game that was then illegal.

Without waiting to discover the truth of the matter, the courtiers cornered Gordon-Cumming, who complained that he had just been using a different betting system and that no one at the table had objected. Forced into a corner, however, he finally agreed to sign a pledge that he would never play the game again in return for total secrecy.

So the matter should have ended if only the other guests at that house party had been able to keep the secret, but the high society aristocrats who formed Gordon-Cumming's circle of friends were not renowned for their discretion. He himself had had an affair with the then mistress of the prince, Daisy, Lady Brooke, known to her friends as 'the babbling Brooke' for her habit of making known every secret and affair that came to her ears. It may well have been through her that news of the scandal got out. When it broke, the furious Gordon-Cumming determined to defend his reputation.

Going to the civil courts, he sued some of the house guests for defamation, regardless of the fact that a trial would reveal that all of them had been playing an illegal game, including the prince. Indeed, Gordon-Cumming even called the prince as a witness at the ensuing trial. Despite a valiant performance, his chances were slim to say the least. The defendants could produce the pledge he had signed never to play again, which looked to all intents and purposes like a confession, and the judge made little attempt to hide the fact that he was on the side of the defendants. It took the jury just thirteen minutes to find in their favour, although those in the gallery smelt a royal cover-up and the verdict was met with hissing.

The next day Gordon-Cumming was dismissed from the army and resigned from his London clubs. The Prince of Wales from then on refused to be introduced to anyone who publicly acknowledged his former friend. Sir William Gordon-Cumming never again returned to the inner circles of society.

The Gowrie Conspiracy

Exactly what happened at Gowrie House on 5 August 1600 is still one of the greatest mysteries in Scottish royal history.

Early that morning, King James VI of Scotland rose early to go hunting in the countryside around Falkland Palace with his friends the Earl of Mar, Thomas Erskine and the Duke of Lennox amongst others. As he set off he was suddenly approached by Alexander Ruthven, the younger brother of the 3rd Earl of Gowrie, who told him a rather tall tale.

He claimed – if we believe the official account of events – that he and his brother the earl had that morning captured a foreigner carrying a large quantity of gold and were holding him at Gowrie House in Perth, some 14 miles away. Would the King come and interrogate him personally? And if so, could he come now and without his entourage? James, initially suspicious, finally agreed to go to Gowrie House after the hunt had finished. Alexander Ruthven asked the King not to tell his courtiers of the plan before dispatching a servant to Gowrie to warn the earl of the King's arrival.

At about 1 p.m. James and a small retinue reached Gowrie House, surprised to find no preparations had been made for their arrival. After an hour's wait, the King was finally provided with a meal in a private room whilst his retainers were offered food in the hall. As they ate, the King was led away by Alexander Ruthven up the main staircase, through several doors and into a turret room, in which there was no sign of the mysterious prisoner or the gold. Instead one of Ruthven's servants was waiting with his sword drawn and the King was told to stay silent if he valued his life. Ruthven left his servant guarding the King and went to consult with his brother.

Meanwhile the Earl of Gowrie spoke to the King's retinue, claiming he had been informed by a servant that the King had already left by the back door. At once they saddled up and prepared to follow their monarch. At that moment, however, there was a commotion. In the window of the tower room the King was suddenly seen struggling with Alexander Ruthven and shouting, 'I am murdered! Treason!' The King's retainers dashed back into the house and found a way into the turret room where Ruthven, grappling with the King, was stabbed and pushed down the stairs. The Earl of Gowrie, who was still in the grounds and apparently unaware of what was happening, now rushed back inside and up to the tower room where, in the mêlée, he too was killed.

That, at least, is the official line on the events of that day. The question that remains is: what really did happen? The official report, commissioned for James, makes it clear that the Ruthvens intended to kidnap the King – a tried and tested tactic over the years for Scottish aristocratic families hoping to increase their influence. The people were less certain, however. Not only was the King known to owe the Gowries a very significant amount of money (around £48,000), but he also quite rightly believed that they were disloyal and vocal opponents of his government. The rumour therefore went round that the kidnapping was a ploy to allow the King to rid himself of a troublesome family. It was said that the Ruthvens had been invited to join the hunt, not that they had invited the King to join them, and that letters to this effect had been found on the earl's body and destroyed. Certainly the surviving royal accounts show payments that month to messengers taking letters to both the Ruthven brothers.

There is also the possibility that the Gowries did plan to kill or kidnap the King. Their father had been executed by James and there was no love lost between the two families. The Gowries represented a pro-English faction in Scotland that wanted to see the Catholic elements of the government removed as well as an improvement in relations with their southern neighbour, where the Protestant Elizabeth still reigned. Kidnapping the King might have seemed a way to achieve this.

The spiriting away of the King whilst his retainers ate, and the strange news that the King had suddenly left, would tally with a kidnap plot although this cannot explain the strange scene in the tower room or the brothers' death. Some scholars have suggested that the King, known to be homosexual, made a pass at the young Alexander Ruthven, causing him to lose his composure and attack the King. Others suggest that when the King arrived with retainers, and not alone as hoped, Alexander knew it would be impossible to kidnap James, so, in his despair, he decided to avenge his family and kill him instead. Whatever the truth behind the plot, James, who three years later became king of England, would never reveal it and the Gowrie brothers, dead on the stairs of Gowrie House, would never be in a position to do so.

11

Secret Tricks

C'est double plaisir de tromper le trompeur.

Jean de la Fontaine, *Fables* (1668)

The Dreadnought Deception

For Admiral Sir William May, the events of 7 February 1910 proved highly inconvenient, even awkward. As he was in charge of the home fleet of the greatest naval power on earth, it was his duty not only to protect Britain, but also to help the Foreign Office with its diplomatic work. And it was this latter role that was annoying him. A telegram had arrived from the Foreign Office that morning, informing him of the visit of 'Prince Makalen of Abyssinia and his suite', who wished to inspect his pride and joy – the vast, state-of-the-art battleship HMS *Dreadnought*, then lying off Weymouth in Dorset.

The whole day had been something of a scramble and the Foreign Office had, typically, not given sufficient warning to those involved. At Paddington railway station in London, Herbert Cholmondley of the FO had demanded a private train for the Abyssinians to travel to Weymouth. However, no one had troubled to inform the railway company. Nevertheless, the stationmaster managed to attach one private carriage to the regular Weymouth service, found some red carpet and arranged a guard of honour made up of his ticket inspectors. That would have to do.

The Abyssinian party headed for Weymouth, the stationmaster waving his top hat as the dignitaries pulled out of his station. At their destination there was more confusion. The officers of *Dreadnought* had turned out in their full dress uniforms to hear the party piped aboard but they hadn't managed to find an Abyssinian flag and none of the marine band knew the Abyssinian national anthem. Instead they hoisted the flag of Zanzibar, whose anthem the band played in the hope that this would be similar enough to pass unnoticed.

It seemed to work. On board *Dreadnought*, the party were apparently very pleased with what they saw, regularly stopping at every new technical marvel, raising their hands in the air and shouting, 'Bunga bunga.' At sunset they asked for prayer mats, which again caused consternation as such things were not normally carried on board British battleships. It was finally agreed that evening prayers could wait until the visit was over, provided the navy agreed to abandon its usual bugle call at this time, which might offend the dignitaries. Finally the party was invited to take tea, at which point their interpreter suddenly announced that the visit was over and they would have to return to their train.

The Abyssinian visit to HMS *Dreadnought* ended without a diplomatic incident and the exotic party waved from the windows of their train at the crowds who had gathered to see them off. By now there was some suspicion on *Dreadnought* that all was not quite as it should be. Why had the party so suddenly left and, as one staff officer pointed out, why did their interpreter have a German accent? Could he be a spy? Should they have shown these people around without first confirming their identity with the Foreign Office?

Of course they certainly should have rung the Foreign Office as they found out the next morning when the story broke in the newspapers. The 'Abyssinians', whom they had so deferentially shown around the world's most powerful warship, were in fact a group of London hoaxers, including the son of a judge, an artist and the writer Virginia Stephen (later Virginia Woolf). With the aid of Sarah Bernhardt's make-up artist, they had fooled the whole British establishment into believing they were the Abyssinian royal family. Their sudden departure from the ship the previous evening had been solely due to the fact that they had been warned not to eat or drink when wearing their make-up as it would come off.

Needless to say, the papers took an absolute delight in ridiculing the Royal Navy, as did the crowds at Weymouth. So embarrassed was the navy that HMS *Dreadnought* was ordered to sea to 'ride out the storm'.

The Campden Wonder

On Thursday 16 August 1660, William Harrison, estate manager for local landlord Baptist Hicks, set out on his rent-collecting rounds to the village of Charingworth. It was a simple, everyday event and so it would have remained, were it not for the fact that Harrison did not come home.

By dusk his wife was worried and sent their servant, John Perry, to search for him. When he too failed to return by daybreak, the now distraught Mrs Harrison sent their son Edward to go looking for both men. On the way to Charingworth, Edward met their servant Perry, apparently coming back from there, having been unable to find his master. The two decided to ask at the nearby villages of Ebrington and Paxford to see whether Harrison had been seen in the area. In Ebrington they were told by a tenant that Harrison had indeed visited the previous evening on his way back from Charingworth, but he had not stayed long and had not been seen since. At Paxford there was no news of William at all. The two headed back to Chipping Campden.

It was on the road home that news reached them that a hat, shirt, comb and collar had been found concealed in a gorse hedge by the road that William would have taken from Ebrington back to Chipping. The hat had slash marks in it, and the shirt and collar were covered in blood.

Fearing the worst, Edward and John Perry immediately began searching for a body. Unable to find one, they returned to Chipping to raise the alarm and seek the help of other villagers. It was during this fruitless search that village suspicion first turned on John Perry. As William was collecting rents he would have had a reasonable amount of cash on him. Perry would have known his master's movements. Had he perhaps arranged a violent robbery?

To test the thesis, Perry was brought before the local magistrate where he produced an unconvincing story. He described having met a man called William Reed the previous evening and returning to Chipping Campden with him as it was too dark to go on without a horse. He then claimed to have spent several hours in his master's hen roost before starting back for Charingworth again on foot, getting lost in the mist and sleeping under a hedge. He had finally reached Charingworth the next morning and met Edward Harrison on his way back.

The Justice of the Peace, unconvinced, remanded Perry in custody, during which Perry announced that he had some grave intelligence for the magistrate if he were to be brought before him once more. Back in court, he declared that he not only knew that Harrison was dead but could identify who had killed him: his own mother Joan and his brother Richard. He had provided them with details of when Harrison would be there, and they had robbed and murdered him.

The claim was extraordinary, not only because it implicated his family, but because he admitted to being an accessory in providing them with the specifics of Harrison's journey – something for which he too would surely hang.

Sure enough, all three were questioned and indicted. When the court reconvened, however, they each declared themselves innocent. John changed his story again, claiming his accusations had been false due to insanity. The jury didn't believe him, nor did they believe his mother or brother. All were convicted of having arranged the murder of William Harrison for his rent money. John's mother was hanged first on the grounds that she was a witch who had led her sons astray. John and Richard then went to their deaths, both pleading their innocence to the last.

And so the story ended, or it would have done, had not the supposedly murdered William Harrison walked back into Chipping Campden two years later. He claimed that on that fateful August day as he went about his rent collecting, he was abducted by three men on horseback, dressed all in white, who took him to Deal in Kent and put him aboard a ship for Turkey. In Turkey he had been sold into slavery but had escaped when his master had died. Finding his way aboard a Portuguese vessel bound for England, he had used a silver bowl that he had been given to pay for his passage home. He had arrived at Dover, via Lisbon, and walked home from there.

Even in an era of highway robbery and piracy, the story seemed fantastical, indeed, far more outlandish than John Perry's tales. With no way of disproving it, however, and with William never admitting to anything different, the case was dropped. No one will now ever know why John Perry brought himself and his family to the gallows for a murder that never happened. Nor can we say what game William Harrison was really playing when he set out on his two-year rent-collection round.

The Smuggler's Friend

The case of the seizing of the *Admiral Hood* off the Goodwin Sands on 17 October 1833 looked cut and dried. At about 3 p.m. the dandy-rigged yawl had been spotted acting suspiciously by the Revenue cutter *Lively*, which had gone to investigate. The *Hood* had tried to escape and a chase ensued in which the Revenue cutter soon began to gain ground. With only a mile or so between them, the smuggler's ship went about and tried to head back to France.

At this point customs officers on the *Lively* noticed men on the deck of their quarry, heaving overboard tubs that were painted dark green to match the sea. A boat was launched and twenty-two of these casks were recovered. Finally, as the *Hood* refused to answer any other signal, the captain of the *Lively*, James Shambler RN, ordered a warning shot to be fired, which cut through the yawl's mainsail and finally forced her to heave to. The ship, the crew and her cargo of brandy were all brought ashore. A surer case of smuggling would be hard to find — until, that is, the case came to court.

At the trial an astonishing turnaround occurred when Sir William Courtenay MP suddenly appeared for the defence. A knight and Member of Parliament defending a group of smugglers was in itself unusual, but there was more to come. Courtenay insisted he had been on the cliffs the day the *Admiral Hood* was intercepted and was absolutely sure that the barrels recovered from the water had been there before the chase commenced. As such, they could not possibly have come from the *Hood*; indeed, he had seen no evidence of anyone throwing anything overboard from that vessel.

This left the prosecution in something of a quandary, but, fortunately for them, not everyone took Sir William at his word and clerks were sent off to investigate the claim. They were wise to check, for Sir William Courtenay had a secret. It was not that he was a smuggler himself, nor was he involved in funding such operations, although many local gentry were. The strange truth was that Sir William Courtenay was not Sir William Courtenay at all – he was John Nichols Thom.

Thom was a little eccentric, to say the least; indeed, his mother had died in the lunatic asylum in their home county of Cornwall. Much of his early life had seemed quite normal. He had married well, worked hard and built a business in Truro as a wine merchant. Then, on a business trip to Liverpool, he had disappeared, bobbing up some time later in Canterbury, telling a story that he had been in the Near East – which he hadn't.

Thom had actually been living in London under the name of Squire Thompson where he had taken to helping Jews in financial trouble. In Canterbury he claimed first to be Count Moses Rothschild, using the name to garner loans that he never repaid, and then Sir William Courtenay, rightful Earl of Devon. Astonishingly, no one bothered to check this out, least of all with the real Earl of Devon. Thom managed to stand as an independent candidate in the general election of December 1832 – on the unlikely promise to abolish most taxes. Although he didn't win, he was taken seriously and began publishing a weekly paper, *The Lion*, which contained a varied mix of wild claims, gross exaggerations and very astute commentary on the problems of high taxation. It was then, perhaps now actually believing himself to be Sir William Courtenay, that he appeared in court for the smugglers.

Just why he chose to do so is anyone's guess. Perhaps he simply enjoyed the power that a pretend dignitary could wield over a local court. What we do know is that he had no known connection to the smugglers; he didn't profit from his story; and he opened himself up to a lot of trouble. Indeed, the prosecution discovered that he was actually at church in Herne Bay at the time of the chase. The smugglers were therefore found guilty and Thom was charged with perjury at the Maidstone assizes, for which he received a three-month prison sentence and seven years' transportation. At this point his wife finally caught up with him and persuaded the court that Thom was a touch unbalanced. He was placed in the Barming Heath asylum instead.

After much petitioning by friends, he was eventually released, having been in the asylum for four years, but continued to maintain he was the Earl of Devon. He also began to identify himself with a still greater personage – Jesus Christ, issuing prophecies and gathering around 100 followers. When an attempt was made to arrest him for taking labourers away from their work, he shot dead one of the officers who was trying to apprehend him and then, as the man lay dying, viciously mutilated his body with a sword, which he said was Excalibur.

The army were called out. Thom and about forty of his followers retired to Bossenden Wood for a last stand. In the short firefight that ensued, Thom was mortally wounded. His reasons for attempting to get the *Hood*'s smugglers off the hook died with him.

Blood's Last Trick

Thomas Blood was someone whom few people chose to trust and quite rightly so. Indeed, his epitaph ended rather rudely with 'Here let him then by all unpitied lie, And let's rejoice his time was come to die', which is certainly not a friendly comment.

One man who did trust Blood was Talbot Edwards, an error that would lead to one of the most famous crimes of the seventeenth century. Blood already had a 'varied' career behind him when the two men first met. Formerly a Royalist in the Civil War, he had later 'converted' to being a Roundhead. He had owned and lost large estates in Ireland, had probably worked as a government agent, had kidnapped and attempted to murder the Duke of Ormond (whom he blamed for his loss of land), and had liberated an old friend on the way to trial, and probably execution, by shooting five of his guards.

Now in April 1671, Blood was planning his greatest escapade of all, and it revolved around poor Talbot Edwards, a former soldier now in his late seventies. Their paths had crossed thanks to an act of charity. Blood and his wife had been inspecting the crown jewels, which Edwards, as deputy keeper at the Tower of London, could show to visitors in return for a small fee. During Blood's visit, his wife had been taken ill and Edwards had offered to take the couple back to his rooms in the Martin Tower, just above where the jewels were kept, to recover.

Blood was very grateful, making Edwards's wife a present of four pairs of white gloves. The two men became great friends, so much so that a marriage was suggested between Edwards's daughter and Blood's 'nephew', a man with a generous private income – or so Edwards thought. In fact, he had been thoroughly hoodwinked. He believed his dear friend was called 'Doctor Aycliffe' and had no idea that the man presented to him as his future son-in-law was in fact Blood's son, Thomas, a noted highwayman. Nor was he aware that every solicitous visit to his home simply gave Blood and his accomplices more intelligence for planning the most audacious robbery in history.

So it was, on the morning of 9 May 1671, after a whirlwind 'engagement', that the marriage day dawned for Edwards's daughter and 'Doctor Aycliffe's' 'nephew'. At about seven that morning, Blood, his son and three friends rode up to the Tower and were allowed in. At the Martin Tower, Blood apologised that his wife had not yet arrived and suggested the party might care to examine the crown jewels whilst they waited. With one of their number posted at the door, allegedly on the lookout for 'Mrs Aycliffe', the rest proceeded into the lowest chamber of the Tower where the jewels were kept behind an iron grating.

It was at this point that Edwards received a rude awakening.

His 'friends' produced pocket pistols, swordsticks and knives. With the door slammed behind him, he was knocked to the ground and a piece of wood jammed in his mouth to shut him up. When he struggled, the aged soldier was stabbed and knocked unconscious. Blood and his gang now set to work with a casual disregard for the awesome majesty of the royal regalia. Taking the crown from its case, Blood beat it flat with a mallet to make it fit under the parson's cloak he was wearing. Another accomplice unceremoniously stuffed the orb down his trousers while Blood's son set to work, sawing the sceptre in two to get it into his bag.

At this point providence intervened. It was at this very moment that Edwards's son returned home from years abroad and rode into the Tower, asking for his family. The lookout on the door alerted Blood and the group prepared to make their getaway, but as they reached their horses Talbot Edwards regained consciousness and began shouting for help. His son soon found him and raised the alarm. All hell broke loose. Blood and his men rode at full speed for the gates but in their headlong flight his son rode straight into a cart and was knocked to the ground. Undeterred, Blood continued, with one Captain Martin Beckman in pursuit. By the time he reached the Tower gates they had been slammed shut and a brief firefight ensued. With nowhere to go, the jewel thieves were finally forced to surrender.

Although it might be imagined that the King would take a dim view of someone attacking his faithful Yeomen Warders and making off with his jewels, astonishingly this wasn't the case. Blood, who could certainly have expected the death sentence, refused to speak of the crime to anyone other than the King who, amazingly, agreed. On 12 May, Blood was taken in chains from the Tower, where he was now a prisoner, and interviewed by Charles II. On 26 August, after a very convivial stay in the Tower, Blood received a full pardon and a grant of Irish lands worth £500 a year.

What passed between the King and Blood has been a matter of speculation ever since. Certainly Blood had powerful allies at court including the Secretary of State, Henry Bennet, and his secret work as a spy for the government may have saved him. It has also been suggested that the King was simply delighted by the sheer audacity of the man and pardoned him for that alone, or even that Charles, being a little short of ready money, had arranged the whole robbery himself. The exact truth will probably never be known.

Although Thomas Blood survived and prospered, having escaped the noose, he was certainly never trusted again. Even when he finally died in 1680 the government arranged for the exhumation of his body – just to make sure this wasn't another of his little tricks.

Mackenzie's Ruse

At the head of the densely forested Glenmoriston, in Ross-shire in the Scottish Highlands, stands a stone cairn to the memory of a soldier whose quick-thinking deception once saved a royal life.

After the battle of Culloden on 16 April 1746, the claimant to the throne, Bonnie Prince Charlie, escaped from the field through Glenmoriston and took refuge in a cave above the river Doe. As he had a bounty of £30,000 on his head, the area was soon crawling with soldiers and informants, all looking for the prince who they knew must still be near by.

Holed up in his cave on an exposed hillside, Charles Edward Stuart had little hope of leaving the area unnoticed. With his supplies running out, the end for the pretender seemed at hand. And so it probably would have been, were it not for the presence of mind of Roderick Mackenzie, the son of an Edinburgh jeweller with what some claimed was an uncanny resemblance to Bonnie Prince Charlie.

Mackenzie, a fervent Jacobite who had fought at Culloden, was in a similar predicament to his prince. He too was a fugitive from the battle, looking for a way out of the glen. It is not recorded whether his attempted escape was a deliberate decoy or whether he was simply unlucky, but as he made his way down the track that is today the A887, he was challenged by one of the many British patrols in the area. As he turned to flee, the redcoats opened fire and he fell to the ground, mortally wounded.

This was the point at which he saved his prince's life. As the patrol gathered round him he summoned up the strength to say just a few words: 'You have killed your prince.'

With that he died. The patrol were absolutely delighted, of course. As far as they knew, they had killed a Jacobite who in his death throes had confessed to being Bonnie Prince Charlie. It is not known whether they had ever seen the prince in the flesh but clearly they thought the resemblance good enough to make it worth their cutting off his head and taking it back to Fort Augustus, in the hope of claiming the huge reward.

At Fort Augustus there was further confusion. The British commander, the Duke of Cumberland, who was familiar with the real prince, was unsure about the head, which, when he had last seen it, had been attached to a body. He therefore sent it to London for identification but the government there sent it back again without confirming – or refuting – the identity. Whilst this gruesome game of pass the head was going on with the noble Mackenzie's mortal remains, the search for the pretender slackened off. In his distant cave, Bonnie Prince Charlie had seen his chance and slipped away across the water to the relative safely of the Hebrides.

The Tartan Forgery

Very little is known of the early life of John and Charles Allen, both of whom were probably born sometime in the 1790s. Although this is partly because of the lack of contemporary records, it is more a product of the elaborate and fantastical web of deceit they spent the majority of their lives weaving around themselves.

We do know that they were the sons of Thomas Gatehouse Allen, a lieutenant in the Royal Navy, but beyond that things start to get a little murky. According to them, their father was not the son of Admiral John Carter Allen, an ancestor, you might think, illustrious enough to suit most purposes, but actually the son of Bonnie Prince Charlie, the Stuart claimant to the English throne. This made John and Charles his direct heirs and hence potential kings of England.

It is unclear exactly when they 'realised' that they were of royal stock. They claimed to have offered their services to Napoleon and even to have fought alongside him at Waterloo, which would be a disappointing trait to find in the sons of a Royal Navy officer. What is certain is that sometime later they appeared for the first time in Scotland, where, in the Highlands at least, many held firm to the idea that the rightful king should be a Stuart and not a Hanoverian.

In Scotland the Allen brothers seem to have decided to become as Scottish as possible, changing their names several times until settling on the surname Hay in the hope that people would think they were related to the Hay Earls of Errol. This was so successful that they were soon regular guests at the homes of some Highland chiefs and came under the personal patronage of the Earl of Moray. Indeed, so much time did they spend deer stalking with their new aristocratic friends that they would later be able to write a whole book on the art, *The Lay of the Deer Forest with Sketches of Olden and Modern Hunting.*

Another book altogether would mark the beginning of their downfall. In 1829 they approached the Scottish antiquary, Sir Thomas Dick Lauder, claiming to be in possession of a late fifteenth-century manuscript known as the Vestiarium Scoticum, which detailed all the various identifying tartans of the Highland and Lowland clans. It was a brilliant opening gambit at a time when there was a huge interest in reviving Scottish history and folklore. Many saw the Allen brothers as the rightful Stuart heirs to the throne, championing the ancient rights and customs of Scotland. The brothers even claimed that some clan chieftains had 'checked' their own tartans against the book, proving their ancient and noble heritage.

Lauder was impressed but needed further proof – after all, he had been shown what was said to be an inferior eighteenth-century copy of the original. So he wrote to Sir Walter Scott, the eminent Scottish historical novelist. Scott was less impressed, pointing out that there was absolutely no evidence that Lowland clans had ever worn tartan or plaid, and noting that even the title of the book was bad Latin. He did, however, suggest that perhaps the original manuscript should be sent for detailed examination by antiquaries. This, of course, the Allen brothers refused to do.

If Scott was sceptical, others were not, and the Allens had soon set up house at the beautiful hunting lodge of Eilean Aigas, on an island in the Beauly river, Inverness-shire, which their new patron, Lord Lovat, had granted them. Here they really did hold court, finally fully declaring their Stuart ancestry and converting to Roman Catholicism (the religion of the Stuarts). With their hopes of acceptance amongst the Scottish aristocracy revived, the brothers published a version of the manuscript in 1842 that included a huge amount of their own research – some very good but a lot of it simply invented. As they gained in confidence, this was followed up by *Tales of the Century, or, Sketches of the Romance of History between the Years 1746 and 1846*. Nominally fiction, it was in fact a barely disguised rehearsal of the Allens' claim to the throne. This little bit of hubris would finally bring them down.

The book drew an anonymous attack in the *Quarterly Review* (now known to have been written by Professor George Skene), which, having quickly dismissed the *Tales*, went on to demolish the scholarship of the Vestiarium, page by page. The author pointed out that the Vestiarium was a fantasy, a book that everyone would like to have existed but which was clearly a forgery. As even the romantic Sir Walter Scott put it, the 'idea of distinguishing the clans by their tartans is but a fashion of modern date'.

With their reputation demolished, the Allen brothers' little court broke up and the family moved to the continent where they hoped their pretensions to royalty might be better received. Twenty years later, and now very poor, they returned to London, where it was said they could be seen daily in the British Library, researching their claims, and carefully making notes using pens surmounted with miniature golden coronets. Perhaps they had the last laugh after all, as the myth that they started – of the ancient clan tartans – is stronger than ever. Today people from all over the world travel to Scotland to discover which 'ancient' tartan their Scottish ancestors once wore.

The Fooling of the Black Legion

It's not unusual for older and more patriotic history books to claim that mainland Britain hasn't been invaded since the Norman Conquest in 1066, but this overlooks a few more embarrassing events that perhaps we would rather forget. In fact, the last invasion of mainland Britain occurred in 1797 just outside Fishguard in Dyfed.

With the Napoleonic Wars in full swing, the French government of the Directory decided that a direct attack on Great Britain might be, at the very least, a good diversion. As most of Napoleon's troops were rather busy elsewhere, the job of invading Britain, destroying Bristol and then marching north across Wales to take Chester and Liverpool was given to a septuagenarian Irish-American colonel and his 1,400 troops, 800 of whom were ex-convicts. These were given the rather grand title of the Légion Noire – the 'Black Legion'.

Whilst Colonel William Tate was certainly keen on the job – he had hated the British ever since his parents had been killed by pro-British Native Americans in the War of Independence – his mission was a tall order. On 18 February 1797 the four ships carrying the invasion force set sail from Camaret in France but were driven past their intended target of Bristol by strong winds. Although Tate now ordered the landings to take place in Cardigan Bay, the element of surprise had been lost. When the flotilla approached Fishguard, the town's fort had to fire only one round to see off the enemy. Fortunately for the people of the town,

William Tate didn't know that one shot was all they had in their somewhat limited arsenal.

Eventually the invaders found an unprotected beach, probably at Carreg Wasted Head (or perhaps near Llanwnda), and made their historic landing. By night they scaled the cliffs and seized Trehowel Farm where they set up Tate's new headquarters. Behind them their ships were already turning back for France, leaving the Black Legion to its fate.

In truth Tate was quite pleased with the initial stages of his plan, which had met with no opposition. His men were also fairly content, having discovered the local houses to be full of port recently salvaged from a Portuguese wreck. From this point on, the invasion began to founder. First, Tate found it harder and harder to control his now drunken men; they had been drawn from the prisons and the worst companies in the French army, and hence were not big on discipline. Second, the Welsh were about to fight back. Baron Cawdor was already advancing on the coast with his volunteers and lead was being stripped from the roof of St David's Cathedral for making bullets.

However, it was the women who, according to legend, would drive off Britain's last invasion. In the first instance one Jemima Nicholas, a local shoemaker, became a national hero when she spotted twelve Frenchman wandering around in a field and promptly rounded them up with a scythe.

Back at the Legion's HQ, things weren't much better. Tate's drunken forces had by now eaten all the food they had brought with them, as well as anything else they could find, and had virtually wrecked the farmhouse by breaking up everything in it that would burn and throwing it on the fire to keep warm. And that was even before local women with scythes intervened.

Tate had had enough and ordered his men to march down on to Goodwick Sands, preparing to parley. One final ignominy awaited. Above them, Baron Cawdor's volunteer troops were gathering, and with them were many of the local people, including hundreds of women dressed in their traditional red flannel shawls and tall black hats. From the beach the befuddled French mistook these women for lines of professional troops in their distinctive red coats and promptly surrendered outright.

On the afternoon of Friday 24 February 1797, in the Royal Oak pub in Fishguard, William Tate signed the surrender note and the invasion was over. The Black Legion were imprisoned and Britain, if it had ever been at risk, was safe once more.

12

Secrets of the Grave

Let's talk of graves, of worms, and epitaphs;
Make dust our paper, and with rainy eyes
Write sorrow on the bosom of the earth.
Let's choose executors, and talk of wills.

William Shakespeare, *Richard II* (1595)

Henry VIII

The Debenhams Mystery

There are many places that claim to be haunted in the UK. Church crypts, graveyards, castles and ancient manors all claim their fair share of spectres and ghouls. Perhaps a less likely location is the Debenhams store in Salisbury, Wiltshire.

Why this innocuous (and modern) building should be haunted is a story that stretches back to the bloody events of 1483. In that year Henry Stafford, 2nd Duke of Buckingham (and one of the main suspects in the disappearance of the 'Princes in the Tower'), rebelled against Richard III in favour of Henry Tudor (later Henry VII). Frankly the rebellion hadn't gone well and on 2 November he found himself on the scaffold in the yard of the Blue Boar Inn in Salisbury, where a headsman soon put paid to his political career.

What then happened to the body of this illustrious duke is a matter of conjecture. Even though he was executed as a traitor, others in his position at least received a decent burial. In the nearby village of Britford there is an elaborate and anonymous tomb of about this date that is sometimes claimed as his last resting place. In the *Gentleman's Magazine* for 1836 an attempt was made by Sir Richard Colt Hoare to decipher the meaning of the strange symbols on the tomb as follows, trying to prove that it was that of Buckingham:

> There are six niches, five of which contain male and female figures; the first is vacant, which I think was designed for the unfortunate Duke. I consider the female figure in the second niche, having a crown on her head, as representing the Duchess, his wife. The next figure is evidently an ecclesiastic, or bishop, deploring the unfortunate fate of the Duke: and at this period Widvile, brother of the Duchess, was Bishop of the See. The fourth figure represents a female crowned like the second, holding a sword in one hand, and in the other a cap or bonnet, probably that of the Duke. The fifth figure represents the Executioner, with

the sword in his hand. The last figure, representing a female, holding up her hand in apparent grief, and with a child in her arms, as alluding to one of the unfortunate Duke's offspring.

It was perhaps a decipherment too far and not everyone agreed with it. In particular, the contemporary document, the Chronicles of the Greyfriars of London, states that the duke was buried in their foundation in Salisbury. It is the third option that takes us into Debenhams.

In 1838, according to the September edition of the *Salopian Journal*, renovations at the Saracen's Head Inn in the city revealed a skeleton, complete save for its head and right arm, buried beneath the floor. The workmen, a superstitious bunch, feared bad luck from uncovering what they thought was an ancient murder victim. They therefore quickly broke up the fragile remains, mixing them with the clay, or as the *Journal* puts it, with a turn of phrase sadly lacking from many modern newspapers, 'knocked about his noble dust, and in a few minutes compounded it with the clay whereto 'twas kin'.

Only later did anyone realise that perhaps these were the remains of the Duke of Buckingham, which had lain undiscovered in his unconsecrated grave for 355 years.

In time the Saracen's Head Inn was demolished, having itself taken the place of the Blue Boar Inn where we know Buckingham died. And in its place? Debenhams, where a blue plaque now marks the site of the execution and where the ghost of the unfortunate duke is said to still walk the aisles.

The Man Who Wouldn't Be King

Henry Fitzroy, Duke of Richmond, holds a peculiar place in British history as one of those 'might-have-been' characters. Had events turned out only slightly differently, he might have been king, instead of which he was secretly buried and quietly forgotten.

Henry Fitzroy was living proof that Henry VIII could father a healthy son. The only problem was that his mother wasn't Henry's legal wife, but his mistress, Elizabeth Blount. The mere existence of young Henry put his father in a quandary. Whilst he knew this meant he could sire children, and boys at that, he also needed a legitimate heir to inherit. Should he keep trying to produce a legitimate son or should he legitimise Henry?

Certainly the young Henry was not hidden away. On 18 June 1525, when he was just six, he was made Earl of Nottingham and, on the same day, received the unprecedented gift of the double dukedoms of Richmond and Somerset, as well as being granted various other honours. His education was carefully attended to by some of the finest scholars of the day, including Richard Croke. The little duke also took after his father in his great love of sports and hunting. Many considered him a youthful version of Henry VIII and there was even talk of making him king of Ireland when he reached his majority. The King further ensured the boy duke had a background in politics, summoning him to parliament, taking him to Calais to meet the French sovereign and arranging for him to reside for a while in the French court. A good marriage was also organised, possibly engineered by Anne Boleyn, who brought together Henry and her young cousin Mary Howard.

In 1536 a new Act of Succession was passing through parliament that would have allowed the King to name his successor as he chose. Before it was made law, tragedy struck. The normally hale and hearty duke was said to have been taken ill with a lung infection. Just two weeks after this announcement was made, he died, on 23 July 1536. He was seventeen years old.

Henry VIII had never officially recognised his son as his potential heir, perhaps always believing he would have a legitimate one, as of course he went on to do with Jane Seymour. Therefore, when Henry Fitzroy died, all plans and thoughts of his possible future greatness died with him. He was now simply a dead, illegitimate child, best forgotten. The Duke of Norfolk was ordered to arrange a secret funeral with as little fuss and attracting as little attention as possible. The body was wrapped in lead and placed in a wooden coffin, which was hidden in a cart-load of straw. It was then taken away for a private interment, accompanied by only two mourners. At Thetford, a good distance from London, Henry Fitzroy was buried in the local priory, his body being moved to St Michael's church in Framlingham when the priory was later dissolved by his father. The man who wouldn't be king was not to be mentioned again.

The Two Graves of Henry Tremble

On 19 August 1876, Henry Tremble, butler to Mr John Johnes, proved conclusively that you really can't get the staff these days when he shot his employer dead. For Cluedo fans the full scenario was Mr Tremble, in the library, with the revolver. Agatha Christie fans hardly need be told that it was the butler who did it.

Henry Tremble had been furious with his master, a former judge of the county court for the counties of Carmarthen, Cardigan and Pembroke, and the lord of the now long-demolished Dolaucothi House. Tremble had been refused the tenancy of the local pub, which Mr Johnes owned. Mr Johnes, for his part, had been of the opinion that it would be unwise to make his alcoholic and rather unstable butler a pub landlord. Within seconds, his opinion was wonderfully justified when Tremble burst back into the room and shot him dead in the chair where he sat. The butler then dashed from the room, shooting at Mr Johnes's daughter en route and wounding the cook for good measure.

From Dolaucothi, Tremble ran to his own cottage in Caeo where he barricaded himself in and threatened to shoot the policemen who subsequently surrounded the building. Eventually thinking better of this, and realising there was no escape, he wrote a confession addressed to the local vicar and shot himself instead.

Although the tragic tale of John Johnes and Henry Tremble should have finished with two funerals and two graves, it didn't. Tremble was buried in the churchyard at Caeo, something that annoyed the locals who objected to having a suicide and murderer in their hallowed ground. However, rather than complain to the authorities, one night they simply dug him up, loaded the coffin on a cart and drove it secretly through the night to the village of Tirabad, 20 miles away. Here, having told the locals the body was that of a pauper who had died at Llandovery workhouse, they buried him in their churchyard.

Of course news of this little wheeze soon leaked out, making the people of Tirabad incensed that the body of a murderous suicide from another village had been dumped in their churchyard. Borrowing a large block and tackle from the local wool merchant in Builth Wells on the pretext of needing it to pull up tree roots, they opened Tremble's grave for a second time, hauled his now well-travelled coffin on to a cart, covered it with hay and set off for Caeo.

Just before dawn the Tirabad parishioners – perhaps the only grave robbers in history to dig up a body they didn't want – arrived at Caeo churchyard where they unceremoniously ditched the coffin and ran away. Reluctantly, the burghers of Caeo were forced to reinter the now badly decayed body of Henry Tremble in their own churchyard, making him the only man to be buried there twice.

Miller's Mausoleum

Amid a row of 1930s bungalows in Craigentinny Crescent, Edinburgh, stands one of the city's more unusual monuments with its own secret history. The Miller mausoleum is an enormous stone structure in the form of one of the grand old Roman tombs on the Appian Way outside Rome, decorated with what are known as the 'Craigentinny Marbles'.

Although this suburban street very definitely isn't consecrated ground, the monument is indeed a tomb and it contains the remains of William Henry Miller, a nineteenth-century book collector and MP. Miller was one of the great collectors of his age, amassing a library that included books from William Caxton's press as well as the cream of the libraries dispersed during his lifetime. He was particularly well known for collecting only very good editions that had not been trimmed but had wide margins, or were, as he put it, 'fine and tall'. To this end he became famous for carrying around a foot-long wooden ruler, which he used to ensure that prospective purchases were indeed as fine and tall as he had been told and this led to his being known as Measure Miller.

Miller died in 1848 at the age of sixty and, during the six-week delay before his burial, a host of rumours began to circulate around Edinburgh as to the cause of the hiatus. Such gossip was not laid to rest when it was announced that he had left a sizeable fortune for the construction of a huge tomb for himself, set up not in a consecrated churchyard but in the grounds of his estate at Craigentinny. The monument itself, which would cost £20,000, was to be designed by David Rhind and would be decorated with two sculptural panels by the famous Victorian artist Alfred Gately, the scenes depicting 'The Overthrow of Pharaoh in the Red Sea' and 'The Song of Moses and Miriam'. It is these panels that led to the monument being called the Craigentinny Marbles, although they're not actually made of marble.

More peculiar than this massive and expensive tomb in a field was what lay beneath it. Miller's will required that he be buried at the bottom of a 40-foot (one account says 20-foot) stone-lined shaft under the monument, with a large slab of stone placed over the coffin lid to ensure it could not be lifted. It was his reason for going to such extreme lengths that had sparked the rumours. Miller's death occurred at a time when Edinburgh graveyards had an unhealthy reputation, due to the 'resurrectionists' who secretly exhumed bodies there to sell to the medical schools for dissection. What was buried in them rarely stayed buried for long. Indeed, only twenty years had passed since Burke and Hare had scandalised society by going one better and murdering victims for the dissection slab.

So was it a fear of ending up the object of an anatomy class that worried William Miller? Possibly, but there was also another rumour. Miller had been known to be excessively secretive, rarely allowing academics (or anyone else) access to his books. *Old and New Edinburgh*, published forty-two years after his death, quotes a contemporary source as saying: 'He was averred to be a changeling – even a woman, a suggestion which his thin figure, weak voice, absence of all beard and some peculiarity of habit seemed to corroborate.'

The Danbury Pickle

The secrets of the grave are often best left exactly where they are but in the eighteenth century, as a new age of antiquarianism dawned, there was a sudden craze for investigating the contents of ancient tombs in churches and cathedrals. It led in one case to the remarkably unsavoury discovery of the secret behind a strange preservation.

Following the successful 'opening' of the tomb of Edward I in Westminster Abbey in 1774, in which the king was found to be richly dressed and crowned, with his facial features 'shrunken but intact', many local historical societies took the opportunity to investigate the more important-looking graves in their own churches.

In 1779 just such an occasion presented itself at Danbury in Essex where excavations for a new burial in the church had led to the discovery of a sealed lead sarcophagus beneath a mediaeval wooden effigy of a knight. With local dignitaries gathered, the workmen were ordered to open the lead box, inside which they discovered an elm coffin almost perfectly preserved. On removing its lid, the spectators were presented with a peculiar and some- what gothic sight: what is described as a 'shell' covering the body, which was probably the vitrified remains of a shroud covered in resin. When this 'shell' was broken open, the gathering came face to face with the occupant, whose preserved flesh was said to be 'exceedingly white and firm', although the face was dark and the throat lacerated.

The investigators' attentions now focused on what had preserved the body so remarkably. The remains were lying in a liquor, containing herbs, feathers and flowers, which an onlooker said reminded him of mushroom ketchup. In the spirit of enquiry, one Thomas White decided to test this observation, in a way that is best left for him to describe, as recounted in the *Gentleman's Magazine* of that year:

> We were presented with a view of the body, laying in a liquor or pickle, somewhat resembling mushroom catchup, but of a paler complexion, and somewhat thicker consistency. As I never possessed the sense of smelling, and was willing to ascertain the flavour of the liquor, I tasted and found it to be aromatic, tho' not very pungent, partaking of the taste of catchup and of the pickle of Spanish olives.

This then is the best description we have of the combination of once exotic herbs and spices used to preserve the body of a mediaeval knight so many centuries ago. With that, the doors of the church were thrown open and the queasy investigators departed, leaving the locals to view the discovery at their leisure.

Henry Trigg's Coffin

A coffin is not the sort of item that usually spends a lot of time on show, unless it's in a particularly unsuccessful funeral parlour. Henry Trigg's final resting place, however, is another matter, being as much on view today as it was when he died nearly 300 years ago. The question is: what is really in his coffin?

Henry Trigg, a wealthy grocer from Stevenage in Hertfordshire, had an unnatural fear of 'resurrectionists'. The story he told was that one night, whilst walking home a shade the worse for wear, he wandered past the local graveyard where he noticed lights. Peering over the wall, he saw to his horror bodysnatchers at work, engaged in their grisly trade of disinterring the recently dead in order to sell their corpses to anatomical schools for dissection.

Henry was so affected by the sight that he determined he would never suffer the indignities of being dug up, going to elaborate lengths to prevent this. Now Henry was a wealthy bachelor so his will carried considerable clout. In it he left everything to his brother, on the condition that he was laid to rest, not in the churchyard, but high up in the rafters of the recipient's barn. If the beneficiary refused to abide by the terms of his will, the money would go to the next most senior family member and, if he refused, to the next and so on down the line.

This put Thomas Trigg in something of a bind as he was the local vicar and might be expected to maintain certain standards. Either from a desire to fulfil his brother's will or an interest in inheriting his fortune, he eventually agreed. Henry Trigg's body was sealed in its coffin, which was hoisted up on to the rafters of his brother's barn, where it remains to this day – apparently.

The coffin of Henry Trigg soon became something of a tourist attraction for travellers changing coach in Stevenage, who had never before seen a man buried in the air. Despite numerous town fires, the coffin survived. In the meantime the building changed in use from a barn to the Old Castle Inn, before becoming a branch of NatWest bank, still with the coffin of Henry Trigg looking down on the depositors.

The question remains, however, as to what is actually in it. There are various stories as to the fate of Henry's bones. We know that his niece Ann left forty shillings in her will of 1769 to finally bury the embarrassing coffin but there is no evidence that the money was spent. Indeed, with such a tourist attraction in the town, why would anyone want to inter it? Certainly in 1831 the new landlord of the pub decided to take a look inside his star exhibit and announced that Henry was very much still there, noting that 'the hair on the skull of the deceased is in a perfect state of preservation'. But then again, he would say that. Another examination by the members of the East Hertfordshire Archaeology Society in 1906 resulted in the announcement that about two-thirds of a human skeleton remained inside.

Where was the rest? It was probably taken as ghoulish souvenirs, a fate that has perhaps overtaken the rest of the body. In 1917 at the last (surreptitious) examination of the coffin, the investigators reported finding only horse bones, confirming in their minds the theory that soldiers stationed in the area in the First World War had taken Henry's own as mementoes. So Henry's greatest fear may well have finally come true.

The Red Lady

In 1823 the Very Reverend William Buckland, Dean of Westminster and noted geologist and palaeontologist, was exploring Goat's Hole Cave at Paviland on the Gower Peninsula in South Wales, in search of fossils. What he stumbled upon was one of the greatest finds in British archaeology, albeit one that would keep its secrets until well after his death.

He discovered that day a human skeleton, covered in a strange red dye and adorned with prehistoric elephant (mammoth) ivory and seashell jewellery. He wrote later that year in his book *Reliquiae Diluvianae* that he found the body

stained superficially with a dark brick-red colour, and enveloped by a coating of a kind of ruddle, composed of red micaceous oxyde of iron, which stained the earth, and in some parts extended itself to the distance of about half an inch around the surface of the bones. The body must have been entirely surrounded or covered over at the time of its interment with this red substance. Close to that part of the thigh bone where the pocket is usually worn, I found laid together, and surrounded also by ruddle, about two handsfull of small shells of the nerita littoralis in a state of great decay, and falling to dust on the slightest pressure. At another part of the skeleton, viz. in contact with the ribs, I found forty or fifty fragments of small ivory rods nearly cylindrical, and varying in diameter from a quarter to three quarters of an inch, and from one to four inches in length.

The skeleton presented Buckland with a number of problems. Despite being Professor of Geology at Oxford University, he was also a cleric and therefore still firmly believed that the timeline presented in the Bible and the story of the flood were literal truths hence the title of his book *Reliquiae Diluvianae* – 'Remains from the Flood'. And so finding a human skeleton together with such extinct animals as mammoths was bothersome.

Like many facing an awkward truth, Buckland's first instinct was to ignore the troublesome evidence. So in his initial conclusions he claimed that the body was male, the remains of a customs officer murdered by local smugglers. Nevertheless the evidence – and the elephant – bothered him and by the time he published his find, his story had changed. Now he claimed the body was that of a woman whose red-ochre covering showed she was, quite literally, a painted lady – a prostitute serving the needs of the Roman garrison on the nearby hill. The mammoth beads were obviously made from ancient tusks dug up by the Romans and the other strange bones in the cave must have been disturbed from lower, pre-flood levels when the poor woman's shallow grave was dug.

The mystery persisted for nearly another century. By the time the cave was re-excavated in 1912, there had been revolutions in the study of geology and natural history. Darwin's works had gained acceptance and the earth was known to be billions, not thousands, of years old. In fact a re-examination of the Red Lady of Paviland showed she was in truth a man and the new finds from the cave proved he was from the Palaeolithic era – the Old Stone Age. It was only with the advent of radio-carbon dating and, indeed, accelerator dating that the true significance of Buckland's mystery woman became apparent.

The Red Lady of Paviland is now known to be the remains of a young man in his twenties from the most distant period of the habitation of Europe, the oldest human burial in Britain, which lay hidden in the Paviland cave for 29,000 years.

13

Secret Places

And above all, watch with glittering eyes the whole world around you because the greatest secrets are always hidden in the most unlikely places.

Roald Dahl, *The Minpins* (1991)

The Secret City

The city of Burlington is in many ways unremarkable. It covers a relatively modest area of 34 acres, criss-crossed with a grid of 60 miles of roads. Water comes from a large reservoir; there are four power stations, plus all the usual hospitals, canteens, workshops, laundries and offices. There is also accommodation for around 4,000 people. That, however, is where the unremarkable side of Burlington ends. What makes this city remarkable is that none of this shows up on any map, nor is there now a single inhabitant in this eerie ghost town.

The city of Burlington, also known at various times by the code names Stockwell, Chanticleer, Turnstile and the more bland but sinister '3-site', began as an idea in the early 1950s. The location had for over a century been the subterranean 'Spring Quarry', a source of fine Bath stone, before being requisitioned as Europe's largest munitions store and then, during the Second World War, it became an underground aircraft factory.

By the 1950s the advent of high-yield nuclear weapons meant that the site was being looked at again for a new reason. Military planners who had been modelling the effects of an all-out nuclear war had estimated that 132 nuclear bombs falling on major British cities would cause hundreds of thousands of casualties and disable all forms of government. In 1955, when William Strath of the Central War Plans Secretariat updated this report to include hydrogen bombs, his estimate for immediate deaths had risen to 12 million (with a further 4 million serious injuries) or around a third of the population. Plans were considered for providing public shelters but the cost appeared prohibitive and it was feared that a construction programme would be taken by the Soviet bloc as an escalation of tensions and a prelude to war.

The answer the Secretariat came up with was to leave the people to their own devices while hiding away a core of government officials and ministers. From a place of safety, these individuals could organise the massive retaliation that the doctrine of

'Mutually Assured Destruction' (or MAD) required and then re-establish contact with the outside world, as well as with their own government, when the (radioactive) dust settled.

Thus was born the plan to create a hidden, underground bunker near Corsham in Wiltshire. In 1957, work finally began on Britain's secret city. Burlington was designed on a grid plan as a small-scale mirror of Whitehall, its streets lined with pared-down versions of peacetime ministries, complete with provision for ministers and civil servants. This miniature government would be equipped with food, water and fuel to last three months, after which it was assumed it might be safe to venture outside.

The whole treeless city was divided into twenty-four areas, designed to offer outside communication and cater for the basic welfare of 4,000 to 6,000 people. Area 21 held the communications offices of the intelligence services that would monitor above-ground events. Here they would communicate with twelve regional bunkers, which in turn would be connected to a network of 1,563 monitoring posts manned by the Royal Observer Corps, who would relay details of the unfolding devastation in all its horror.

Elsewhere, Area 8 contained the second-largest telephone exchange in Britain, which would be manned by GPO staff. Area 16 contained the BBC broadcasting studio from where the Prime Minister would update his or her people on the progress of the war. Area 12 housed the industrial ovens of the kitchens, making meals from the long-life foodstuffs stockpiled in Area 9, which also housed a fully operational hospital and dental surgery. Area 6 housed the bakeries and canteens. It was a bleak and utilitarian world at best, the only concession to the life left behind being the provision of a pub, the 'Rose and Crown', on 'Main Street'.

At the centre of operations was Area 17 where politicians and senior officials would live and work, centred on the 'Map Room'. Here the Prime Minister had the only en-suite bedroom in the entire complex. Notably, there was no accommodation included for their, or any other official's, family members. Indeed, it was only with the declassification of the site in 2002 that many civil servants even knew they had a desk reserved for them in Burlington. Had the warning come, they would have been expected to immediately leave their families to their fate, take the special train that branched off just before the tunnel at Box in Wiltshire and dive underground to their new home. With the blast doors sealed and protected by the living rock of the quarry, as well as by 100-foot-thick reinforced concrete walls, it was expected that they would survive what was estimated as a two-day 'destructive phase', followed by the 'survival phase' of a month. The 'reconstruction phase' was rather optimistically scheduled to last just a year. Precisely what the inhabitants of Burlington hoped to 'reconstruct' afterwards remains unclear.

Burlington was finished in 1961 and was put in a state of readiness. Journalists who were invited into the bunker after its declassification forty years later noted piles of chairs and tables still in their wrappings, thousands of toilet rolls, reams of paper and rows of 1960s telephones still in their boxes – all stockpiled for the unthinkable event. Fortunately, that event never came. When Margaret Thatcher was presented with an estimated bill of £40 million for renovating the site in 1989, she deemed it unnecessary as the threat from the Soviet bloc had disappeared. In 1992 the last few maintenance officers left Burlington and the 'city that never was' was quietly forgotten.

The Hidden World of Welbeck Abbey

The 5th Duke of Portland was a man wealthy enough to indulge his hobbies as he saw fit and his decision to indulge them secretly is not in itself that peculiar for a nineteenth-century aristocrat. The peculiarity lies in what those hobbies were.

John Cavendish-Scott-Bentinck had started life in the manner of many a noble of his day. He courted a celebrity (in his case a famous singer), to no avail; he served in the army (the Grenadier Guards); he inherited a title (Marquess of Titchfield); and he served as a Tory MP (for King's Lynn). On 27 March 1854 he succeeded to the dukedom of Portland. If anyone in London expected the new duke to become a major society figure, they were much mistaken.

Few had failed to notice that, now aged fifty-four, he had never married, and it was widely known that he was something of a recluse, shunning the parties, balls and dinners that people of his class (and wealth) were expected to both give and attend. The 5th Duke was, by all accounts, someone who didn't do the normal society things. However, society had no idea about what he *was* actually doing.

The duke's real – indeed, perhaps his only – love was his estate at Welbeck Abbey, yet even here he shunned company, reputedly ordering his servants never to acknowledge his presence, should he wander by, on pain of dismissal. His gardens were a particular passion, being famous for producing exotic fruit from what were said to be the finest hothouses in the country. He also, like his peers, loved riding and built a 121-metre-long riding house, lit by 4,000 gas jets. Nor did he forget his staff, having a roller-skating rink built for them when the craze took off.

The house itself made for quite a contrast. The building's interior was in a state of dangerous disrepair, there not being the money to maintain the whole of it. The duke had most of the rooms stripped of their furniture, save for a small suite in the west wing where he lived. All the rooms in it were painted pink and an unscreened commode placed in each. Only his valet was allowed into his presence and all his business, private and public, was conducted by letter.

Yet even this wasn't the Duke of Portland's real secret. That lay beneath the abbey. Under the house and grounds, the duke had excavated an astonishing 15 miles of passages and rooms, many connecting above-ground features to the house so that the duke could access them hidden from prying eyes. This included a 910-metre tunnel to the Riding School – a building he never actually used. Another ran to the East Lodge at the edge of his estate, allowing him to cross his grounds unseen, via a private railway installed in the tunnel. At the lodge he could take his carriage to Worksop where it would be loaded on to a train to take him to London and hence to his house in the capital, without his ever stepping into the open air.

Of the subterranean rooms – all of which were painted pink like those in his wing in the house above – the Great Hall, which could also double up as a huge ballroom, was particularly fine. An unconfirmed report claims that a hydraulic lift, able to carry twenty people from the surface to the hall, was installed for balls, but as the duke never held a ball this remains unproven. Other subterranean rooms included a library, a billiard room and, most eccentrically, an underground observatory, with a glass roof to reveal the stars above.

No one knows why the 5th Duke built this underground domain or what he wanted it for, as no one was ever invited there to find out. The duke died in 1879 in London, wishing in death to retain the anonymity he had sought in life. He was buried without pomp, in a plain grave in Kensal Green cemetery. His legacy was a mysterious subterranean world, a lifetime of charitable giving and a whole generation of employment for the workmen and builders of Welbeck – even if they had no clue as to the purpose of their labours.

The Warkworth Hermitage

On the north bank of the Coquet river in Northumberland, near the village of Warkworth, stands a small stone building partly cut out of the living rock of the cliff face. It is an isolated site; to reach it you must climb down the opposite cliff and ring a bell to attract the attention of the ferryman who will take you across. The building, consisting of just a few small rooms and a chapel, was constructed at some point in the late fourteenth century as a hermitage. At the time there were many such cells where religious individuals might escape from the worldly life but there is a unique story behind how the Warkworth hermitage came to be tucked away in this forgotten spot.

It is told in the ballad 'The Hermit of Warkworth', published in 1771, by Thomas Percy, bishop of Dromore, the first man to collect together all the ancient, and not always wholly reliable, ballads of England. According to this, in the time of Edward III, Earl Percy (the owner of Warkworth Castle) had in his service a knight, Sir Bertram of Bothal, who was engaged to Lady Isabel, the daughter of Lord Widdrington. Having been badly wounded while fighting the Scottish Earl Douglas, Bertram sent for his sweetheart. She never arrived. When he had recovered enough, he and his brother set out for her home to discover why she had not come, only to find she had already left and must have been kidnapped en route.

In the manner of all great chivalric quests, Sir Bertram and his brother swore to disguise themselves (for reasons best known to themselves) and go their separate ways in search of the lady. Whilst journeying across the land, Sir Bertram heard of a beautiful woman kept prisoner in a nearby tower. He rushed to the scene just in time to see a figure in Highland garb carrying her away. Enraged, he dashed forward, shouting her name. On hearing his voice, Isabel turned and called out that it was his brother in disguise, but it was too late. As she stepped in front of her rescuer, Sir Bertram lunged forward with his sword, running through his lover and his brother with a single thrust and killing them both.

Desolate, Sir Bertram returned to his master's castle at Warkworth. There, he gave away his lands and wealth, and asked his lord to grant him some isolated spot where he could spend the rest of his life in solitude. Earl Percy granted him the inaccessible cave on the river bank, which, over the years, he turned into Warkworth hermitage with his bare hands. Over the doorway he is said to have carved the legend: 'My tears have been my meat day and night.'

The Town Beneath the Sea

According to the Anglo-Saxon historian Bede, writing in the eighth century, Siegebert, ruler of what was then the kingdom of East Anglia, invited St Felix of Burgundy to visit his realm in AD 632. The bishop was permitted to set up a new diocese at 'Donmock'.

Such events usually marked the beginnings of greatness for the places chosen. The bishops and archbishops of Canterbury, London, York and Winchester all brought prosperity to the cities they chose as their home, yet if you walk through the streets of 'Donmock', or Dunwich as it is now, you might be forgiven for wondering exactly what went wrong here, for today Dunwich is just a small village. This, however, was not always the case.

St Felix's diocese thrived and eventually East Anglia became absorbed into the kingdom of England. By the time of the Norman Conquest, Dunwich had three churches. Just a century later there were at least eight and perhaps as many as eighteen, with a rising population estimated at more than 3,000. By then Dunwich was also one of the major ports on the North Sea coast and, for the standards of its day, might be considered a city. In 1199 the King recognised its importance by granting it a Royal Charter, making it a borough with elected council members, magistrates, bailiffs and a coroner. Along with trade, shipbuilding and defence became important industries for Dunwich; in 1205 five royal ships are recorded as being anchored in the port – the same number as for London.

By 1229, King Henry III could demand from the town forty ships 'well equipped with all kinds of armament, good steersmen and mariners' (although the thrifty burghers got away with sending only thirty). When a French invasion was imminent in 1242, putting the same burghers' livelihoods at risk, Dunwich managed to rustle up a more impressive eighty ships to defend the seas. Just over fifty years later, the town received a further honour, being enfranchised to send two Members of Parliament to London. However, by this point Dunwich was teetering quite literally on a precipice.

The success of the town was its location. A long gravel spit, known as King's Holme, stretched down from Southwold past Dunwich, protecting the harbour and ensuring that all ships sailing from Southwold and Walberswick had to pass by Dunwich, where the inhabitants levied a very lucrative toll. Early in 1250 all that changed. An unusually high tide, combined with strong north-easterly winds, shifted the gravel of King's Holme, blocking the harbour mouth completely. In order to prevent the town's trade from dying, the people of Dunwich went to extraordinary lengths to cut a new channel to the sea, demolishing their own houses where they stood in the way of the proposed watercourse.

However, the damage to King's Holme was not Dunwich's only problem. The town itself was built on the same soft gravel and sand as the spit. In March 1286 a high tide and a strong easterly wind again beat on the coast. This time it was not the spit of King's Holme but the town itself that suffered, as a huge swathe of land on the eastern side of Dunwich was simply torn off and swallowed up by the sea, carrying away houses, churches and a small monastery. Much of the rest of the town also flooded as the waves crashed over the Holme, opening a new entrance to the sea nearer to the rival village of Walberswick.

The final nail in Dunwich's coffin was driven home on the night of 14 January 1328, when one more huge storm hit the coast, destroying much of the soft cliff on which the town stood. According to the contemporary bailiff's rental notes, nearly all the houses in three parishes had been destroyed, a windmill had collapsed, and the church of St Leonard's, which the townsfolk had already stripped of its fittings as it teetered on the edge of the cliff, had finally disappeared completely into the sea. Worse still, the storm drove the gravels of King's Holme decisively against the harbour entrance, sealing it for ever.

Dunwich staggered on, but its population was now divided geographically and its prosperity at an end. The sea continued to eat away at this once great port and by the eighteenth century the sole evidence of its former glory was the fact that this almost entirely abandoned place could elect two MPs – making it notorious as a 'rotten borough'. By the time of the 1832 Reform Act, which abolished such anomalies, Dunwich had only eight residents.

Today it is just a small village, the last vestige of whose most inland parts are now themselves on the edge of the sea. All that remains of its heyday are the ruins of a leper hospital and the Greyfriars priory – and the legend that on stormy nights the bells of long-submerged mediaeval churches can still be heard ringing beneath the waves.

The Orford Ness Pagodas

The shingle spit of Orford Ness on the Suffolk coast is today a National Nature Reserve and a designated Area of Outstanding Natural Beauty. As the largest vegetated shingle spit in Europe, it is a wild and unspoilt habitat, yet for a large part of the twentieth century it was one of the most secret military test sites in the country.

Orford Ness first came to the attention of the armed forces in 1913 when much of the area was drained to make way for the airfields of the Central Flying School's Experimental Flying Section, which helped to develop new aircraft, the parachute, gunsights and aerial photography. In the 1930s the site also hosted the first experiments involving the technology that would become radar. However, it was the construction here of an Atomic Weapons Research Establishment (AWRE) base in the early 1950s that marked the beginning of the most secret chapter in this wilderness's strange history.

The Ministry of Defence site at Orford Ness was first earmarked for hosting Britain's most sensitive military tests in 1953. In the following year it became the centre for testing the country's nuclear deterrent. Orford was obviously not a suitable place to actually test nuclear material – these tests would take place many thousands of miles away – but its relative isolation did make it the perfect base for something equally important. As Britain's nuclear arsenal grew, so did concerns about potential accidents. The detonators in nuclear devices were conventional explosive charges, albeit highly sophisticated and delicate. If a bomb were mishandled, dropped, overheated or in any other way mistreated, this charge might explode, spreading fissile material over a huge distance – effectively making it a 'dirty bomb'. Orford Ness would be where they ensured that this would never happen.

Testing nuclear casings and initiators would require subjecting them to the very worst conditions that might be imagined, for which a series of remarkable buildings began appearing on the site. In all, six test labs were constructed in which bombs could be heated past boiling point and frozen colder than the deepest winter. In one, a centrifuge could exert 100 g on a test casing; in another, huge electronic vibrating devices (effectively massive amplifiers) shook the bombs to breaking point. On an outside test bed, a rocket sledge accelerated bombs into concrete targets to ensure the devices would not fire prematurely.

From the outside there was, at least in the early stages of research, precious little to show for what was happening at the Ness, which, no doubt, was just how the AWRE liked it. In 1960, however, a new type of strange structure could be seen growing on site – something that locals would soon dub the 'pagodas'. By then, Orford was a world leader in what was known as the 'environmental testing' of nuclear devices and at this time it was also given a new challenge. Britain had opted to use a US nuclear bomb, code-named WE177, but this device was not 'single-point safe', as they put it. In plain English, this meant that the conventional explosive was liable to detonate in an accident, spreading radioactive debris.

In response, the teams at Orford started work on three new labs. These would have to be strong enough to survive an accident, should one of their tests actually set off a bomb. Tests with a model had shown that their previous designs would simply be obliterated by the new device. So the mysterious pagoda shape was settled upon. The test beds in the pagodas sat in a reinforced concrete cell beneath a huge roof supported on pillars – like a pagoda. In the event of a minor explosion, the cell would direct the blast up at the 3-foot-thick concrete roof, which would deflect it down again, between the pillars and harmlessly out on to the shingle of the Ness. In the case of a massive explosion, the roof – which was not actually attached to the pillars but simply balanced on them – would lift off and crash back down, shattering the columns and sealing the test cell below.

In the fifteen years of nuclear-trigger testing at Orford, no such accident, as far as we know, ever happened. By the time the work there finished in 1971, Orford had helped to put itself out of business, having made nuclear missiles, paradoxically, safer. Nevertheless, in the light of the government's recent admission that there have been two cases of nuclear bombs being dropped by accident, it's worth remembering how Orford's pagodas secretly helped stop those accidents becoming environmental and human disasters.

The Safest Place

The role of Chislehurst in saving London, or rather Londoners, from the Blitz is one of the least well-known stories from the home front, but for much of the war this Kent village was home to a completely subterranean town sheltering 15,000 Londoners.

Chislehurst caves are a man-made marvel – 22 miles of underground chamber and tunnel carved out of the chalk by flint makers and lime burners over hundreds of years. By the 1830s they had become redundant and it was only with the advent of the railways that the caves became a weekend tourist attraction, as well as a rather damp concert venue. During the First World War the caves had come to the attention of the government and were requisitioned as a storehouse for the Woolwich Arsenal, during which time a small railway was installed in the tunnels to move around the 100,000 pounds of high explosive kept there. With the coming of peace the caves returned to private hands and, for a while, became home to a mushroom farm. At the start of the Second World War no further use was found for them.

Fortunately the owner was an enterprising chap who saw a gap in the market. With easy access to London, the Chislehurst caves might become the largest air-raid shelter in England. Putting up adverts around the capital, he offered the security and safety of the caves for a penny a night (or sixpence a week) for adults, with children allowed in free. By the autumn of 1940 the caves were becoming London's most popular 'night out', and Southern Railway frequently had to post notices at its stations saying 'Caves Full'. With 15,000 people soon crowding on to trains each evening to escape the Blitz, strict rules had to be introduced to the subterranean city by the newly formed cave committee. Each 'guest' was allocated a pitch by a 'cave captain', which they had to keep clean, and they had to be in by 9.30 p.m. Lights out was at 10.30 p.m. after which absolute silence was to be maintained. No pitch could be sold or exchanged and no unauthorised goods could be traded. If you spent four consecutive nights away from your pitch, you lost it.

Initially, conditions in the caves were certainly primitive, until the government realised the value of the shelter and provided thousands of bunk beds. Electric lighting was also installed, along with running water and toilet facilities. Strangely, whilst the threat of bombing decreased as the war went on, the popularity of the caves continued to soar and the sophistication of the subterranean city grew. By 1945 the caves boasted their own shops, offices, canteens, workshops and even a chapel. A fully functional hospital was also built, complete with seven wards and an isolation unit, all manned by one Red Cross doctor and two nurses. Fortunately the hospital never had to deal with any emergency more challenging than the one single birth that took place in the caves. The grateful parents named their child Rose Cavena Wakeman in memory of this unusual start in life.

By the end of the war Chislehurst caves were a complete underground community, entirely hidden from view, but when the hostilities ceased the project was quickly mothballed. As the last of the cave-dwellers drifted away, the grateful owner was able to write the government a goodwill cheque for £10,000 from the profits of running England's underground city.

The Deserted Villages

In 1948 the son of a warehouse manager published an article pointing out something that had apparently passed unnoticed by everyone who had walked through the British countryside for the previous five hundred years. Using maps and aerial photographs to prove his point, he showed that the ridges and furrows that still scarred many hillsides were the ghosts of another era – the remains of mediaeval open fields. And where there were fields, surely there would have been villages too?

Maurice Beresford was one of the first historians to use maps and the then newly available aerial photographs to study the British landscape for clues to how we used to live, and his work uncovered a whole class of settlement that no one previously knew was there. It was whilst he was studying a field system in the district of Harborough in Leicestershire that he came across a series of humps and bumps in a field that didn't appear to be farming ditches. Having carefully mapped the strange undulations and compared them with photographs of the site, he came to an extraordinary conclusion. What he had found was a village – or it had been at the time when the fields he had been surveying were in use. By matching details of the site with surviving mediaeval records, such as the Domesday Book, he was able to give the place a name. Those mossy mounds were the wraith of the village of Bittesby – its house platforms and sunken roads, even the remains of its chapel, all of which had been lost since 1494.

Over the next half-century, Beresford would go on to discover over 100 other deserted mediaeval villages in Warwickshire alone and nearly 3,000 across the country as a whole. Here at last was an explanation for those lonely churches apparently stranded in the middle of nowhere that in fact had once been at the heart of thriving communities. The question remained: what had happened to the settlements themselves?

Some answers came from Beresford's most famous discovery, the deserted village of Wharram Percy, tucked away in a remote valley of the Yorkshire Wolds. Here Beresford, his friend J.G. Hurst and a host of volunteers and students spent forty seasons excavating houses and streets, the ruined church and even the graveyard, which produced one of the best samples of mediaeval skeletons we have. This work started at a time when it was generally considered pointless to excavate 'poor' sites with meagre finds and an apparent lack of major historical significance. Through half a century of perseverance, Beresford and his team revealed a different, secret history every bit as valuable as any major chronicle.

Wharram Percy was for many years a survivor. It had originally been laid out some time in the tenth century, before the Norman Conquest, and received a mention, albeit a brief one, in the Domesday Book. Perhaps thanks to its tucked-away position, the village had survived William the Conqueror's 'Harrying of the North' and even the cold hand of the Black Death, which for many years was assumed to lie behind the desertion of mediaeval villages. Life in these hamlets had indeed continued after 1500 and was finally brought to an end, not by disease, famine or war, but by sheep.

As landlords realised they could make more money from pasturing sheep than renting fields to peasant farmers, so the villagers at places like Wharram, and thousands of others, were thrown off the land. Their centuries-old villages were left to crumble back into the earth, their roads and houses becoming grown over with grass where livestock now grazed, and their isolated churches left to tumble into ruin. At Wharram the final death knell came in 1517 when a document shows that Baron Hilton evicted the last four families and demolished their houses to make way for his sheep. Here then was the story of a whole way of mediaeval life, hidden for centuries beneath the grasslands of England and only rediscovered thanks to a warehouse manager's son who liked to walk in the countryside.

The Royston Enigma

In August 1742 the 'Mercat House', where the butter and cheese market was held in the Hertfordshire town of Royston, was undergoing improvements. In the course of this, a workman was digging down to find good footings for a new bench for the traders and their customers when he hit a millstone.

Digging through the central hole in the stone, he was amazed to find that a great cavern opened up beneath it. The millstone was duly levered aside and a small boy 'volunteered' to be lowered on a rope into the chasm below. The boy reported that he could descend 16 feet on to an earth floor, a finding confirmed by a 'thin man' who was persuaded to go down and check the truth of the boy's excited claims. Having widened the entrance, the workmen, encouraged by the local bailiff George Lettis, began removing the soil from the chamber floor, in the belief that there might be treasure at the bottom. By the time they had finished, they had removed 8 feet of soil from the cavern, which, according to the local antiquarian, the Reverend George North, included a human skull, some copper plate, other bones and a small earthenware cup, all of which were cast aside in the desperate hunt for gold. At the bottom, though, they found nothing. The disappointed workmen were left with merely the chamber itself, although this was extraordinary enough.

In the dim light of their candles they could make out that they stood in a large room hollowed out from the chalk of the bedrock, 17 feet wide at the base and 10 feet high. The lower portion was cylindrical and the upper part bell shaped, but what was most surprising was the frieze of strange figures carved into the chalk between the two levels. Their exact meaning has been a source of contention ever since.

By 1790 a new entrance to the cave had been cut and its guardian, Thomas Watson, had finally found a way to extract gold from the empty room, by charging a hefty sixpence apiece for visitors to see the marvel. This, he told them, was variously considered to be a Roman tomb, a monastic storehouse, a mediaeval hermitage or, most exotically, a secret meeting place of the militant monastic order of the Knights Templar.

The true use of the building depends upon how the strange carvings of the frieze are interpreted and what date can be given to them. The scenes are undoubtedly religious in character, with a crucifixion clearly visible. Some saints are recognisable from the items they carry – St Lawrence with the gridiron on which he was martyred, St Catherine of Alexandria with the wheel on which she was broken. Other carvings are much less clear and it is uncertain to what extent some may have been added to or adapted by early guardians of the cave, keen to exploit its mysterious connotations.

Neither is the date of the carvings certain. The images are crudely formed, apparently by many different hands, and have been dated from the eleventh to the sixteenth century. The only actual dates carved on to the walls, 1347 and 18 February 1350, are in Arabic numerals, which were highly unusual at that time and possibly 'altered' from '1547' and '1550'.

Whilst some still see images of the pagan goddess Astarte, Richard the Lionheart and even a naked mediaeval figure (known as a Sheela na gig), perhaps the most likely explanation for the cave can be found in the records of the churchwarden of the parish of Bassingbourne. Under the date 1506 he records: 'Gyft of 20d. recd. Off a Hermytt depting at Roiston in ys pysh.'

This suggests that the strange cave was home to a late mediaeval hermit, who carved his own devotional images on its walls. We know that a local hermitage was acquired by Robert Chester at the Dissolution of the Monasteries. It was he who built the Royston market house and he may well have taken the precaution of first filling the cavern to above the level of the carvings, which would undoubtedly have been considered undesirably 'popish' at the time. With any surviving archaeology thrown away in the initial scramble for gold, however, the mystery may never fully be solved.

14

Secret
Meanings

Some word that teems with hidden meaning – like
Basingstoke.

W.S. Gilbert, *Ruddigore* (1887)

The Snowdrop Inn

Many inn names hide a secret or a forgotten meaning. A case in point is the inordinate number of Marquis of Granby pubs, their name deriving from that military marquess's habit of setting up in business as publicans former NCOs. Behind the romantic-sounding Snowdrop Inn in Lewes lies a more tragic tale.

The pub on South Street does not get its name from the spring flower but from an extraordinary event that took place on 27 December 1836. That winter was particularly cold, the weather taking a turn for the worse on Christmas Day, when the pioneering dinosaur collector and Lewes local, Gideon Mantell, wrote in his diary: 'A snowstorm, begun last night, has continued through the day, and everything is most dreary and wretched.'

In fact this was something of an understatement. Snow had actually started to fall on 21 December and by Christmas Day most roads in the South of England were impassable. Snowdrifts tens of feet thick were reported on the South Downs and the mail service had ground to a halt.

At that time, on the place now occupied by the Snowdrop Inn, stood a row of workmen's cottages, known as Boulder Row, no doubt from their position at the base of a large chalk cliff. On this clifftop the snow had been piling up for nearly a week, until, at 10.15 on the morning of the 27th, it suddenly gave way, releasing the largest avalanche in British history straight on to the cottages of Boulder Row.

The snow and rubble that crashed down on to the street trapped numerous families in their cottages and the townsfolk spent a frantic day trying to dig out the engulfed and injured. By the evening it was known that eight people had died in the avalanche.

Despite being described by every newspaper of the day as the worst disaster in a catastrophic winter, the story melted away almost as quickly as the snow. Avalanches simply don't happen in Britain and little more was said about the event. Today, over 170 years later, the only clues to this almost unique episode are a white dress in the local museum worn by two-year-old Fanny Boakes, who happily was dug out alive from the snow; a small plaque to the dead in South Malling Church; and the name of the pub that now stands on the site of the calamity – the Snowdrop Inn.

Thomas Hollis's Fields of Dreams

The names of fields often have meanings that are obscure to us today but in the Dorset villages of Halstock and Corscombe they hold a clue to the secret burial of one of the greatest academic patrons of the eighteenth century.

Thomas Hollis was a very unusual character for his age. As a libertarian and a firm believer in democracy, he was of the opinion that the people had every right to depose a tyrant. As a republican, he was all in favour of the increasingly independent noises coming out of the British North American colonies. Like his great-uncle before him (another Thomas Hollis), he was also a major benefactor to the fledgling country's academic institutions, making huge bequests to the library of Harvard College (later Harvard University), whose online library system has been named after him (Harvard OnLine Library Information System).

Having dedicated his life to helping the poor and promoting the arts, Hollis brought his philosophy to bear closer to home. He had inherited large tracts of land from various relatives and he renamed them in honour of his heroes and beliefs. Where some villages had 'Apple Tree Farms' and 'Hillside Farms', Hollis's were named Liberty Farm, Locke Farm (after the philosopher John Locke) and Marvell Farm (after the satirist Andrew Marvell). Nor could his workmen avoid his influence in the fields, where it was possible to walk from Socrates field to Constitution field, passing on the way 'Plato', 'Brutus' (honoured for killing the tyrannical Julius Caesar), 'Toleration', 'Confucius', 'Education' and the very splendid 'Reasonableness'.

Of course, in the intervening centuries these names have

themselves been corrupted – Massachusetts Field becoming 'Massy Field', for instance, and many of the others have disappeared altogether.

Beneath one of these fields still lies Hollis's last secret. Often accused of atheism, and certainly a rational dissenter at the very least, he did not believe in the pomp and ceremony of church burial or the vainglory of memorials. On 1 January 1774, whilst giving orders to workmen in one of his fields at Urless Farm, Corscombe, he suddenly announced: 'I believe the weather is going to change; I am exceedingly giddy,' and, with that, dropped dead. In line with the wishes of his will, he was buried where he had died, 10 feet down, and the land was immediately ploughed over so that no one would ever know in which of Thomas Hollis's exotically named fields he lay buried. And there he remains to this day.

The Green Church

On the last Sunday in August each year, the parishioners of the little Derbyshire village of Eyam gather for a unique event in Cucklett church, tucked in a small, steep valley known as the Delf. But Cucklett has to be one of the most peculiar churches in Britain as it has neither windows nor doors – not even a single wall. It is simply a piece of open ground. The secret of how it became known as a church goes back to the terrible events of 1665.

In the summer of that year, George Viccars, a journeyman tailor, was lodging in the village with Jonathan and Edward Cooper and their mother. At some point over that hot summer, he received a package from London, a parcel of cloth, which unknown to him was infested with fleas. The cloth was damp and it was hung out to dry by a fire, releasing the parasites. One bit him and he fell sick, dying just days later from the disease they had brought with them from London – bubonic plague.

From that one incident in what is now known as the 'Plague Cottage', the infection spread rapidly, killing the Cooper brothers and spreading down the street. In an age with little understanding of how disease was transmitted, panic ensued. It was halted only when the local vicar, William Mompesson, suggested an extraordinary scheme. Although it may have saved the cities of northern England from a similar fate to that of London (where at its height the plague killed 6,000 every week), the plan would require an unheard-of level of sacrifice from his parishioners.

Helped by the former vicar, Thomas Stanley (who as a Puritan had been ejected from the post at the Restoration but had stayed in the village), Mompesson suggested a three-point plan. First, all victims were to be buried as quickly as possible near to where they had died, not in the consecrated ground of the churchyard. Second, all church services were now to be held in the open air at the 'Cucklett church' in the Delf, so that parishioners didn't have to come into close contact with one another. Finally, and most terrible of all, the village was to cut itself off from the outside world so that no one might carry the disease elsewhere.

Quoting the gospel of St John that 'Greater love hath no man than this, that a man lay down his life for his friends', Mompesson persuaded the terrified villagers to isolate themselves while they waited for the plague to wreak its havoc and die away naturally.

Of course, the people of Eyam would still have to eat. It was therefore agreed that villagers from the nearby settlements of Grindleford and Bakewell would leave food and other provisions at collection points on the village boundary. In return, the people of Eyam left money at these same points, on one of which, 'the Boundary Stone', can still be seen the small holes that were filled with vinegar for 'disinfecting' the coins before they were picked up. Greater local landlords such as the Earl of Devonshire also sent food to the village in thanks for the people of Eyam not bringing plague to their estates.

Although the plague died down in the winter of 1665, it flared up again in the village with a breathtaking new savagery in the spring of 1666. Many tales survive of that time. Rowland Torre of Stoney Middleton would shout across the Delf every day to his Eyam sweetheart, Emmot Sydall, until one day she failed to come. She and all her family, with the exception of her mother, were dead. The entire Talbot household of Riley Farm succumbed and were buried in the orchard there, save for one son who was away from the village.

From here the disease spread to the Hancock family in August 1666 where their two children, John and Elizabeth, died on the 3rd. Four days later, their father and two more children were dead. Two days later, another daughter joined them and the remaining daughter the day after that. Only Mrs Hancock was left to drag the bodies outside, dig the graves and bury her family unaided. The stones now known as 'The Riley Graves' once marked where they were interred.

There were also some surprising survivals. Marshall Howe, who took to burying the dead when there was no one left to do this, seems to have been immune to the disease and survived, despite being surrounded by its victims. William Mompesson also outlived the plague, although his wife did not, and he had himself written letters of farewell in the belief that he too would soon succumb.

Finally in the autumn of 1666, after several weeks with no further deaths, Mompesson ordered the survivors to fumigate their houses and there was a 'great burning' of anything that might harbour disease. The quarantine was over. Four in ten of his parishioners were dead, a total of 259 men, women and children. Had the villagers dispersed, they might well have escaped the close proximity to the rats that carried the disease and cheated death. However, in doing so they might equally have brought plague to the villages and towns of the North. Their sacrifice, in remaining in their plague-stricken village, is what is still remembered every Plague Sunday in Britain's most unusual church, the Cucklett church at Eyam.

The Gates of Nagapattinam

You would be perfectly within your rights to expect to find the gates of Nagapattinam in the walls of the city of Nagapattinam in the Indian state of Tamil Nadu. Which is why it's all the more surprising to find them in the Highlands of Scotland.

How a vast monument bearing this name came to stand on the summit of Fyrish Hill in the Highlands is all thanks to General Sir Hector Munro. Born in 1726, Munro was said to have got his first army commission after rescuing the Duchess of Gordon when her drunken coachman had got her lost and didn't seem too bothered about it. His rise thereafter was rapid. Having helped to apprehend some of the Jacobite rebels in Scotland, he was posted to India.

There, his early successes against both native rulers and the French were legendary and on his return home in 1768 he was elected to parliament for the Inverness Burghs. Ten years later – and perhaps to the surprise of his constituents, whom he continued to 'represent' for the next twenty years – he was back in India as commander-in-chief of Madras. This time, luck was not with him. The plaudits he'd previously won were quickly replaced with reproach when he was defeated by Haidar Ali and his son Tipu Sultan (who celebrated the death of Sir Hector's son in 1792 by commissioning the famous automaton known as Tipu's Tiger).

For this reverse Munro lost his command. Nevertheless, he remained in the field and at Nagapattinam seized one last chance to revive his fortunes when he stormed the Dutch base there. On his return home again, he found he had been dismissed from the service of the East India Company. So he travelled back to Scotland to console himself by improving his estates at Novar. And there was certainly a need for improvement, as any of the local people would have told you. Munro was a vigorous proponent of the introduction of sheep in the Highlands, creating violent opposition from his tenants who stood to lose both their livelihood as arable farmers and their rights to common grazing.

With unemployment spiralling due to the Highland clearances, Munro felt he should do something to at least temporarily alleviate the problem that he had undoubtedly helped to create. Did his thoughts focus on rehousing his tenants on new farms? No, they did not. They reverted instead to his last great victory at Nagapattinam. On a hill over his estate, the men who had once farmed his land were put to work, building a full-scale model of the gates of that faraway city to forever remind the general of his triumph, and of their loss.

Beeswing

In Dumfries and Galloway in the parish of New Abbey, between Dumfries and Dalbeattie, stands the tiny hamlet of Beeswing. Its name is not a corruption of an old Gaelic word, nor has it any topographical meaning, either in English or in any other language, so for those who pass this way it is something of a mystery. In fact, the village is named after a horse.

Originally known as Lochend, the small hamlet was home to a solitary inn which was bought in the mid-nineteenth century by the racehorse owner Robert Orde. Wishing to bring a bit of glamour to the place, he decided to rename the building after his brother's most famous steed, Beeswing. Beeswing was one of the most outstanding thoroughbreds of the nineteenth century, racing sixty-three times between 1835 and 1842 and winning an astonishing fifty-one of those races, including the Ascot Gold Cup in 1842. Of the six others that she finished, she was placed lower than second only once.

Orde's pub, like his brother's racehorse, proved to be a success. The small hamlet duly grew, the fame of the inn soon outstripping the rather dull and very common name of 'Lochend' until the settlement itself was generally known as Beeswing. Eventually it simply became easier for locals to refer to their village as Beeswing and the name was officially adopted. Only the local church, perhaps unhappy about being renamed after something associated with gambling, held out. Today it is still known as Lochend church.

As Old as the Hills?

Few great hoaxes leave a lasting legacy but one that began in Denmark in 1747 can still be seen on any map of England today.

In the previous year a young English teacher at the Royal Marine Academy in Copenhagen, Charles Bertram, had begun a long correspondence with William Stukeley, the most famous English antiquary of his day. The two became enthusiastic correspondents. Then in mid 1747, Bertram wrote, saying, rather casually, that he had in his possession a copy of a manuscript fragment of a work by Richard, a mediaeval Westminster monk. This fragment included some ancient geographical information in the form of itineraries supposedly made by a Roman general, a mediaeval history of ancient Britain and a map.

Stukeley was, of course, fascinated and begged to see this manuscript. At the time it was a matter of much debate how Roman Britain had been divided up and ruled, and what the provinces and towns had once been called. Although a few ancient authors mentioned Britain, their information was sketchy. This document appeared to open a new and detailed window on to our own early history.

Bertram hesitated, pointing out he had just a copy but hoped to soon get the original (which, he claimed, had been stolen from an English library). In the meantime he agreed to send Stukeley a transcript and his own copy of the map. Stukeley was delighted – the map was everything he had hoped it to be – and, by chance, he discovered that there had been a monk at Westminster at the right time by the name of Richard, some of whose other writings had survived. Surely this proved the map's authenticity? Stukeley, however, was being deceived. The supposedly mediaeval map of ancient Britain was in fact a clever forgery by Bertram, carefully compiled from genuine information in ancient and mediaeval sources, and liberally sprinkled with his own inventions.

Bertram's clever decision to arrange for his 'discovery' to be published in an edition with two genuine early manuscripts under the snappy title of *Britannicarum Gentium Historiæ Antiquæ Scriptores tres: Ricardus Corinensis, Gildas Badonicus, Nennius Banchorensi* added further credence to the find. With the support of the widely respected Stukeley, little thought was given to the apparent inconsistencies in the text.

And what a find it seemed to be. Stukeley wrote enthusiastically that it was 'the completest account of the Roman state of Brittain, and of the antient inhabitants thereof; and the geography thereof admirably depicted in a most excellent map'.

The forgery seemed to fill in so many gaps in our knowledge of the period, adding over sixty new Roman locations, giving the names of all the tribes of Britain, and filling in the parts of the map that other Roman writers had failed entirely to mention, like northern Scotland. Soon the place names were finding their way on to Ordnance Survey maps and into common parlance. It is here that Bertram's legacy still remains.

It is in *De Situ Britanniae* that the central spine of England's mountains first gets the name 'Pennines'. Recent research has shown that the name occurs no earlier and in no other source that wasn't dependent on this. In short, the name, which Bertram simply 'borrowed' from the Italian Apennine range, is entirely his own fabrication.

Bertram's forgery survived largely unchallenged for a hundred years, pervasively infiltrating every book and map that dealt with the period. It was only in 1845 that the German writer Karl Wex finally exposed the work and it was not until 1867 that it was finally conclusively debunked in Britain by B.B. Woodward. Over the next century the influence of *De Situ Britanniae* was slowly weeded out of the literature. Nevertheless, the name Pennines has stuck and so Bertram's forgery lives on.

The Oldest New Town

The idyllic village of Milton Abbas in Dorset holds a secret that belies its apparently ageless charm. The name might suggest an antique place, a settlement that grew up around some ancient religious foundation, but for all its rustic charms it is, in truth, a relatively modern confection as well as perhaps the first planned community in England.

The earliest settlement in the area had been Milton Abbey, founded by King Athelstan in AD 938, around which had grown a thriving town and grammar school. The abbey itself had later fallen prey to the Dissolution of the Monasteries, being granted to one of Henry VIII's lawyers. In 1771 it had finally come into the hands of Joseph Damer, later Earl of Dorchester, who had inherited a fortune from his great-uncle, a successful moneylender in Ireland.

What Damer found at Milton, or Middleton as it then was, was indeed a mediaeval village huddled around an abbey, but it was not particularly to his liking nor was it in the tastes of his day. Gentlemen of wealth wished to have large, modern houses, surrounded by naturalistic parks designed by such luminaries as Capability Brown. Damer had a decaying mediaeval abbey, with a town and a school on its doorstep.

Work began in 1753 to build a new and more suitable mansion, the architect chosen being John Vardy, who would later build Lord Dorchester's London residence (now rebuilt as the Dorchester Hotel). Damer seems to have changed his mind during construction, however, and this Gothick design was abandoned in favour of a Palladian structure designed by Sir William Chambers. Work for this began in 1771 but the problem of the town remained. It was smelly, noisy and, according to Damer's garden designers, ruined his view. And so he decided simply to erase it from history. Over the next nine years, as leases became due, Damer kept hold of the properties in his town, transferring his tenants to his new 'model' village of Milton Abbas, tucked away on the other side of the hill where it didn't impede his outlook.

By 1780 the settlement of Middleton was a virtual ghost town and demolition was well under way. The mediaeval houses, the town cross, the King's Arms, the Red Lion and George inns, the wide Market Street were all gone. Only William Harrison who owned four leases in the town held out. Damer showed his opinion of Harrison by having the sluice gates of his ponds opened to flood one of these properties, but Harrison, a lawyer by training, sued him and won. Damer was forced to wait for Harrison to die, which he eventually did, before removing the last of the old town, save for one rustic cottage, which Capability Brown kept as a decorative feature. The Tudor grammar school survived for a few more years before Damer introduced a Bill in Parliament in 1785 to get it moved to Blandford Forum. The whole site was then submerged beneath a large artificial lake, leaving the soon to be Lord Dorchester free to enjoy an uninterrupted panorama.

Thomas Hardy later noted that, according to local tradition, the irreverent treatment meted out to the bones in the old church-yard, which Damer had converted to lawns, drew down a curse on him and he died of 'a gruesome disease'.

The Name of the Cave

In the heart of the Peak District in Derbyshire, beneath Peveril castle in the village of Castleton, lies what was once said to be the gateway to the underworld and the home of Britain's last cave-dwellers. Today 'Peak Cavern' is one of the most famous cave systems in the country but its modern name belies it true past.

The earliest story about Peak Cavern, which has the largest cave entrance in Britain, dates to the mediaeval period, when it was said that one winter a swineherd working for the lord of Peveril followed his pregnant sow into the bowels of the earth. As is the case with most such tales, he claimed he had emerged into a wonderful land where it was late summer and the people were gathering in the harvest. Here he met the lord, who graciously returned to him his sow (and the piglets she had since been delivered of) and sent him back through the cave to the wintry landscape of Derbyshire. This sort of thing happened a lot in mediaeval caves.

From before 1600 the cavern had been home to a troglodyte colony, the last member of whom left only in 1915. For over 400 years this subterranean village earned a living making ropes for the lead miners of the Peaks. Behind this legitimate and industrious community, further down into the caves – through Lumbago Walk, the Great Cave and Roger Rain's House, to Pluto's Dining Room – lay a haven for bandits and outlaws, protected by the perpetual darkness and the fiercely independent lead miners. Here in the early Tudor period, it was said, in the physical underworld, the secret language of the criminal underworld – or thieves' cant – was created at a meeting between Cock Lorel (the mythical leader of the rogues) and the King of the Gypsies, 'to the end that their cozenings, knaveries and villainies might not so easily be perceived and known'.

Certainly there is one piece of euphemistic language that can be associated with the cave. Many subterranean chambers were believed to be routes to the underworld and often retained quite 'earthy' names, given them in the mediaeval period. When Queen Victoria visited the cavern for a concert in 1880, she was told that the place was simply known as 'Peak Cavern'. What her delicate ears had been protected from was the fact that the cave had always previously been known as 'The Devil's Arse'.

15

Hidden Secrets

A valet, of stealthy step, thence conducted me, in silence, through many dark and intricate passages in my progress to the studio of his master.

Edgar Allan Poe, *The Fall of the House of Usher* (1839)

The Mystery of the Lang Pack

The story of the Lang (long) Pack is a splendidly gory tale that has no doubt been liberally added to over the years, but at its heart lies a memory of what must have been a type of 'country-house heist' common in the eighteenth century and earlier. In this case it was a heist with a decidedly bloody ending.

The tale in its basic form states that the events took place in the winter of 1723 at Lee Hall, near Bellingham on the banks of the North Tyne. It being winter, the owner of this impressive pile, Colonel Ridley, had shut up the house and moved south to his London residence for the season. At the Hall he had left a skeleton staff of three servants to ensure the place came to no harm, all with strict instructions to allow no one into the house. No one whatsoever.

Late one afternoon, however, a traveller came calling. He was a pedlar – a poor man dressed in rags, carrying a large pack – and he asked for shelter for the night. Winters on the Tyne can be hard and that year was no exception, but the staff had their orders, so they told the man he would have to find shelter else-where. Before he left he begged one small favour. Could he leave his heavy pack with them overnight? This seemed the least they could do and so the servants agreed, taking the large parcel and placing it in the kitchen.

Hours later, when night had fallen, a maid by the name of Alice was in the kitchen fetching candles when she thought she saw the object move. Terrified, she called for the other servants. Initially they were reluctant to open the pack as it was not, after all, theirs. Alice was clearly alarmed and, perhaps with an eye to earning her undying affection, a young footman, Edward, announced he would fetch his gun (to which he gave the grand name of 'Copenhagen').

And so the suspicious staff sat in the kitchen, waiting, until suddenly the pack twitched again. Impulsively, Edward fired at it. To their horror there was a scream and blood began to seep from

255

the pack. The three immediately set to unwrapping it and inside they found a small man, now dead, with a silver whistle around his neck.

It did not take long for it to dawn on the servants what had been planned. The pedlar who had come to their door was in fact a burglar and inside his pack was an accomplice. When the household was asleep he would have broken out of the pack, drawn the bolts on the doors and used the whistle to summon his partners in crime to rob the house. It would be fair to say, however, that the villains' plan had misfired.

Summoning some heavily armed friends and neighbours from Bellingham, the staff staked out the Hall. Late in the night, having doused the lights, they blew the whistle. The other robbers, believing their friend had opened the Hall doors, rode out of the undergrowth, only to be met by a hail of gunfire that left four of them dead. The rest fled, taking with them the bodies of their compatriots. Only the mysterious man in the Lang Pack was left, stone cold, on the floor of the kitchen. He was later buried in Bellingham churchyard.

Jack Cade's Caverns

In 2002 a large hole opened up in the A2 road as it passes over Blackheath in South London and, for a brief moment, a light was shone on to one of the most scandalous locations in Georgian England.

The hole was caused by the partial collapse of a cave beneath the heath. Indeed, the heath is riddled with man-made caverns, which legend has it were dug as a hiding place by Jack Cade, the leader of a popular mediaeval revolt, who brought 5,000 protestors to Blackheath in June 1450.

In truth the caverns were cut from the rock in the seventeenth century by lime burners who quarried chalk there. So eager were these miners that in 1677 one William Steers was fined a very hefty £40 for 'undermining the King's highway and causing wagons to overturn' – a collapse not unlike the one 325 years later on the A2. By the end of the century all the readily available chalk had been quarried out. Perhaps fearful of more collapses, the mining was brought to a close and the caves were abandoned.

So they remained until 1780 when a local builder discovered a vertical shaft in his garden, leading down into these by then forgotten caverns.

Having explored this huge underground network, and being an enterprising chap, he resolved to turn them into one of South London's first tourist attractions, cutting forty steps down into the bowels of the earth and charging fourpence for a short candle-lit tour (sixpence for the full works). Business thrived until a nineteen-year-old girl, Lucy Talbot, fainted on one of the tours, apparently overcome by noxious vapours. By the time she was returned to the surface, she was dead. The tours were brought to an abrupt end.

Such a money-spinner would not remain idle for long, however, although there were some problems to sort out first. In order to prevent further suffocations, the owners drilled a large ventilation shaft and placed a pumping house over it to pump fresh air down into the Stygian gloom. Of course, manning this pump was expensive so the caves would have to turn more of a profit. With this in mind, the tours were abandoned in favour of the installation of a bar, complete with glass chandelier, turning the caverns into London's first underground nightclub.

With only minor setbacks (subsidence led to another hole opening up in the road in 1798, swallowing a horse in the process), the club thrived and, in the dark and febrile atmosphere of the caves, its reputation for immorality grew. By the mid nineteenth century the caverns were notorious. The titillating rumours around the more prudish parlours of Victorian London were that these hellish grottos were the haunt of prostitutes and gamblers, where women walked naked amongst the binge-drinking rakes who hid their famous faces in troglodytic shadows.

With everyone apparently having so much fun, the only sensible

Victorian solution was to shut the place down. In 1854, the entrances were sealed and once more the caverns were quickly returned to their former oblivion. In 1906 the council toyed with the idea of opening them again but concerns for safety prevented the work going ahead and the caves drifted further into obscurity.

Finally on a foggy October morning in 1939, a party from the council gathered in the backyard of 77 Maidenstone Hill to see whether the rumoured caverns under the heath existed and, if so, whether they might be used as air-raid shelters. When a shaft was sunk 32 feet down, a short passage was discovered. A workman volunteered to go down, reporting back that the walls were carved with many names and dates, and that the floor was strewn with ancient broken bottles. Even the old brass suspension ring for the great chandelier still hung in position.

The caves proved unsuitable for air-raid shelters and the site was sealed again. Today there is no evidence on the surface at 77 Maidenstone Hill for the 1939 entrance to the caves and so what was once London's most notorious nightclub is again slipping out of popular memory.

The Woman in the Wall

During the short and bloody reign of Mary Tudor, in which Catholicism was re-established as the official religion of England, it might certainly have been said that walls had ears. In one exceptional case in London, for a while they could also speak.

On 14 March 1554, people began gathering outside a house on Aldersgate Street in London. What drew them there was the news, then racing around the city, that an invisible angel had begun talking from the wall, which was soon dubbed 'the spirit in the wall'. This was extraordinary enough but what made it all the more sensational was what the spirit was saying. In an era when Protestants were being burnt at the stake for their faith, the voice in the wall in this reformist part of town was uttering unspeakable heresies. It threatened terrible calamities if Queen Mary married

Philip of Spain, or gave the Pope any further jurisdiction in the country, and it railed against Catholic rituals such as the Mass and confession. Its darker utterances were interpreted to the crowd by two clerks, who moved amongst the entranced throng, ensuring they hung on every word of what was now said to be an angel.

By the second morning the crowd numbered 17,000 by some accounts, all attracted by this boldly anti-Catholic spirit. Some hazarded to shout, 'God save the Lady Elizabeth,' in reference to Mary's Protestant sister, later Elizabeth I. In reply, the spirit in the wall said, 'So be it,' suggesting it supported whatever moves might be afoot to replace Mary.

Eventually the Lord Mayor was dragged into the business and charged with revealing the cause of all the trouble. Being of a practical bent, he arranged for the wall to be knocked down, upon which it was discovered that it was actually a false wall with another behind it. There in the gap, bedusted and bewildered, was the wretched form of Elizabeth Crofts, an eighteen-year-old serving maid.

Elizabeth was arrested and admitted to the fraud. She had been approached by a man called 'Drake', probably a servant of one of the Protestant nobility, and persuaded to shout anti-Marian propaganda from her hiding place. After questioning, during which the terrified girl also denounced the clerks who had 'interpreted' her utterances for the crowd, she was taken on 15 July to St Paul's Cross to atone for her sins. Here, on the scaffold used by preachers, she confessed to having offended God and the Queen.

It was never disclosed who put Elizabeth up to this elaborate scheme, although there are two theories: that it was part of a serious plot to remove Mary from the throne, and also that it was a simple hoax that got out of hand. Either way, the authorities chose not to be overly harsh with the spirit in the wall. When Elizabeth Crofts finished her penance at St Paul's she was returned to prison but very shortly after released. She was never heard from again.

Britain's Secret Treasure House

It would be fair to say that there are very few mines in Britain in which you could find diamonds, let alone a Titian, and yet the Manod Slate Quarry at Blaenau Ffestiniog in Gwynedd can justifiably make that claim.

The secret history of Manod began in 1940 during the Blitz on London. With nightly bombing it was soon clear that the nation's treasures were at risk, particularly the collections of art in the National Gallery. Its director, Kenneth Clark, drew up a plan for the evacuation of the paintings. Initially they would simply be moved away from London and then finally, he hoped, across the Atlantic to Canada, well beyond the range of bombers and safely out of the reach of any invading army, should one arrive. His plans were sent to Winston Churchill, who had also expressed worries about the contents of the London museums and galleries and – most importantly, as he saw it – the crown jewels. Getting them out of London was clearly a priority but, equally, if everything of value was shipped abroad it might cause panic, making people think all was lost and that the establishment was packing up and leaving.

His response to the plan came in a short telegram, ordering Clark to 'bury them in caves or in cellars, but not a picture shall leave these islands'.

Of course, cellars and caves do not necessarily make very good homes for rare paintings, but fortunately one exception came to their notice. The Manod mine was one of the deepest of its type in the world, containing huge caverns that could house thousands of pieces of art. Work immediately started in turning it into Britain's secret treasure house. Behind a vast steel door, a tunnel 250 metres long led to a series of vaults 60 metres high, each of which was fitted with heated ventilation controls.

Then, when the site was finished, and much to the surprise of the people of Ffestiniog, a steady stream of chocolate delivery vans began heading for the mine. However, these disguised vehicles carried not chocolate but Rembrandts, Titians, da Vincis and Gainsboroughs, and, in one, the crown jewels.

Back in London, Kenneth Clark was faced with the awkward job of directing a gallery with no paintings in it. He arranged instead for Myra Hess to give free daily piano recitals to keep visitors' spirits up. The following year it was also arranged for one picture a month to be returned from Manod so that the gallery at least had something to show.

So a Welsh slate mine kept the nation's treasures safe for the entirety of the war. Indeed, so successful was the site that the government retained the lease throughout the Cold War, paying two local brothers to maintain the ventilation systems for another forty years in case nuclear war ever required a further evacuation of art. During the Cuban Missile Crisis, plans were actually drawn up for the removal there of London's treasures for safe keeping but then abandoned, as it was quite rightly felt that the sudden disappearance of the contents of museums and galleries might suggest a nuclear attack was imminent and thus inspire a panicked exodus from the capital.

The caves were finally given back to their owners in 1983 but the effects of Manod are still felt in every gallery today. It was discovered after the war that the very even temperature and humidity maintained at Manod provided the perfect conditions for conserving the collection, which directly resulted in the opening of the first air-conditioned gallery in 1949.

The Escape from Scotney

There are many tales of how English Catholic priests hid and sometimes escaped from government searchers during the sixteenth and seventeenth centuries, and many an old manor has a secret room known as the 'priest hole' where such men were supposedly concealed. Some of these stories are undoubtedly true; many others have a basis in truth but have been greatly embroidered. One, however, whose precise details vary from telling to telling, gives a great flavour of the dangers and daring of the time.

Richard Blount was a typical English Jesuit. Well educated in Protestant England, he had slipped abroad to join those Catholic Englishmen who studied at various colleges in France, Rome and Spain. For some this was a life of exile but for others, like Blount, it was a training ground where they took holy orders before returning to England to minister secretly to the Catholics who remained there.

Even getting back into England was not easy in the 1590s, yet Blount managed to disguise himself as a survivor from the Earl of Essex's disastrous 1589 expedition against Spain. Hiding amongst the returning sailors, he was interrogated for three days by a suspicious Lord High Admiral, finally managing to persuade him that he was a recently released prisoner. He was freed to go to Scotney castle, home of the Catholic Darrells.

Life at Scotney was not easy. The Darrell family were suspected of harbouring priests and the penalty for priest and master, should they be found, was death. It was an era of suspicion, when neighbours informed on neighbours, servants on lords. The government pursuivants, employed to flush out priests, had free rein to arrest, imprison and search. To protect themselves to some degree against these incursions, the Darrells had installed two hiding places in their house, one in a roof space and the other in the thickness of an old stone wall.

Searches usually followed the same pattern: the male members of the household would be arrested and taken away. Meanwhile, the women and children would be removed to another house while searchers, carpenters and stonemasons used their skills to try to locate priests hidden in these concealed places.

On the first occasion, this happened whilst Blount was at Scotney in 1597. He and a servant, Bray, managed to reach the hiding place in the eaves, just large enough to hold the two men, which was rediscovered in 1860. They remained here for a week whilst the search took place. These were often long-winded affairs, not simply because the houses of magnates were large and rambling, but because a week in a hiding place was usually enough to bring out a priest who by then might be starving. By the end of their seven days in hiding, Blount and Bray were indeed starving but thanks to Bray's quick thinking he managed to save his master. Emerging at night from the hole, he gave himself up, pretending to be the priest. The search was called off and Blount escaped. Bray was interrogated but, as it became patently clear that he wasn't a priest, he was eventually released.

It was Christmas the following year that the second raid took place. Having surrounded the house in the night, the searchers stormed in at first light to surprise the family, a maid barely having time to shout a warning. Blount and Bray once again dashed for a priest hole, this time in the thickness of a stone wall, and so the whole procedure began again. How long they remained there is a matter of debate – some sources say ten days – with only a loaf and a bottle of wine between them. At some point they were discovered, thanks to a piece of Blount's girdle that had become trapped in the secret door and was dangling out into the garden. According to the family tradition, just as the masons began prising open this door a torrential rainstorm drove them indoors, giving Blount just enough time to come up with a plan.

Blount and Bray escaped from their hiding place and headed for the south-eastern tower where Blount proposed to swim across the moat. He dived into the icy water and managed to make his way to the other side, hiding in the woods opposite, but Bray could not swim. According to legend, the resourceful servant wrapped a cloak around himself and ran into the hall, where the searchers and guards were drying off, shouting that thieves were in the stables taking the horses. The guards ran out, opening the gates as they went. Bray slipped through and away into the night.

Of course, the exact nature of their escape may not have been quite as swashbuckling in reality, but the priest holes are very real. Blount certainly did make his getaway, probably in a manner not dissimilar to the story. After his flight from the moated fortress of Scotney, he was posted as one of the most wanted men in the country, eventually becoming head of the Jesuits in England and dying some forty years later.

The Deadly Curiosity of Robert Tresilian

Sir Robert Tresilian had to tread carefully. As a lawyer and advisor to the young Richard II, he was in a powerful position to make money – and enemies. In 1381, as Chief Justice of the King's Bench, he had been given the job of presiding over the trials of the leaders of the Peasants' Revolt and he became famous for his savage treatment of them. His undoing, however, would be not the peasantry, but his own desire to spy on his enemies.

Having fought against parliament's attempts to restrain the King's advisors, Tresilian was in a precarious situation when those same powerful lords he had thwarted rose against the King. The Lords Appellant, as they were known, nominally appealed to the young Richard II simply for good government, yet their true aim was to destroy the coterie of nobles that surrounded the King, including Tresilian.

The late fourteenth century was a turbulent time and such sudden changes in political fortune were not unusual. For Tresilian this would seem a good time to escape abroad and wait for the political wind to change – he was, after all, rich from royal favour and the sale of justice (trial rigging for which he had received a royal pardon). Tresilian, fatally, chose not to run.

On 4 January 1388, the Lords Appellant ordered Tresilian to be imprisoned at Gloucester, but by then he could not be found. Rumour had it that he had gone to Bristol to see the King or had fled abroad. In fact, he was probably already in London where the machinations of his adversaries, including his own trial in absentia, so intrigued him that he could not help but put them under surveillance: his own.

Disguised in a false beard and wearing an eccentric collection of shabby clothes, he took rooms in a house that overlooked

Westminster Hall. By climbing on to the roof of an apothecary's

Westminster Hall. By climbing on to the roof of an apothecary's house and then down the gutter, he could see who passed through the gate and into the council chamber. Perhaps he hoped to see former friends go in and thus get an early warning of their betrayal. Given that he had been condemned in his absence, exactly what he hoped to do with such information is unclear. He was also not quite as well disguised as he thought.

During one session, one of the Lords, or possibly one of their squires, looked out of the window and saw Tresilian peeping in. According to the chronicler Froissart, the startled man announced, 'Methinks I see yonder Sir Robert Tresilian.' This rather surprised everyone but, keen to investigate, a party of guards was sent to search the house. They scoured the building, finding no one other than the owner, on whom they decided to put a bit of pressure. On pain of death, he announced that the man they were looking for was hiding under the table. The guards yanked the wretched Tresilian from his hiding place by his heels.

The guards, no doubt amazed by this turn of events, hurried into the Palace of Westminster, dragging Robert Tresilian behind them with cries of 'We have him!' An equally amazed group of Lords Appellant met them and asked Tresilian why justice should not now be done on him. According to the records of state trials, Tresilian was dumbstruck, unable either to escape or to explain why he had taken the reckless step of spying on his opponents. He was taken to the Tower of London, with his wife and children following, in tears. Not wishing to give their foe a chance to change his mind about fleeing abroad, the Lords ordered Tresilian to be immediately tied to a hurdle and dragged behind a horse to the execution ground. A great crowd followed the former Chief Justice, still in a false beard and rags, still dumbstruck, through the streets.

At the gallows Tresilian refused to climb the ladder, apparently claiming he 'could not die'. He was then stripped to reveal that he was covered in amulets and magical spells designed to protect him. These were stripped away, he was hauled up the ladder and hanged. To ensure he was dead, his throat was cut and the body left on the gallows overnight. Robert Tresilian would never be overcome by his curiosity again.

The Hidden Friends of Lady Lisle

The fate of Lady Alice Lisle at the Bloody Assizes of Judge Jeffreys shows how dangerous it can be to hide fugitives in your house, even if you're doing it for all the right reasons.

Lady Alice had, indirectly, been closely linked to the main events of the English Civil War. Her husband, John Lisle, had been one of the signatories to Charles I's death warrant and a grateful Cromwell had elevated him to the upper house in his Commonwealth government. At the Restoration in 1660, naturally enough, their fortunes had turned. John and Alice had chosen to flee rather than face the Royalists. However, the Royalist cause followed them to Switzerland and John was assassinated on his way to church.

Lady Lisle returned to England around 1665 and took up residence at Moyles Court, her father's old house, where, having reached the age of fifty, she hoped to quietly live out the rest of her days. Indeed, she had every reason to think she would remain unmolested. She had never directly been involved in politics and although she remained a pious Protestant she never spoke out against the accession in 1685 of James II, the Roman Catholic brother of Charles II.

Not everyone took the accession of James so well. Within days of its taking place, a full-scale rebellion broke out when the Protestant Duke of Monmouth, an illegitimate son of Charles II, claimed the throne. The rebellion proved abortive. After the battle of Sedgemoor, Monmouth was captured and beheaded, and his supporters were mercilessly hunted down. It was at this time that the now elderly Alice Lisle was approached by James Dunne, a baker from Warminster, who was carrying a note for her from one John Hicks, asking her to shelter him and his friend Richard Nelthorp. Hicks, a Nonconformist minister, was well known to Alice. She agreed to lodge the men and hide them as necessary.

What she almost certainly hadn't been told, and didn't know, was that the two men were more than just Nonconformists sheltering from religious persecution; they were fugitives from Monmouth's defeated forces at the battle of Sedgemoor.

It was not long before the presence of the two men at Moyles Court was public knowledge. A local farmhand, John Barter, saw them and reported them to Colonel Thomas Penruddock. He made a surprise search of the house and arrested Hicks, Nelthorp and Lady Alice. All three were taken to Winchester to one of the most notorious special commissions in British history, set up by a fearful sovereign anxious to root out and punish any who had, in thought or deed, supported Monmouth. Presided over by the zealous Judge Jeffreys, the commission would soon gain another title – the Bloody Assizes.

The treatment of Lady Alice, the first person to be tried at these assizes, was considered excessive even by the standards of the day. Now almost deaf, she had to have the proceedings relayed to her by her friend, Matthew Brown, who stood beside her through-out her six-hour trial. Although the original transcripts don't survive, accounts made from them suggest Jeffreys badgered and interrupted her witnesses. When the baker James Dunne was subjected to a prolonged cross-examination, he panicked, fearing he might himself be implicated, and denounced Alice. She calmly admitted that she had hidden Hicks, but only as a Nonconformist preacher, not as a traitor.

Alice was nonetheless condemned by a jury unnerved and overawed by Jeffreys' ferocity. She was sentenced to the stan-dard punishment for female traitors at that date – to be burnt at the stake – but put in an appeal for clemency to King James. The King, in a move that gained him widespread condemnation, merely altered her sentence from burning to beheading. Lady Alice Lisle was executed in the Market Square at Winchester on 2 September 1685, going to her death insisting that her only 'crime' was to 'entertain a Non-Conformist minister'. She was seventy-one years old.

The Capture of Roger Mortimer

The tragic tale of the life and death of King Edward II is told by the rather hysterical but splendidly enjoyable Latin chronicler, Geoffrey le Baker of Swynbroke. His description of how the weak king was brought down by his own wife, Isabella, and her lover, Roger Mortimer, includes graphic details of how, at their command, the poor man was finally dispatched, in 1327, by being stabbed with a red-hot plumber's iron 'in the fundament', as Geoffrey delicately put it. *

What happened next is not so widely known, however, perhaps because nothing is quite as memorable as reversing on to a red-hot poker. For a while it appeared that Isabella and Roger had got away with their crime. As the new king, Edward III, was still only fourteen, he came under the control of the murderous couple who acted as regents. Roger began to sequester estates and consolidate his own power, alienating many at court, but as the king was still a minor there was precious little anyone could do. For his part, Edward was reduced to smuggling a message to the Pope, warning that only messages containing the words 'Pater Sancte' in his own hand could be taken as expressing his true desires; everything else he would have been forced to write.

By 1330 there were rumours that Mortimer was planning to seize power before Edward came of age when, in all likelihood, the young king might exact revenge, not only for the murder of his father but for the many slights he had received as a child. Certainly when the royal couple arrived at Nottingham in October of that year for a parliament, it was noted that Roger seemed already to have taken on a rather royal bearing, walking beside or even in front of the king, when it was traditional for everyone to walk a little behind the monarch. Geoffrey le Baker was also outraged to note that Mortimer suffered Edward to stand in his presence, as though he were the king and the king were his subject.

Perhaps with the regency firmly in his hands and Edward still only seventeen, Mortimer felt secure enough to behave like a king,

* I have read a book — name forgotten — years ago claiming that this did not happen — just a legend, but that the king was tucked away in a prison.

or perhaps power had simply gone to his head, but either way it's never a good idea to annoy teenage boys. Edward was indeed planning his revenge.

Roger was not an idiot of course. He had already been locked up in the Tower once (from which he had escaped by holding a party for his guards and getting them drunk) and he knew he was unlikely to win any popularity contests, so he did take precautions. On the night of 29 October, he and Isabella were safely locked in the royal apartments of Nottingham Castle, a formidable structure perched on a huge sandstone outcrop. The doors were bolted and guards had been posted. Furthermore, at least according to one source, Isabella had taken the extra precaution of asking for the castle keys and placing them under her pillow for safe keeping. What harm therefore could possibly befall them?

Castles are generally considered to be secure structures, one of their main purposes being to keep out unwanted sorts. Nottingham, however, was the exception that proves the rule. Its gates and walls were strong enough but, rather peculiarly, the whole edifice sat on a rock that was as riddled with tunnels and passages as a Swiss cheese – as Edward III knew well. He, and his friends (which meant just about everyone, as no one liked Roger), had been talking to Robert de Heland, who had once been constable of the castle. De Heland had pointed out to the young king that the gates to Nottingham Castle were somewhat superfluous as there was a secret passage that led from near the river right up into the inner bailey.

That night Edward, de Heland and their supporters crept through the overgrown passage and into the sleeping castle. Having dispatched a couple of guards, Edward, not wanting an awkward family scene, discreetly waited outside the royal apartments while his friends burst in. Isabella and Roger were taken entirely by surprise. Guessing her son was near by and perhaps wishing she'd been nicer to him in previous years, Isabella called out to him, begging for mercy for her lover.

It was not forthcoming. Isabella was taken off to Castle Rising where she spent the rest of her life under house arrest. Roger was returned to the Tower where he met with the same summary justice that he had wielded against his enemies. Without trial or opportunity to defend himself, and just a month after his capture, he was sent to the gallows of common thieves at The Elms and there hanged, drawn and quartered. Thus began the personal reign of one of England's greatest mediaeval kings.

16

Secret Signs

Laughter is the cipher key wherewith we decipher the whole man.

Thomas Carlyle, *Sartor Resartus* (1833–4)

The Extraordinary Machines of Tommy Flowers

The invention of the computer will undoubtedly go down in history as one of the most pivotal events of the twentieth century, yet the story of its birth amid the secrecy of code-breaking in the Second World War is only now coming to light. The work of one of the men who might rightly be called its inventor is still almost entirely unrecognised.

Thomas Flowers, the son of a bricklayer, had as a boy an uncanny facility for engineering. In 1926 it led him to join the Post Office as an electrical engineer and, four years later, to transfer to their experimental laboratory in Dollis Hill, constructing the first automatic electrical switching equipment for the burgeoning telephone service. *radio Tubas, as called in Canada and U.S.A.*

Flowers' work using valve technology first came to the attention of the secret wartime code and cipher school at Bletchley Park (near Milton Keynes in Buckinghamshire) in 1942. The codebreakers there had been using electromechanical devices, know as 'bombes', to help crunch through the huge numbers of combinations needed for cracking German codes. These proved highly effective at attacking the morse code 'Enigma' messages used by much of the German military, but had hit something of a brick wall when it came to breaking another group of even more important codes.

Since 1942 it had been noted that the German High Command were using a new teletype code machine, the Lorenz SZ. Unlike Enigma, this was a bespoke system (Enigma had been available on the open market since 1923), offering 5 trillion times more combinations than the 157 trillion already offered by Enigma. The intelligence intercepted from this system was assigned the name 'Fish' by the British. Attacking the code, and in particular the High Command variant known as 'Tunny', seemed almost impossible until Max Newman – a member of the group, who was given the task of breaking it in 'Hut F' at Bletchley – suggested that high-speed machinery might help crunch the data by comparing messages. And who better to build such machines than the electrical engineers of the Post Office, who were already used to making high-speed switching equipment for automatic exchanges?

So Tommy Flowers was set to work, designing and building these early machines, known as 'Heath Robinsons' after the English cartoonist famous for drawing impossibly complicated devices. A problem quickly emerged. Heath Robinsons could not store the contents of the Fish messages in order for them to be analysed, which slowed down the code-breakers greatly. Flowers suggested that, provided the machine was always left on and undisturbed, he could build a machine where electronic valves stored the data for processing.

The response was generally sceptical, as it was assumed that fragile valves could never take the strain of being on continually. Flowers was therefore left to devise and develop his system in his spare time and largely at his own expense. He started in February 1943, working at a blistering pace, and his first machine was ready for testing on 8 December of that year. For eight hours the 1,500 thyratron valves performed faultlessly, immediately silencing his critics. One man who witnessed the operation was particularly excited. The brilliant mathematician and cryptanalyst Alan Turing realised that this was not simply an electromechanical calculator; its capacity to store data made it something entirely new. Whilst it could not store a program internally (it had to be physically reconfigured for this), nor was it a general-purpose machine, it was undoubtedly the first electronic computer.

The device was immediately set to work on Fish intercepts. It also gained a new name, thought up by the members of the Women's Royal Naval Service (known as Wrens) who operated the 1-ton, room-sized behemoth – Colossus. Another 2,500-valve version was immediately ordered and entered service just four days before D-Day, providing crucial decrypts of Tunny messages in the lead-up to the invasion. Indeed, it was said that Eisenhower had a Tunny decrypt, courtesy of Colossus, in his hand at the moment he gave the order to launch Operation Overlord.

By the end of the war there were ten Colossi at Bletchley, but with the surrender of Germany their work suddenly came to an end. As they had clearly been instrumental in winning the war, precisely what they did and how they did it was deemed top secret. Eight of the machines were destroyed and the other two secretly moved to the peacetime government intelligence centre, GCHQ, where one remained in operation into the 1960s. Flowers was given £1,000 compensation, much less than he had personally spent on developing Colossus, and was sent back to the Post Office – where he built ERNIE, the Premium Bond selecting machine – with a reminder that he could never talk about what he had done.

Gagged by the Official Secrets Act, Flowers was prevented from telling anyone about his machines until 1983 and even then he was banned from explaining how they were employed at Bletchley. As a result, the designer and builder of what was effectively the world's first electronic computer never received the credit he deserved. Nor indeed did he receive even a small fraction of the staggering financial returns that commercial computing brought some. Tommy Flowers died in 1998 still largely unrecognised and unrewarded.

The Code-Breaking Bishop

The world of cryptography is a dark one and its prizes are rarely revealed to any outside the craft, as code-breakers, by their nature, tend to prefer anonymity. That is, unless you were Edward Willes, one of the greatest cryptographers of his generation, whose rewards were decidedly public and surprisingly holy.

As Willes was the son of a village rector, it is hardly surprising that a career in the Church awaited him. Whilst at Oxford University, however, he was distracted from the usual clerical trajectory – towards securing a comfortable country living – by a meeting with William Blencowe, decipherer to Queen Anne. A fine linguist, Willes quickly picked up the skills of the code-breaker, eventually coming to the attention of the newly installed Hanoverian monarchy and being appointed decipherer to George I in 1716.

It was a very different life for someone who had expected to be a vicar, working in the 'secret office', intercepting, decoding and secretly reading foreign correspondence. It was also rather well paid, at £200 a year (nearly £300,000 in comparison to modern average earnings). This was a great time to be a cryptographer; the Hanoverians were attempting to establish themselves on the throne in the face of continual attempts by the Jacobites to restore the Stuart monarchy. Alongside such factional internal politics, external European powers also used the situation to interfere in the hope of gaining an advantage. Indeed, Willes was instrumental in bringing the Swedish ambassador to London to be tried for pro-Jacobite intrigue, having cracked that country's diplomatic cipher.

How was the government to show Willes its appreciation? Willes had been trained in the Church and it was through the Church that he wished to be rewarded. He was given the very comfort-able living of Barton-le-Clay, Bedfordshire – his first church.

Other cryptographical triumphs were to follow. His decoding skills brought to light the Jacobite sympathies of the bishop of Rochester, for which his recompense was being made a canon of Westminster and then dean of Lincoln. Two more livings followed in 1734 in recognition of his government work. Nor were his clerical appointments simply honorary – they were financially valuable. As the vicar of various churches, a dean and a canon, in addition to his labours for the state, he was earning £500 a year.

Provided his code-breaking skills didn't fail him, only one reward that was of any value to him still remained. In 1742, with much of the day-to-day work of cryptography now in his sons' hands, he finally accepted the bishopric of St David's. The following year, he was given the even more profitable bishopric of Bath and Wells, making him the only spy to ever rise to such a high ecclesiastical position. However, to be fair, Willes was never simply 'on the make'. Unlike many of his day, he took his cler-ical appointments seriously, handling much of the work himself rather than harvesting the income and delegating his own duties to vicars. This alone was popularly thought to account for his rise to the position of bishop.

Although a steady stream of intercepted messages made their

way to the bishop's palace at Wells right up until his death in 1773, his secret work remained entirely unknown to his flock as his evidence in court was always given in private to protect his identity. No one who attended communion in Wells each Sunday knew that the man who sat in the *cathedra* before them had risen to such heights as much by ciphers as by sermons.

Florence Hensey's Lemon Juice War

Florence Hensey did not have a particularly high regard for the English. This had nothing to do with being teased about his rather mediaeval Christian name but was due in part to the failure of his London medical practice and equally to his upbringing as an Irish Catholic.

Hensey's opportunity to change his impecunious circumstances occurred suddenly in 1756 with the outbreak of the Seven Years War between France and England. Hensey, who had studied and travelled extensively on the continent, received news that a fellow student from Leyden University had just been appointed to a job in the office of the French Secretary of State. In sending his congratulations to his old friend, he dropped the hint that he'd be delighted if he too could be of any service to the French state.

A reply came quickly and in the affirmative. In return for a substantial fee of nearly £25 a month, Hensey was ordered to 'send complete lists of all our men of war, both in and out of commission; their condition, situation, and number of men on board each; when they sailed, under what commanders, from what ports, and their destination; an account of the actual number of our troops, what regiments were complete, and where quartered or garrisoned'.

In short, the French wanted to know everything about the British military build-up in preparation for war. All Hensey had to do was provide details. As a doctor, however, he was not in a particularly good position to acquire secret information. He tried chatting to the clerks from public offices but this simply put them on their guard, not surprisingly, so he settled on a much simpler plan. Each day he would make the rounds of the London coffee houses used by Members of Parliament and just listen in to their loud and boastful conversations. The French were so enchanted with the quality of the intelligence that Hensey drew from loose-tongued MPs that they gave him a pay rise.

Meanwhile the British government remained entirely oblivious to the operation. Indeed, it would be not government agents but a postman who would eventually bring Hensey down. Obviously Hensey could not correspond directly with France, so he posted his letters there via Holland. His instructions were sent back from France via Switzerland and delivered to a coffee house in the Strand, where they were collected under an assumed name. The postman delivering these frequent dispatches became suspicious of such regular mail from Switzerland but, when he held up the letters to the light, as postmen sometimes do, he could see only a few lines of text on each.

He lost no time in informing his superiors of his misgivings. Accordingly, the secretary of the Post Office ordered one of the dispatches opened. Although it contained just a few lines of widely spaced and apparently innocuous text, the wily Post Office clerks had seen this sort of thing before. When they held the text over a candle, the true message soon began to appear – having been written between the lines in every schoolchild's favourite invisible ink: lemon juice.

Hensey was followed, arrested and tried for high treason, putting up a valiant if rather misguided defence. Having been caught red-handed, he first pleaded that he couldn't be tried in London, the site of the Post Office headquarters, as he'd written the letters in Middlesex – something of an admission of guilt. He then argued that writing a treasonable letter was not an act of high treason in itself unless it were published. The court ruled, however, that the posting of the letter was an act of publication. Hensey finally claimed that, as he had addressed his treasonable letters to an intermediary in Holland, he was corresponding only with the Dutch (with whom England was not at war) and not the enemy. The prosecution replied that as one of his letters contained an overt invitation for France to invade England, it was reasonable to assume that the letters were indeed addressed to the enemy.

It will probably come as no surprise to learn that Hensey was found guilty and sentenced to death, but luck was with him right to the end. His brother was by this time chaplain to the Spanish ambassador at The Hague and his intervention, through his counterpart in London, reached the ears of George II. On the morning of his scheduled execution, Florence Hensey was granted a respite and later a reprieve at the King's pleasure. Under no circumstances could George II be persuaded to pardon the man who had compassed his death but by the time George III acceded a more forgiving attitude prevailed. Hensey was pardoned, having given security for his good behaviour, and was not heard from again.

Fitton's Finest Hour

Michael Fitton managed to start a war thanks to a single eagle-eyed exploit in uncovering a damning secret one morning in September 1780.

Fitton had entered the Royal Navy in June of that year as servant to a family friend, George Keppel, then captain of the 28-gun frigate *Vestal*. With the American Revolutionary War raging, the vessel was sent to intercept American shipping and so fell in, on Sunday 3 September, with the US privateer and packet *Phoenix* and its convoy off the Newfoundland banks. *Vestal* easily got the better of these small ships, firing several shots across their bows and through their rigging. Eventually the Americans began to heave to and struck their colours.

It was at this point, as the two ships came alongside, that Michael Fitton – who at the time was up the mast, furling the fore-top-gallant sail – noticed a man fall into the sea from the *Phoenix*. He shouted, 'Man overboard!' and the crew of the *Vestal* immediately set to, retrieving the seaman from the water. What they found, however, was not a sailor but a bag, filled with papers and lead shot, which had hastily been thrown over the side. Because of the air still in it, the bag had floated.

Now another discovery was made. On board the innocuous *Phoenix* was a certain Henry Laurens, former President of the Continental Congress, the first ever national government of the United States. He was on his way back to America from Amsterdam. What was recovered from the bag was the reason for his trip: a secret treaty between the USA and the Dutch – the document whose publication would lead to the outbreak of the Fourth Anglo-Dutch War. Laurens was, for his part, taken prisoner and eventually sent to England, where he became the only American ever held captive in the Tower of London. From there he was eventually exchanged for the British general, Lord Cornwallis.

Fitton gained some fame, if little reward, from this exploit and eventually deserted the service when a new captain replaced his friend Keppel. He later returned to the navy, commanding several vessels, but, given only the command of tenders and the rank of lieutenant, he never received the prize money he deserved for a long and illustrious life's service. He died a pensioner of the Greenwich hospital in 1852.

The Nether Silton Code

In a field behind All Saints church at Nether Silton in North Yorkshire stands a mysterious, tall stone carved with the following inscription:

HTGOMHS
TBBWOTGWWG
TWATEWAHH
ATCLABWHEY
AD 1765
AWPSAYAA

The meaning of the stone confused the many nineteenth-century antiquaries who visited the site, having an obvious date (AD 1765) but no apparent method behind the code. Many an amateur cryptographer mused over the text. Was it coded with a substitution cipher, perhaps, or a transposition cipher? No amount of frequency analysis would make it yield. It was not an anagram, nor a foreign language known to any.

Eventually the answer to the riddle that had confounded many a gentleman with time on his hands was found, rather splendidly, by the compilers of the *Victoria County History*, who simply 'asked a local'.

They were told that the stone was not code at all but a joke set there by an eighteenth-century landowner, Squire Hicks, to confuse just such people as themselves. In fact, each letter is the first letter of a word and the whole inscription reads:

Here The Good Old Manor House Stood
The Back Beams Were Oak, The Great Walls Were Good
The Walls At The East Wing Are Hidden Here
A Thatched Cottage Like A Barn Was Here Erected Year
AD 1765
A Wide Porch Spans A Yard And Alcove

And so the Nether Silton code is nothing more than a memorial to the old mediaeval manor house, which was probably torn down by Hicks to build the current manor, marked now only by a single enigmatic stone.

The Mystery of the Dark Lady

In 1609 a small book was published entitled *Shakespeare's Sonnets*. It in were 154 poems by the great playwright on themes of love, politics and morality, probably written at different times in his life. In it also lay a coded mystery that has yet to be solved and that continues to obsess writers and historians.

The sonnets contain references to two unidentified people who clearly played pivotal roles in the bard's life but about whom we can only speculate. The book is dedicated to a 'Mr W.H.', whom the publisher calls 'the onlie begetter of these insuing sonnets'. The first seventeen sonnets are addressed to a young man, urging him to marry and have children so that his beauty will not die with him. The next 109 express the poet's love for this unidentified person, usually referred to as the 'Fair Youth'.

From this point onwards, the sonnets are no longer addressed to the young man but to the poet's mistress, whose relationship with him ends when she has an affair, perhaps with the 'Fair Youth'. Four hundred years after the book's publication, the question is still being asked: who were these two characters?

The main candidates for 'Mr W.H.' are Shakespeare's patrons, Henry Wriothesley, 3rd Earl of Southampton, and William Herbert, 3rd Earl of Pembroke, both of whose initials would fit, provided you're not too worried about the letter order. Oscar Wilde thought he saw something in the sonnets that suggested 'W.H. was a young actor called "William Hughes"', although we have no evidence that such a boy ever existed.

It is the mistress, often referred to as 'the Dark Lady', who has created the most puzzlement. Of the few candidates about whom we know anything, perhaps the most intriguing is Mary Fitton.

Mary was a young maid of honour at the court of Elizabeth I in the late 1590s, placed by her father under the care of the Comptroller of the Royal Household, Sir William Knollys. Knollys promised he would be 'the Good Shepperd and will to my power defend the innocent lamb from the wolvyshe crueltye and fox-like subtletye of the tame be[a]sts of this place'.

In fact he fell in love with Mary who was thirty years his junior. As he was already married she rebuffed him. 'Mistress Fitton', as she was known, was also coming to the attention of others at court. William Kempe – a clown with Shakespeare's acting troupe, the Lord Chamberlain's Men – dedicated his book, *Nine Dayes Wonder*, to her (although he embarrassingly confused her name with that of her sister). His affections could hardly compete with those of William Herbert, eldest son of the Earl of Pembroke and a good candidate for 'Mr W.H.', whose mistress she became. When

Mary became pregnant the following year, Elizabeth dismissed her and sent William, now 3rd Earl of Pembroke, to prison, but he refused to marry his mistress.

After the birth of her son Mary retired in disgrace to the country, where she became the mistress of a vice admiral whose own wife had been declared insane. They had a daughter together, shortly after which he died of smallpox. Then, in 1606, when Mary was still only around twenty-eight, she married Captain William Polewhele, for whom she bore a further three children. After he too died, she married former MP John Lougher and gave birth to another three children.

Is Mary Fitton Shakespeare's Dark Lady? She certainly had a powerful impact on the men at court and was well known to members of Shakespeare's company, although we have no proof that she and the bard ever met. We know too that she had an affair with a 'W.H.', who was also Shakespeare's patron. There is a telling reference in one sonnet:

> Whoever hath her wish, thou hast thy 'Will,'
> And 'Will' to boot, and 'Will' in overplus;

Some claim this is a series of puns on the three 'Wills' in her life – William Knollys, William Herbert and William Shakespeare. Furthermore, her reputation was rather lively, her affairs scandalising her family and the court. However, the sonnets describe the Dark Lady as having black hair and dark-brown eyes, whereas we know Mary Fitton had brown hair and grey eyes. So the mystery of the Dark Lady remains.

Catherine's Cipher

Catherine of Aragon was a princess of Spain, the daughter of Ferdinand II of Aragon and Isabella I of Castile and León. Betrothed at an early age to a future king of England, she might be expected to have been bred into the world of court intrigues, where codes and ciphers were commonplace. Yet her own attempt at secrecy illustrates how primitive espionage could be, even at the beginning of the sixteenth century.

Catherine had come to England in 1501 to marry the son and heir of Henry VII, Prince Arthur, but shortly after their marriage, on 2 April 1502, her young husband had died. Henry VII, reluctant to return the large dowry he'd received from Ferdinand, prevaricated, keeping the young Catherine a virtual prisoner in Durham House in London whilst suggesting a possible second marriage to his younger son, the future Henry VIII.

It was a painful situation for the daughter of one of the most powerful families in Europe to find herself in and, not surprisingly, she looked to her father for help. She wrote to him, complaining of having been given so little money to pay her servants that she had been forced to pawn some of her own jewellery. Nor was she even regularly allowed to see her putative new husband, Henry. This situation remained unchanged until 1509.

Naturally enough, such a difficult diplomatic problem could not be discussed openly, so Ferdinand sent his daughter a cipher to use, as was routine for important diplomatic correspondence. What he perhaps did not realise was that his daughter, stranded in England, had no confidential secretary to help her with the decoding and encoding of letters. In a time when it was not always even considered necessary for a noble to be literate, this was a terrible blunder.

Catherine, receiving advice from her father in code, was forced, excruciatingly slowly, to decipher the text herself – but that was the easy part. She then had to write her replies by hand and encode them. Knowing, as for any diplomatic correspondence, that there was every chance it could be intercepted, decoded and read, she did her best. Fearful, however, of a mistake that would render her dispatches unreadable, she made one blinding error. She included an uncoded version of her letter with each coded one, just in case her father couldn't understand them, in the process instantaneously sabotaging both his and her own efforts at secrecy.

17

Commercial Secrets

The secret of business is to know something that nobody else knows.

Aristotle Onassis, quoted in *The Economist* (November 1991)

The London Ghost Train

Just outside Waterloo station in London stand the remnants of the city's most unusual railway terminus. You might well ask why anyone would want to build a station right next to Waterloo. Furthermore, a casual glance at this railway's books would reveal another mystery – an unusual number of single (and very expensive) tickets sold for the short trip to this line's sole destination. The answer to these puzzles was once written in bold letters over the station entrance, although the sign has long since been removed. It read: 'London Necropolis Railway'.

By the mid nineteenth century, overcrowding was becoming a real problem in London and not just for the living. With space at a premium, the tiny graveyards of the city's mediaeval churches were overflowing, sometimes scandalously, with human bones being unearthed by accident and scattered about indiscriminately. What was needed was a new burial ground that was large enough and affordable enough for ordinary Londoners. The newly arrived railway service appeared to provide an answer.

Just four years after Waterloo station was finished in 1848, the London Necropolis and National Mausoleum Company was formed. It had bought 2,000 acres of land from Lord Onslow at Brookwood near Woking in Surrey, of which 500 acres were landscaped as a cemetery. Being so far out of town, the land was cheap, so that even the poor would be able to afford their own plot (as opposed to having to share communal ones in the City), but the coffins and mourners would still need transport to get there. This was where the railway came in.

The management of the London and South West Railway were unsure about having funeral parties on their trains, fearing that the new breed of train traveller that they were encouraging onto their still novel form of transport might be put off by sitting in a carriage that had previously held a coffin. Then there were the concerns of the bishop of London, who warned that it would be highly inappropriate to convey the coffins of working-class people in the same carriage as respectable folk. Similarly, the mourners from different classes should never be allowed to mix.

It was decided to address all these issues by creating special funeral trains with their own stations, so as not to spook ordinary travellers. Funeral parties, both living and dead, were to be divided up into three classes and two types (Anglican and Nonconformist). At the London Necropolis terminal, first-class mourners could enjoy the privacy of their own dedicated waiting room, from which they could watch their loved one's coffin being loaded on to the reserved first-class section of the mortuary car, whose more elaborate doors helped to justify the increased cost for carrying a first-class corpse. First-class Nonconformists could travel in similar luxury but in a different compartment.

After the fifty-seven-minute journey, the train would arrive in turn at each of two specially built stations, one on the south side of the cemetery for Anglicans and another on the north for Nonconformists. Here first-class mourners would disembark with their own chaplain, who would hold a private service in the station chapel before moving on to the interment. Afterwards there was time for a drink and perhaps lunch in the refreshment room, followed by a walk around the grounds, before the train returned the mourners to London.

For third-class mourners, there were less-elaborate arrangements. They warranted only one communal service said at the chapel over all the coffins collectively, rather than over each one individually (although Nonconformists and Anglicans still had separate services). Third-class mourners also had to make do with a communal waiting room, rather than a private room for each funeral party.

The Necropolis railway opened on 13 November 1854 but was never the great success its founders had hoped. Other railways offered competing services, some with cemeteries much closer to London, and only 3,200 burials a year took place in the first twenty years of the service. At the turn of the century, the Sunday service was abandoned and by the 1930s there was just one Necropolis train a week.

Nevertheless the end of the line for the London Necropolis railway was not the result of its unpopularity. On the night of 16 April 1941 its London terminus was bombed, destroying the mortuary, workshops and entrance. The bespoke funeral carriages in a nearby siding were also wrecked.

In the cold light of day it was realised that, even with compensation, it was uneconomic to revive the service. Today only the London frontage of the terminus remains. At Brookwood cemetery the railway tracks have been taken up, the station buildings have gone and only the platforms and station chapels survive as a last reminder of London's ghost train.

The Elusive Mrs Cathcart

Helen Cathcart was one of the most popular royal biographers of the twentieth century, writing with a gentle, old-fashioned deference far removed from modern royal biographers. Titles such as *Charles: Man of Destiny* and *Her Majesty: A Biography of Queen Elizabeth II* sold in their thousands to mainly female audiences who imagined Mrs Cathcart as the last representative of a bygone era. That was certainly the image she wished to project whilst hiding all the while a lucrative commercial secret.

For her fans Mrs Cathcart could be a fugitive heroine. Requests to give speeches or open fêtes were always met with a demure and polite refusal, penned on her behalf by her literary manager Harold Albert. Although Mrs Cathcart was delighted to be asked, her only interest was in promoting the royal subjects of her books, not herself, so she had to decline. Rumour had it that she had once been on George V's staff, which perhaps explained her dignified reticence.

For those who wanted to know her opinions, however, she was very present in the letters pages of the *Daily Telegraph* and later as a regular columnist for *Majesty* magazine, although no one other than Harold Albert and his wife Winnie – who would occasionally receive acknowledgments in Cathcart's books – ever met her.

The elusiveness of such a famous author naturally roused suspicions. It was only on the death of Harold Albert in the late 1990s that the truth finally emerged. He was Helen Cathcart.

Albert had led an extraordinary life. Having run away from home to escape his violent stepfather, he had started his writing career as a journalist for the *Evening News* and the *Daily Mirror*, using a variety of pseudonyms. It was here that he had begun writing profiles of famous people, securing interviews with Clark Gable (on the set of *Gone with the Wind*), Hitler and Mussolini amongst others. The Second World War nearly put a stop to his career as Albert was a conscientious objector. Claiming he would serve his country only by writing to amuse the troops, he was convicted of inciting others to fight whilst refusing to do so himself and sent to Wormwood Scrubs on a sentence of hard labour.

With this sort of record, work proved hard to find after the war so, in the late 1940s, Albert came up with his great plan. In the colonial twilight of the British Empire he would write biographies of members of the royal family, detailing their lives, their houses and hobbies – if not always entirely accurately, at least without the venom of the scandalmongers.

The one difficulty was that the target audience for these books was almost entirely female and Albert thought that a male author would put them off. So Britain's most secretive author was born and Helen Cathcart made her debut. For fifty years she would remain one of the country's best-loved, if least-seen, authors, finally dying with her inventor, Harold Albert, on 20 October 1997. A lady's age is, of course, never discussed as that would be impolite, but Harold was eighty-eight.

The Name of the Game

You might expect the Littlewoods business empire to have been named after someone called Littlewood – a person who would rightly want their name at the forefront of one of Britain's greatest and most lucrative brands. In fact the name was simply a ruse to cover the tracks of a secret business that initially looked as if it might never get off the ground.

John Moores was a working-class lad, the son of a bricklayer. Despite having to leave school at thirteen to go out to work, he trained at night school to become a telegraphist. After serving in the First World War, he got his first taste of business success while running the 'Waterville Supply Company', a business providing a strange combination of books and golf balls for the community around the Commercial Cable Company (CCC) relay hut in Kerry, where he was based. This was, of course, not strictly legal as he had a full-time job with the CCC that precluded his taking on other work. It was also not to last as after eighteen months he was posted back to Liverpool.

It was here that Moores first heard about a man in Birmingham who ran a football pools operation – a form of betting on the outcome of football matches in which the winner received all the cash staked minus a deduction for administrative costs. It seemed like a licence to print money. Soon Moores had persuaded two friends to invest in their own pools business. They had to be sworn to utter secrecy as the CCC would fire them all if they found out. This new business would not only have to print its own coupons but would also have to have a respectable-sounding name that at the same time didn't attract attention to any of them. Moores considered calling it the John Smith's Pool but rejected this as sounding a shade dodgy, as indeed it did.

The solution came from one of the partners, Colin Askham. He had been brought up by his aunt and had taken her surname, but had been born Colin Henry Littlewood. Nobody would guess the connection. The name was settled upon.

This would prove ironic in future years as the initial business was a disaster. Having invested £50 each, the partners rented a small office and printed 4,000 coupons, which they distributed outside Old Trafford before one Saturday match in 1923. Only thirty-five coupons came back. Thinking it was just a matter of scale, the next time they printed 10,000 coupons, which they handed out before a Hull game. On this occasion, just one came back.

A crisis meeting was called in the canteen of the CCC. By this point all three men were now £200 out of pocket. Moores asked the other two what they would like to do. Askham and his fellow investor said it was hopeless – after all, the Birmingham operation had folded as well – so they should cut their losses. Moores disagreed and offered to buy them out. So John Moores, later Sir John Moores, went it alone, backed only by his family (who marked the coupons at weekends) and his wife, who was reported to have said of the decision, 'I'd sooner be the wife of a man who has gone broke than a man who is haunted by regret.'

The rest is history. The Littlewoods Pools and subsequent catalogue business went on to become one of the most successful UK businesses of the twentieth century, bearing not the name of its founder but the secret surname of a man who bailed out just before it all started to make money.

The Leinster Gardens Illusion

London's early underground railway lines, the first of which opened in 1863, were created in an era before tunnel-boring equipment. The train company therefore had to buy the land above the proposed route, knocking down the houses, digging a trench to put in the line and then filling it back in again. This process quite literally cut a swathe through parts of London, leaving roads and squares with unsightly holes where the line had been excavated. To add further insult, at regular intervals on the route large open-air sections had to be allowed to vent the fumes from the steam-driven trains.

So it is hardly surprising that when the South Kensington extension to the tube reached the elegant Leinster Gardens in Bayswater in 1865, the train company was told in no uncertain terms that it would not be allowed to disfigure the area, damaging the value of other houses there, by knocking down a couple and replacing them with an open-air section of track. If the train company wanted to dig a tunnel near Leinster Gardens, it must hide the fact. Thus was created one of London's strangest secrets.

To all appearances, from the front Leinster Gardens is today still a perfect row of five-storey Georgian townhouses, with Doric porches and sash windows. All, that is, except numbers 23 and 24. To anyone passing, they look no different from their neighbours although a closer inspection shows that the windows are not real, but simply painted on. Nor do the front doors lead anywhere, for these houses are no more than façades. Behind their genteel plastered exteriors lie just buttresses and the ventilation shaft for the tube line below. They are nothing more than walls, designed to restore the look of the terrace for the benefit of its wealthy residents.

Rumour has it that these illusory houses have played a role in falsifications of another kind. One story tells how a confidence trickster in the 1930s sold 10-guinea tickets to a ball to be held at 23–24 Leinster Gardens; as a result, a large number of well-dressed couples learnt, to their acute embarrassment one evening, that they had been knocking at a fake front door. The address is also popular with pranksters, receiving more than its fair share of pizza deliveries and young apprentices sent on bogus errands.

The Secret of Pimm's

James Pimm originally came from Kent where he had started his adult life as an oyster dealer, selling what was then one of the 'fast foods' of nineteenth-century London.

Dealing in oysters was not as profitable as actually selling them directly to Londoners. By 1824, Pimm had gone from being a dealer to a vendor, opening his first oyster bar, initially in Lombard Street and then later at larger premises on Poultry in the City. James Pimm's Oyster Bar was by no means unique; indeed, the City was full of such bars in which the hungry gentlemen of the square mile could enjoy a cheap and quick lunch of oysters, lobster or other shellfish. It was traditionally washed down with a pint of stout or a grog composed of water, rum and fruit juice, which went by the more appetising name of 'house cup'.

By the 1840s drinking tastes had changed in favour of the once-notorious gin. In the first half of the eighteenth century the production of cheap gin (initially encouraged by the government) had been seen as the scourge of the working class, leading to the introduction of the Gin Acts and the creation of Hogarth's famous engraving *Gin Lane*, showing the horrors of alcoholism. Now, with the invention of the column still, a 'drier' type of London gin was becoming fashionable, although there was still the problem of its bitter aftertaste, no doubt partly due to the fact that it was regularly adulterated with turpentine or even sulphuric acid.

To provide his customers with the modish drink of the day, whilst wanting to spare them the bitterness, James Pimm set to work creating his own new 'cup'. By blending fruit extracts, liqueurs, herbs and spices, he created what became known as Pimm's Cup, pints of which soon became a great hit with his customers. Further experimentation led him to develop two new versions, the No. 2 Cup, made with Scotch whisky, and the No. 3 Cup, based on brandy.

By the time Pimm died in 1866, his invention was selling to clubs and bars well beyond his own oyster bar, for three shillings a bottle. The business was later taken over by Horatio David Davies who kept the name and expanded the business into five bars, the last of which survived into the 1960s, although Pimm's formula was eventually sold on to larger drinks corporations. The current owners and manufacturers claim they continue to make Pimm's No. 1 Cup to James Pimm's original recipe, which remains a secret known to only six employees.

The Hand of Glory

There are many versions of the tale of the Hand of Glory, all centring on the creation of a ghastly but powerful talisman, the secret weapon of generations of cat burglars who once stalked the more remote houses and inns of Britain. Of these, the most detailed revolve around the events at the Old Spital Inn in Stainmore, near Bowes in County Durham, in 1797.

The Old Spital Inn was a lonely place, a long, narrow stone hall far from the nearest habitation, standing on the York to Carlisle road as it climbs over Stainmore. Its usual visitors were the travellers who frequented that road. On this particular night in October no wayfarers had passed by. The curtains had been drawn, the bolts on the door had been thrown and landlord George Alderson and his family sat around the fire, having supper. Outside a gale was blowing over the moor, lashing the windows with rain, when suddenly there was a knock at the door. The Old Spital Inn had always been a travellers' refuge and George was quick to let in the mystery visitor. It proved to be an old woman, heavily cloaked and hooded, and soaked to the skin, who was swiftly ushered near the fire. She thanked the landlord but refused a change of clothes or a bed for the night, saying she would sleep by the fire until morning when she was duty bound to make a start at first light.

Out of consideration for the old woman, George asked Bella, their maid, to sleep on the settle in the main room to keep the woman company, as well as to make her a bowl of porridge before she set off in the morning. With that, the family retired to bed and Bella was left with the stranger. At some point the maid became suspicious of the traveller. She seemed surly and silent, refusing to talk, and when she stretched her legs out before the fire Bella was sure she saw trouser bottoms peeking from beneath her skirts – which was a little unusual.

It now being late, Bella laid a blanket on the great oak settle by the fire and lay down but instead of sleeping she determined to watch the old woman. Her vigilance was rewarded. When the mystery guest thought Bella was asleep, she rose from her chair and cast off the heavy cloak to reveal she was not an old lady but a young man. He reached into the folds of the cloak and produced a grisly object – a withered and dried human hand, its fingers closed around the stub of a candle. Quickly the man lit the candle and, moving close to Bella, waved the talisman over her, softly repeating the words:

> Let those who are asleep be asleep,
> And those who are awake be awake.

At this point the story very definitely enters the realms of myth, although the ghoulish object, known as 'the Hand of Glory', was a real enough talisman for Georgian burglars and many believed in its strange powers.

To make a 'Hand of Glory' – and recipes still exist for exactly how to go about this – it was first necessary to cut the hand from a freshly hanged criminal, severing it at the wrist with a sharp knife. The hand should then be drained of blood and packed in an earthenware jar with salt, saltpetre and pepper, and left for two weeks. After this it should be cleaned of salt and dried in a hot oven with twigs of fir and vervain for an hour. The still-flexible fingers should then be shaped around a candle and left to set. In the really gruesome versions of the story, the candle is itself made from the rendered fat of an executed criminal.

This talisman supposedly gave a burglar the power to prevent the household he was robbing from waking, and it is with that in mind that we should return to the Old Spital Inn on that night in October 1797.

With the Hand of Glory lit and the incantation chanted, the story has it that the thief was so convinced of the efficacy of his charm that he opened the front door and called to his gang. Of course what he didn't know was that Bella was still awake. She leapt up and pushed him in the small of the back as he stood in the doorway, propelling him out into the stormy night before closing and barring the door behind him.

He now turned on her in fury, beating at the door with his gang, demanding not money but the return of their precious

Hand. Bella, for her part, dashed upstairs to wake the house but was unable to rouse them. Realising they were under a spell from the Hand, she raced back to the kitchen and fetched a pail of skimmed milk with which she doused the candle clutched in its dead fingers. The household immediately awoke and the gang were driven off.

Various versions of the story give different fates for the Hand (and the gang). One says the Hand remained for decades above the fireplace in the Old Spital Inn as a grim reminder; another that the landlord threw the evil charm into the fire. And the gang? In some versions they were shot and killed by the landlord's son, in some they escaped and in one they were caught and hanged. In a macabre postscript, this last version adds that the next day their bodies were found with the hands hacked off.

The Dark Arts of John Harries

Anyone who has watched the movie *Witchfinder General* will tell you that it was, historically, a very bad idea to declare yourself a witch – or a wizard for that matter. Things tended to hot up for you rather quickly and quite literally. Yet witches are not confined to the mediaeval imagination. They could be found in business well into the nineteenth century, making a very good living from their unique combination of skills.

John Harries's father, a wealthy yeoman farmer in South Wales, had had the means to send his son to Haverfordwest grammar school and then to an (unknown) medical school, from where he moved to Harley Street to practise medicine. In around 1825 this respectable forty-something returned home to Caeo where he again set up in practice.

However, John Harries conducted his Welsh business in a very different way. He claimed to be an astrologer, wizard and surgeon, and soon had people flocking to him for some highly unusual cures. In particular he was said to be good with lunatics, whom he would invite to the edge of a lake or river and then suddenly fire a gun over their heads. The panicked patient would fall into the water and the shock would, so it was said, cure them.

Harries's powers also extended far beyond physical cures, making him what locals called a *dys hysbys* (cunning man). He claimed to be able to recover lost items, fight evil spirits and predict the future. Locals said he possessed a magic mirror in which he saw visions and that he could conjure benign spirits. His son, who was of a more practical bent, maintained that he could divine the future fame – or infamy – of a person without seeing them, advise on marriage, provide investment tips and suggest the best times for playing the lottery, all of which might prove lucrative.

More sinisterly, Harries could also identify secret crimes. His most famous case concerned a missing local girl who, he announced, was dead. He then predicted exactly where the body would be found and pointed the finger of blame at her boyfriend. His predictions proved completely correct. The grateful locals immediately had him arrested as an accessory to murder – after all, how could he have known all that without being involved himself?

Fortunately for Harries, he was cunning enough to wriggle out of the charge. When brought before the local justices, he offered to prove his supernatural abilities by predicting the exact time of death of the two magistrates. It seems they were less than willing to hear such unwelcome news and dismissed the case.

So did John Harries really have secret, supernatural powers? The last, rather bitter, laugh must go to him. As well as predicting the fate of others, he predicted his own violent death and even its date. Having announced that he would die by accident on 11 May 1839, he wisely decided to spend that day in bed. During the night a fire broke out at his home of Pant-Coy and he was roused to help fight it. Stepping on to a ladder, he slipped and fell to his death. He was fifty-four years old.

The Undermining of Hallsands

In 1897 the Board of Trade issued a licence to Sir John Jackson for the removal of sand and gravel from the Devon beaches of Hallsands and Beesands for use in the expansion of the Royal Naval dockyard at Devonport. Although the villagers might have wished to have been consulted since the licence was for an area below the high-tide mark, the land belonged not to them but to the Crown, so they weren't. Indeed, no one would be willing to consult them at all, even when things began to go very badly wrong.

If there was anything unusual about Sir John Jackson's gravel extraction, it was the sheer industry of the man, whose workforce soon began removing up to 1,600 tonnes of material a day from the beach, an amount that, it would be fair to say, the locals found alarming. By the winter of 1900 severe storms were already undermining the sea walls and scouring the cliffs behind. Locals were assured of the safety of the operation right up until 1902, when buildings started collapsing into the sea and the licence was finally revoked. By this point the villagers had noticed that the beach level had dropped by over 3 metres. Two years later it was recorded that the beach had dropped another 3 metres and that, thanks to more dredging and subsequent storms, some 97 per cent of it was missing altogether.

Not surprisingly, there were calls for action and later that year an embarrassed government provided a sea wall for the village, which seemed to prevent further erosion – that is, until 1917. On the night of 26 January an unusual easterly wind began blowing up the Channel at the same time as a peak high tide. Soon waves as high as 12 metres were piling over the paltry remains of the gravel beach, which had for centuries protected the town, and lashing against the sea wall, which had always been designed primarily to shield the village from the prevailing westerlies. By midnight the wall had been breached and four houses had collapsed. By dawn, the 128 villagers standing on the relative safety of the clifftops could see that half their village had simply vanished. Another spring tide during the day brought about the collapse of the other half, bar one solitary house. Twenty-nine homes had disappeared for ever into the sea and the village of Hallsands had been completely wiped off the map.

ACKNOWLEDGMENTS

This book is a collection of historical curiosities that I have gathered over the years as I went about writing books, making documentaries and advising on films. As such it includes the thoughts and suggestions of hundreds of people whom I've been fortunate enough to work with along the way. I hope you will forgive me if I don't list you all.

Writing stories is a pleasure but researching tales back to their source requires tenacity and a willingness to cast aside a wonderful anecdote when, after a long pursuit, you find it to be nothing more than a house of cards. That has been the task Stephanie, my wife, has undertaken on this and many previous books, following often tortuous paths back to obscure documents in the hope of finding a gem. If there are gems in these pages they are hers and she is mine. It takes a rare historian to set out into the wilds of the British history and come back still smiling.

For suggesting particular stories for this book I should add my special thanks to my father, Steve Maher, Dr Matt Lee and Stuart Hill. Once again I am fortunate to have the best team in the business behind the book too – Roland Philipps, Helen Hawksfield and Anna Kenny-Ginard at John Murray, my copy-editor Celia Levett, Julian Alexander at LAW and Richard Foreman at Chalke. It is also nothing short of a privilege to have my words illustrated by Martin Haake.

Finally, as always, I want to thank Connie, who very patiently puts up with a father who drags her round dusty museums and decaying buildings and whose smile alone provides him with more inspiration than she can possibly know.

INDEX

Read more . . .

Justin Pollard

THE INTERESTING BITS: THE HISTORY YOU MIGHT HAVE MISSED

Did you give your school history lessons your undivided attention?

Even if you did, you're probably none the wiser as to how Henry II of France came to have a two-foot splinter in his head; or where terms like bunkum, maverick and taking the mickey come from; or why Robert Pate hit Queen Victoria on the head with a walking stick. Relegated to the footnotes, history's little gems are often forgotten. But *The Interesting Bits* rights this wrong; it is a veritable treasure trove of all those surprising, eccentric, chaotic, baffling asides that make history fun.

'Newsflash: history can be entertaining *and* interesting . . . an energetic, colourful book' *Easy Living*

Order your copy now by calling Bookpoint on 01235 827716 or visit your local bookshop quoting ISBN 978-1-84854-100-9
www.johnmurray.co.uk

Read more . . .

Justin Pollard

CHARGE! THE INTERESTING BITS OF MILITARY HISTORY

A cornucopia of military blunders from one of the writers of *QI*

War brings out the very best and worst in people although, frankly, it's usually the latter. But for all our thousands of years of practice at this most dangerous art there is precious little evidence that we're either outgrowing it or getting any good at it. It is an occupation filled with heroism, genius, hubris, idiocy and blind panic all bought on at least in part by large measures of astonishingly good and bad luck – and they're all here in *Charge!* This is not a book filled with battle diagrams, swarming with arrows or 100,000 word descriptions of the tactical basis for the Pastry War.

It is a book about the smaller tragedies and triumphs that actually make up the big picture – toilets that sink U-boats, unsporting attacks on Christmas Day, armies that stop for tea, bombs on renegade balloons, drunk soldiers, blind kings, blind-drunk generals, circular warships, and all the joy and misery that such things bring with them. And an interesting bit about the Pastry War.

'Barmy Armies: tales of derring-do (and derring-don't)' *Independent*

'Even if this book can't eliminate all future military blunders, it will be invaluable for preparing witty after-dinner speeches' *Diplomat*